RAYS OF THE RISING SUN

RAYS
OF THE
RISING SUN

ARMED FORCES OF JAPAN'S ASIAN ALLIES 1931–45

Volume 1: China & Manchukuo

Philip S. Jowett

**Uniform plates by
Peter Abbott**

**Aircraft profiles by
Richard Humberstone**

HELION & COMPANY LTD

Dedication:
To my family

Helion & Company Limited
26 Willow Road
Solihull
West Midlands
B91 1UE
England
Tel. 0121 705 3393
Fax 0121 711 4075
Email: publishing@helion. co. uk
Website: http://www. helion. co. uk

Published by Helion & Company Limited 2004

Designed and typeset by Carnegie Publishing Ltd, Lancaster, Lancashire
Printed by The Cromwell Press, Trowbridge, Wiltshire

© Helion & Company Limited 2004
ISBN 1 874622 21 3

British Library Cataloguing-in-Publication Data.
A catalogue record for this book is available from the British Library.

For details of other military history titles published by Helion & Company Limited contact the above address,
or visit our website: http://www.helion.co.uk.

We always welcome receiving book proposals from prospective authors.

Front cover: A Manchukuoan soldier standing to attention armed with a Japanese-supplied Arisaka 38 rifle (right); a march past of smartly-dressed Nanking Army soldiers wearing German M35 steel helmets (left) (both Philip Jowett collection).

Rear cover: Propaganda postcard of the Manchukuoan Emperor Pu Yi; the front cover of *Shashin Shuho*, 24 March 1943 – a Nanking Government soldier enjoys a cigarette with his Imperial Japanese Army comrades during a military operation; a propaganda postcard issued by the Inner Mongolian Government bearing the slogans "Anti-Communism" and "New Discipline in East Asia". Besides the flag of Japan, the card also features those of (top to bottom) Manchukuo, Inner Mongolia and the five-barred flag used by both the Provisional and Reformed governments of China (all Philip Jowett collection).

Contents

Author's Note
and Acknowledgements

The author has decided to use the older and now 'out of use' Wade-Giles form of translation from Chinese to English instead of the Pin-Yin system in common usage for the following reasons. Most people reading the book will be unfamiliar with the Pin-Yin translation of Chinese names. For instance, most readers would be familiar with the Wade-Giles form for Chiang Kai-shek, but would not recognise the Pin-Yin form. The author hopes that this the use of Wade-Giles does not cause any problems for any of the readers.

Finding information/photographs on the little-known and historically almost completely ignored subject of 'Japan's Asian Allies' has been difficult. The author would therefore appreciate any information or corrections which could be addressed to him via the publishers.

Photographs

The author would also like to briefly comment on the poor standard of a few of the photographs used in the book. It has proved extremely difficult to find photographs of some of the subjects covered in the book, with much of the material being destroyed at the end of the Second World War. Photographs of China during this period are often wrongly captioned and it had taken a great deal of effort to locate some of the images. For this reason he has decided to include photographs that are not really up to the standard that he would normally set for himself. His policy has been however that even a poor quality photograph of a subject is preferable to no photograph at all.

Acknowledgements

Lennart Andersson, Timothy Brook, Ian Carter of the Imperial War Museum, the late Peter Chick, Richard Fuller, Kevin Mahoney, Jurg Meister, John Spellman, Toshio Tamura, Akira 'Taki' Takizawa, Paul. V. Walsh, Stanley Zielinski, and all others who have helped gather information over the years of research. Particular thanks to Colin Green, Minoru Kamada and Alfred Weinzierl for their help with translations and to Masuo Fujita with photographs. Special thanks to Peter Abbott for his uniform plates and to Richard Humberstone for his aircraft profiles.

CHAPTER ONE

Introduction

This volume sets out to describe the armed forces of the various 'puppet' governments of mainland China and Manchukuo from 1932 to 1945. These forces were raised by the Japanese directly or were recruited by 'client' or 'puppet' states. Client governments were under the complete control of the Japanese occupying forces even though they were allowed a semblance of independence. The military forces of the 'puppet' states were by definition 'puppet' troops and obeyed the orders of their Japanese masters even if these were issued through a 'puppet' officer. Although in most cases these 'puppet' forces were of poor combat value they did perform valuable roles for the Japanese Imperial Army. By taking over the anti-guerrilla and security roles of the Japanese they allowed thousands of their troops to be transferred to the more pressing Pacific Theatre. This transfer of Japanese resources allowed the Empire to resist the Allied advances from 1942 for a little longer. This fact and the sheer number of the 'puppet' forces raised during the 1937–45 period means that they are certainly worthy of further study.

With over a million men under arms in 'puppet' armies, navies and air forces they really are one of the unknown elements of the conflict in the Far East. During first, the Sino-Japanese War from 1937 to 1941 and then the wider world war until 1945 they played a significant and largely forgotten role.

Before starting a history of the 'puppet' forces in China and Manchuria we should give a brief summary of the state of the country at the beginning of this period.

China in the late 1920s was a land of turmoil and civil strife, which had only just been forcibly united by the Nationalist Government of Chiang Kai-shek in 1928. After the fall of the Imperial Dynasty in 1912 the country had been blighted by civil wars, with weak central governments and large parts of the country ruled by provincial governors or 'warlords'. The only real unifying influence in China during this time was provided by the Chinese Nationalist Party founded by Sun Yat-sen who advocated Western style democracy. Sun and his Kuomintiang Party had participated in the first attempts at democratic government in 1911 which failed dismally. By the time of Sun's death in 1924 the Kuomintiang or KMT, now under the leadership of Chiang Kai-shek, had decided that the only way to defeat the Warlords was by military means.

The KMT formed their own revolutionary army and trained their officers at the Wampoa Academy with the help of Soviet advisors in the same year. By 1926 they were ready to advance northwards from their Canton base and launched their Northern Military Expedition on 1 July 1926. After two years of hard fighting the warlords of central and northern China were either defeated in battle by the better-trained and motivated KMT, or brought over to the Nationalist side by negotiation. By 1928, China was, at least outwardly, united under a central Nationalist government in Nanking. In reality however, much of the country was still in the hands of warlords who had little real loyalty to Chiang Kai-shek and his government. Some of the most prominent provincial KMT leaders were looking for the first chance to rebel against the Nanking regime. After a series of rebellions from 1929 to early 1931 Chiang seemed to have finally secured the country when the next threat to his government came from a foreign source.

A weak and divided China was ripe for exploitation by Imperial Japan, which had been going through a period of empire building ever since its first victory against the Chinese in the first Sino-Japanese War of 1894–5. Japan had been trying to expand its territory and acquire more 'living space' for its ever-growing population. At the same time Japan needed to acquire badly needed resources for its growing industrial capacity. China, with its unlimited land and natural resources, was the obvious target for Imperial Japan's expansionist dreams.

The first piece in the imperialist jigsaw took place on 18 September 1931, when an incident occurred on the Japanese-owned South Manchurian Railway near Mukden. An explosion charge placed by Japanese soldiers was blamed on Chinese anti-Japanese agents. This gave the Japanese Kwangtung Army a pretext for a full scale invasion of Manchuria which, on the orders of Chiang Kai-shek, was only slightly resisted. Chiang wanted the Japanese to take the whole blame for any aggression and ordered the local commander, Chang Hsueh-liang and his troops not to resist. This allowed the Japanese to quickly disarm the Chinese defenders and by February 1932 they had control over most of Manchuria, which was then proclaimed as the state of Manchukuo (Land of the Manchu's), with the last C'hing Emperor of China, Henry Pu-Yi, as first a figurehead 'Chief Executive' from 1932, and then from 1934 as Emperor of the Empire of Manchukuo. This new nation was soon encouraged to raise its own army, navy and air force with all the trappings of an independent state, while under the firm control of the Japanese.

After the establishment of their first client state the Japanese did not sit back on their laurels and in 1933 invaded the province of Jehol, which was quickly added to the territory of Manchukuo. At the same time various Japanese intrigues were set in motion with a view to encouraging the genuine Chinese opposition to Chiang Kai-shek's government. These usually took the form of locally organised mini-states in northern China, which were intended to be short term irritants to the Chinese government.

Other Japanese schemes included short-lived regimes in the Province of Chahar, part of Inner Mongolia, and two campaigns in 1935 and 1936 to conquer the Province of Suiyuan. Japanese military and secret service personnel were involved in these intrigues in which they waged 'war by proxy' with the Chinese government by using satellite and 'puppet' troops. These troops were fighting for the independence of Inner Mongolia under the leadership of Prince Teh Wang who had recently thrown in his lot with the Japanese.

All the pretence of the undeclared war between the Japanese and Nationalist Chinese ended with the Marco Polo Bridge Incident of 7 July 1937. A minor skirmish between Japanese and Chinese soldiers was exploited by the former to begin a full-scale invasion of Northern China. The Japanese quickly swept all before them, soon leading to the fall of Peking (31 July) Shanghai (November) and Nanking (13 December). As the Imperial Japanese Army advanced southwards through Northern China and down the Eastern seaboard in late 1937 and into 1938 they set up committees or associations in every city or town they occupied. These committees were made up of local Chinese dignitaries who were willing to co-operate and collaborate with the Japanese. Many of the Chinese were elderly former officials of the pre-1928 period who came out of the woodwork tempted by the chance to once again hold office, even if that meant under the Japanese. Japanese military authorities were happy to use these committees and their members until some more substantial form of 'puppet' government could be put in place.

The first major 'puppet' government was inaugurated in Northern China, in Peking, in December 1937, under the title of the 'Provisional Government of China'. This new government under the leadership of Wang Ke-min, a pre-1928 politician, set the tone for future states. It was sponsored by the local Japanese military command with little reference to their own government in Tokyo. After the fall of Nanking in December 1937 a rival government to the Peking regime was inaugurated in that city under the title 'Reformed Government of China'. Both the Provisional and Reformed governments were allowed to raise limited military forces of 41,000 and 10,000 respectively. Both these governments were made redundant by the establishment of the Wang Ching-wei regime in Nanking in March 1940. Meant to be the new national regime of China, the so-called Reorganised Government of China was given much more support by the Japanese than the previous incarnations. The Reorganised or Nanking regime survived until the surrender of Japan in August 1945. During its lifetime the Nanking Government had at least 500,000 men in its armed forces and even had the temerity to declare war on the Allied Powers in 1943. All the 'puppet' governments died with the fall of Japan but many of their army's soldiers went on to fight in the armies of both the Communists and Nationalists. The Communists especially were pragmatic enough to realise that most 'puppet' troops had fought to fill their rice bowls and most ordinary soldiers went unpunished. Their political leaders fared rather worse with nearly all of them facing show trials under the returning Nationalists and then, when found guilty, facing the firing squad.

Chronology

1931

18 September: Japanese invasion of the Chinese province of Manchuria following the Mukden Incident. By February 1932 they control most of the province including all the towns and cities.

1932

18 February: Proclamation of new state of 'Manchukuo' with ex-Chinese Emperor, Henry Pu Yi as 'Chief Executive'. Throughout 1932 and into 1933, large numbers of anti-Japanese resistance fighters struggle in Manchuria against the Japanese invaders against the orders of, and without the support of, the Chinese Central Government.

1933

January–March: Japanese invasion of Chinese province of Jehol, which is added to the territory of Manchukuo. Manchukoan units take part in the campaign under Japanese command.

31 May: Signing of Tangku Truce which set up a 'De-Militarised Zone' in the area north of the Great Wall. All Chinese and Japanese troops were to withdraw from the region and it was to be policed by a 'neutral' force.

1934

Coronation of Henry Pu Yi as Emperor of Manchukuo.

1935

25 November: Inauguration of East Hopei State under the leadership of Jin Ju-keng

1936

Prince Teh Wang's declaration of the Inner Mongolian 'puppet' state. Suiyuan Campaign – Inner Mongolians with Japanese support fight against Chinese Central Government forces to try and take control of the province.

1937

14 December: Inauguration of 'Provisional Government' of China in Peking with Wang Ke-min as president.

1938

28 March: Inauguration of 'Reformed Government' of China in Nanking with Liang Hung-chih as Chief.

1939

Nomonhan Incident between Japan and Soviet Union involves Manchukuoan units.

1940–45

The situation in China stabilises with the country divided into zones controlled by the Communists, Nationalists and the Japanese with their Nanking 'puppets'. A substantial increase in Communist guerrilla activity in Manchukuo and the north of China during this period leads to a much greater role for 'puppet' troops in the fight against them.

1940

30 March: Formation of 'Reorganised' Government of China in Nanking under Wang Ching-wei which officially unifies the former Provisional and Reformed Governments into one body. In reality the Provisional Government under Wang Ke-min retains much of its power under the title of 'North China Political Council'.

1941

Formation of Nanking Government Air Force.

1943

9 January: The Nanking Government, under heavy pressure from Japan, declares war on the Allied powers, Great Britain and the United States.

1944

10 November: Death of Wang Ching-wei in a Tokyo clinic, he is succeeded by his deputy Chou Fo-hai, who continues to run the Nanking regime in the same vein.

1945

8 August: The Soviet Union informs Japan that a state of war exists between them; this is followed 70 minutes later by the invasion of Japanese-controlled Manchukuo. The Soviet invasion force consists of 1,600,000 men, 5,550 tanks, 28,000 artillery pieces and 4,370 aircraft. In a blitzkrieg campaign the 1,000,000 poorly equipped men of the Japanese Kwangtung Army and the 200,000 strong Manchukuoan Army are easily defeated.

2 September: Formal surrender of Empire of Japan means swift collapse of all 'puppet' governments in China. Nanking, Peking and all major cities of China are retaken by Nationalist and Allied forces often with the co-operation of former 'puppet' troops. Manchuria is largely taken over by Communists who absorb large numbers of former Manchukuoan troops into their army.

Chinese 'Puppet' Soldiers 1931–45

For centuries the soldiery of China had one of the lowest statuses in society and were regarded by the rest of the population as at best a necessary evil. Military service was often a last resort for Chinese peasants, and con-scription and press-ganging had to be employed to fill the ranks. Soldiers were often nothing better than bandits in uniform and the average 'puppet' soldier was regarded as the lowest of the low.

The term 'puppet' soldier was the general name given by the Chinese to any man who served in an army which fought with or on behalf of the Imperial Japanese Army from 1931 to 1945. Another term often used to describe these men was 'traitor' because that was how the vast majority of Chinese people regarded them. Whether the soldier was fighting in the Army of the Empire of Manchukuo, the Army of the Nanking Government of Wang Ching-wei or in any of the five or six other armies described in this book, he would be called a 'puppet'. The governments that these men fought for were called 'puppet' governments and their armies were therefore called 'puppet' armies. The term 'puppet' referred to the fact that these governments had no real power, with their masters the Japanese holding all the power and 'pulling their strings', hence 'puppets'. When well treated, trained and motivated the average Chinese soldier was a match for the combatants of any nation. Unfortunately, neither the Chinese 'puppet' governments or their Japanese masters were willing to pro-vide much in the way of training and motivation. What they were willing to provide in most cases was the rice to fill the soldiers bowl when the rest of the population was starving and a uniform when most of the population were wearing rags.

The average 'puppet' soldier had no great dislike for the Nationalist and Communist forces that they were supposed to be fighting. Most of them were recruited to fight for the Japanese-backed government after service in the Nationalist Army or were brought over en-masse by their defecting commanding officer. The Chinese sol-dier had always had a history of personal loyalty to his commander which often outweighed any loyalty to the central government. Soldiers who defected to the Nanking Regime were not usually expressing any great affec-tion for the Wang-Ching wei government but were often making a rational decision to survive. Service with a 'puppet' army meant that at least they would be clothed and more importantly fed. By joining the Nanking Army they were guaranteed to have their rice bowl filled. Others were bribed or threatened into fighting for the Japanese and were sometimes sent to serve far from home.

Some soldiers were recruited in Manchukuo to serve in China and the methods used to recruit them were often unsavoury. The families of the men were kept back in Manchukuo where they were under the control of the Japanese. Families of soldiers were virtual hostages and ensured the 'loyalty' of the men when serving far from home. On one occasion a unit of Communist guerrillas were surrounded by a battalion of Manchukuoan soldiers. During a verbal exchange between the guerrilla leader and the Manchukoan commander the

Communist tried to persuade the 'puppet' soldiers to desert. The Manchukoan officer explained that when they were recruited by the Japanese all the men's families had been registered. He further explained that if his men refused to fight or deserted to the Communists their families would all be killed. Although the 'puppet' battalion could not be persuaded to join the guerrillas they sent them on their way with the warning, "Do not go in that direction; there are machine gun nests there and the gunners are Japanese."

On another occasion in southern Manchukuo a Communist guerrilla unit wished to occupy a town which was garrisoned by a few hundred Manchukoan soldiers. The guerrilla leader sent a message to the Manchukoan commander stating that his men wanted to rest in the town for a while and that he had no desire to fight the 'puppet' soldiers. He advised them to withdraw temporarily while his men entered the town and the Manchukoan commander replied that he needed 30 minutes to evacuate his men to the mountains on the outskirts of the hamlet. The guerrilla force then entered the town and spent the day relaxing and giving political speeches to the civilian population. As dusk fell the Manchukuoan soldiers grew anxious that the Japanese might discover their actions and began continuous whistling as a signal that they would like the Communists to go on their way. The guerrilla commander then ordered his men to march out of town, but not before leaving a message for his Manchukuoan counterpart thanking him for his hospitality.

The Communist and Nationalist soldiers and guerrillas often had so called 'Live and Let Live' agreements with the 'puppet' soldiers operating in their areas. These agreements proved that the majority of 'puppet' troops had no real desire to fight their countrymen. Many instances of how this 'Live and let Live' policy worked can be taken from eyewitness accounts. One instance involved a unit of Communist guerrillas whose machine gun was broken and who sent a farmer to ask the local 'puppet' unit to loan them one of theirs while it was repaired! The 'puppet' troops agreed as long as the machine gun was returned to them before the next Japanese inspection. On another occasion a unit of guerrillas came under fire during a night operation near a 'puppet' outpost. The next day a messenger was sent to the guerrilla encampment to apologise and to explain that the 'puppet' soldiers had to fire because they had Japanese troops with them and they hoped that none of them had been hurt. On another occasion in North China in 1938 a 'puppet' unit involved in a fight with a guerrilla force fired into the air so as not to hit their opponents. By accident one of the 'puppet' soldiers fired too low and actually managed to hit one of the guerrillas, killing him. A few days later the 'puppet' troops sent a delegation into guerrilla territory to apologise profusely for this 'terrible' mistake.

Some 'puppet' soldiers had been duped into joining the Nanking Government forces and in her book *Battle Hymn of China*, published in 1943, Agnes Smedley relates an interview she had with some 'puppet' soldiers captured by the Communists:

Chinese traitors were brought in every week and in the middle of February I talked with twenty 'puppet' soldiers who had been captured in a battle between the guerrillas and a 'puppet' army commanded by Wang Bu-ching. The captured 'puppet' soldiers were sad-eyed, dreary looking men who said that they had been forced into the 'puppet' army. After the capture of Hankow, one said, the Japanese had come to his village in Hwangpei and burned it to the ground, Hearing that coolies were wanted to build a Chinese railway, he and five friends had gone to a Chinese recruiting agent; they were led up the Han River to Churhushan and then told they were in Wang Bu-ching's army. They knew nothing at all about political matters but Commander Wang had delivered a speech in which he said that his chief, Wang Ching-wei had really been sent by Generalissimo Chiang Kai-shek to make peace with the Japanese, and that was why Wang Ching-wei was in Nanking. He also told them that a representative of the Central Government served in his headquarters as an adviser. The soldiers said that they had had no way of knowing if such things were true or not.

An example of the attitude of 'puppet' soldiers to their Japanese masters was provided by two Europeans who escaped from detention in Peking. During their escape they lost their way and stumbled into an area controlled by 'puppet' troops. They were arrested by a 'puppet' sentry whose attitude changed when he realised that the two men were Allied nationals. He then surprisingly warned them that the village he was guarding had a Japanese garrison. After hiding the two men he contacted a local guerrilla group who took them to a safe area. One guerrilla leader who was trying to make his way from Manchukuo to the Peking region by train rather naively asked a 'puppet' policeman for directions to guerrilla territory! He was helped out of Peking by 'puppet' soldiers and directed on his way to a Communist 8th Route Army controlled area. When he arrived in Communist territory he was promptly arrested as they did not believe his far-fetched story.

The Japanese operating in the Chinese countryside were notorious for their treatment of any civilians who they captured. Most male captives would be killed and in many cases all captives, including women and children, were slaughtered. Some reports of the period state that on some occasions the Chinese 'puppet' troops were even more brutal than their Japanese masters. One Chinese eyewitness of late 1943 in Western Hupeh claimed that the 'puppet' soldiers laid waste to the area they were operating in and killed anyone who fell into their hands. Two Western missionaries working in the province of Shansi during a two year period in the early 1940s also bore witness to this brutal behaviour by 'puppet' troops. The reputation of Chinese soldiery during the first half of the 20th Century was always bad and the military were generally looked down on by the rest of the population. Soldiering was considered a lowly profession throughout Chinese history, and military men who were also considered traitors by the vast majority of the population would have been particularly despised.

Contribution of 'Puppet' Troops to the Japanese War Effort

When gauging the the contribution that the Manchukuoan and Chinese 'puppet' troops made to the war effort of Imperial Japan we can take into account various factors. The fact that there were over a 1,000,000 'puppet' soldiers under arms means that by sheer weight of numbers they must have had some effect. One comparison we could make is with the Russian and Baltic volunteers who fought for the German Army on the Eastern Front from 1941–45. At first the German High Command was loath to employ 'racially inferior' volunteers, no matter how anti-Communist they were, to fight for them. But as the German manpower shortage and military reverses began to take effect as the war continued they had to change their attitudes. In the same way, the Japanese Imperial Army had the same racially superior attitude towards their Chinese and Manchukoan volunteers. In fact the Japanese attitude to the Chinese under their command was even more superior as they regarded themselves as God's chosen race and everyone else, especially their fellow Asians, as inferior. As their occupation of China wore on, and more Japanese units had to be transferred to the Pacific Theatre, they also had to rethink their policies. They decided that their 'puppet' troops would have to be used in a pro-active role to help combat the increasing Communist guerrilla resistance. Although they were usually not very effective in their role, the 'puppet' soldiers at least gave the Japanese additional manpower to try and govern the vast territories they controlled.

CHAPTER TWO

The Manchukuoan Army 1932–45

When the Japanese invaded Manchuria in September 1931 they almost immediately set up the 'puppet' state of Manchukuo, which was duly proclaimed on 18 February 1932. As soon as they had consolidated their hold over the country they began to raise an army to help them control the population. The first recruits for the Manchukuoan Army came from the former soldiers of the pre-invasion ruler of the province, Chang Hsueh-liang. Because Chiang Kai-shek wanted the blame for the invasion of Manchuria to fall fully on the Japanese he had ordered Chang's troops to offer little resistance to the invasion. This lack of resistance by the Manchurian soldiers meant that large numbers of them were captured and disarmed by the Japanese. In time-honoured Chinese fashion many of the defeated soldiers were recruited, either individually or more commonly *en-masse*, into the new Manchukoan Army.

The first volunteers to fight for Japan in Manchuria were groups of irregular horsemen who attached themselves to the invading army in late 1931 and acted as scouts. These volunteers were unofficially raised by the local Japanese commanders and were made up usually of deserters from the Nationalist Army or were ordinary bandits looking for a new employer. One such unit was under the command of the former Nationalist commander of Taonan in Heilungkiang Province, Chang Hai-pong. He was persuaded by the Japanese to command a Frontier Public Security Corps as well as acting as Governor of Heilungkiang Province. After receiving arms and ammunition from the Japanese, Chang changed sides again on 19 November. Another unit was attached to the 77th Infantry Regiment in November 1931 and were photographed in action by the Japanese press on the 26th of that month.

After the successful invasion of Manchuria the Japanese soon began to plan the formation of some kind of army for the new state of Manchukuo. The Manchukuoan Armed Forces were formed officially with the proclamation of the Army and Navy Act of 15 April 1932. This act called for the peace of the state of Manchukuo to be maintained by the Manchukuoan Army and Navy. These Armed Forces were to be formed from amongst the former Army and Naval forces of the 'Young Marshal' Chang Hsueh-liang. According to the Organic Law of the new government the post of Chief Executive held by Pu Yi was to have "The Supreme Command of the Military, Naval and Air forces". Approximately 60,000 of the Young Marshal's former troops gave themselves up to the Japanese and many were absorbed into the new Manchukuoan Army.

The early Manchukuoan Army was regarded by the Japanese as totally unreliable and during the early anti-bandit operations it performed badly. In May 1932 a 2,000 strong force of Manchukuoan troops were operating against a group of 'bandits' at Nungan, 35 miles north of Changchun. Eyewitnesses present at the time noted that the soldiers were "driven like sheep" by the guerrillas. Manchukuoan soldiers in the early days of the state were mainly recruited from the former forces of the Young Marshal Chang Hsieh-Liang. Although Chang Hsieh-liang's Army was large in number, many of its soldiers were of poor quality and doubtful loyalty. Although the Japanese would have been fully aware of the Manchurian Army's unreliability they did provide them with a ready trained pool of men which meant that they could quickly raise a Manchukuoan Army.

The Emperor of Manchukuo, Pu-Yi is pictured at the time of his coronation in 1934 wearing his dress uniform. As the last emperor of Imperial China until his overthrow in 1911 he wears a mixture of Chinese and Manchukuoan decorations. Dress uniforms worn by the Emperor and his entourage had a 'comic opera' appearance and further reinforced the outside world's image of Manchukuo as a puppet state.

Masuo Fujita

The Young Marshal's Army was made up mostly of raw recruits and irregulars and a high proportion of them were opium addicts. These same men were now serving in the Manchukuoan Army and it is hardly surprising that they did not make the best fighting material. The loyalty of the men was constantly called into question and this was demonstrated by the number of mutinies that took place at this time. For instance in August 1932 a unit of 2,000 men mutinied at Wukimiho and went over to the guerrillas. Around the same time the whole of the 7th Manchukuoan Cavalry Regiment was reported to have deserted to the anti-Japanese fighters. The first few years of the Manchukuo regime's life were spent in fighting large number of 'bandit' groups. The Manchukuo Army was regarded as a good supply of arms and ammunition by the bandits and a Japanese officer Fujimoto said "Unfortunately one of the main sources of supply of weapons and ammunition to the bandits is the Manchukuoan Army. There have been cases where the Manchurian troops to all appearances went out to battle with the enemy, but in reality handed over their weapons to the opponent".

The Manchukuoan Army was divided into an Independent Cavalry Corps to provide the capital a garrison; a special Guard Corps was formed in February 1933 as part of the capital garrison and this was recruited from men of Manchu ancestry, and a 'Provincial Guard Corps' was raised in each of the 7 provinces of the new state. The new army was reduced from the pre-Manchukuo days of 300,000 under the command of the Young Marshal to a more manageable 111,000 men. Soldiers who had served in the Young Marshal's Army were regarded as unreliable and would be replaced by more reliable recruits when circumstances allowed. In 1934 a new law was proclaimed which ordered that from now on only officers who had training organised by the Manchukuoan Government could serve in the Army. This law was instituted to try and expel all the former officers of the Nationalist Army of the Young Marshal. After the takeover of Manchuria in 1931 many of the commanders of the Nationalist Army simply continued in their former command under the new 'puppet' state. The old system of army commanders acting as 'warlords' over the area they controlled and using their command area as a personal fiefdom continued at first. This law would, the Japanese hoped, give them a legitimate excuse to get rid of these corrupt officers and replace them with their own reliable candidates.

Establishment of Manchukuo Army 1932	
Fengtien Guard Army	**20,541**
Headquarters	678
1st Teaching Unit	2,718
1st Mixed Brigade	2,467
2nd Mixed Brigade	2,104
3rd Mixed Brigade	2,467
4th Mixed Brigade	1,755
5th Mixed Brigade	1,291
6th Mixed Brigade	2,238
7th Mixed Brigade	2,014
1st Cavalry Brigade	1,098
2nd Cavalry Brigade	1,625
Jilin Guard Army	**34,287**
Headquarters	1,447
2nd Teaching Unit	2,718
Cavalry Detachment	1,295
Infantry Detachment	1,163
4th Infantry Brigade	3,548
5th Infantry Brigade	3,244
2nd Infantry Brigade	2,343
8th Infantry Brigade	2,301
3rd Infantry Brigade	2,496
1st Infantry Brigade	2,301
7th Infantry Brigade	2,343
4th Cavalry Brigade	2,037

1st Cavalry Brigade	1,867
2nd Cavalry Brigade	1,598
3rd Cavalry Brigade	1,598
Yilan Unit	706
North Manchuria Railway Guard Force Headquarters	151
Sanrin Unit	1,452
Heilongjiang Guard Army	**25,162**
Headquarters	1,016
3rd Teaching Unit	2,718
1st Cavalry Brigade	2,244
2nd Mixed Brigade	3,085
5th Mixed Brigade	1,934
1st Mixed Brigade	3,085
3rd Mixed Brigade	3,085
4th Mixed Brigade	3,085
2nd Cavalry Brigade	2,244
3rd Cavalry Brigade	2,666
East Hingganling Guard Army	1,818
North Hingganling Guard Army	874
South Hingganling Guard Army	1,682
Rehe Guard Army	**17,945**
Headquarters	301
Artillery Unit	854
Cavalry Unit	172
Infantry Unit	1,294
Chengde Area Forces	4,783
Chifeng Area Forces	3,414
Chaoyang Area Forces	3,977
Weichang Area Forces	3,150
Seian Army 'Fangtien'	3,760
Xinjing Cavalry Brigade	2,018
River Fleet	640
Total	**111,044 men**

At the Coronation of the Manchukuoan Emperor Pu-Yi in April 1934 a line of Imperial Guard Cavalry stand to attention. They are dressed in uniforms made of Japanese khaki with a peaked cap, high collared tunic and breeches worn with high leather boots. Their lances have the pennant with the colours from the fly of the Manchukuoan flag on a field of yellow

Philip Jowett Collection

In August 1934 a major reorganisation of the Manchukuoan military establishment took place with five administrative districts being formed, each divided into 2 or 3 zones. Each zone had 1 or 2 Mixed Brigades with a higher ratio of cavalry and artillery in each brigade and after this reorganisation the Manchukuoan Army's formation was as follows.

Establishment of Manchukuo Army 1935

1st District Army 'Fengtien'   12,321
Commanding Officer: General Yu Chih-shan
HQ
1st Teaching Unit
1st Mixed Brigade
2nd Mixed Brigade
3rd Mixed Brigade
4th Mixed Brigade
5th Mixed Brigade
6th Mixed Brigade

2nd District Army 'Kirin'   13,185
Commanding Officer: General Chi Hsing
HQ
2nd Teaching Unit
7th Mixed Brigade
8th Mixed Brigade
9th Mixed Brigade
10th Mixed Brigade
2nd Cavalry Brigade
3rd Cavalry Brigade
4th Cavalry Brigade

3rd District Army 'Qigihar'   13,938
Commanding Officer: General Chang Wen-tao
HQ
3rd Teaching Unit
11th Mixed Brigade
12th Mixed Brigade
13th Mixed Brigade
14th Mixed Brigade
15th Mixed Brigade
5th Cavalry Brigade

4th District Army 'Harbin'   17,827
Commanding Officer: General Yu Cheng-shen
HQ
4th Teaching Unit
16th Mixed Brigade
17th Mixed Brigade
18th Mixed Brigade
19th Mixed Brigade
20th Mixed Brigade
21st Mixed Brigade
22nd Mixed Brigade
23rd Mixed Brigade
6th Cavalry Brigade

5th District Army 'Chengde'   9,294
Commanding Officer: General Chang Hai-peng
HQ
5th Teaching Unit
24th Mixed Brigade
25th Mixed Brigade
26th Mixed Brigade
7th Cavalry Brigade

Other Units

East Hingganling Guard Army	929
West Hingganling Guard Army	858
North Hingganling Guard Army	656
South Hingganling Guard Army	1,052
Seian Guard Army ' Fangtien'	2,769
1st Xingjing Cavalry Brigade	2,311
River Fleet	719

Total   **79,329 men**

Organisation of Units in Manchukuoan Army
Mixed Brigade (A) Version:
2,414 men – 817 horses, Headquarters, 2 Infantry Regiments, 1 Cavalry Regiment,

Mortar or Artillery Company
Mixed Brigade (B) Version:
1,515 men – 700 horses, Headquarters, 1 Infantry Regiment, 1 Cavalry Regiment,

Mortar or Artillery Company.
Cavalry Brigade (A) Version:
1,500 men – 1,500 horses, Headquarters, 3 Cavalry Regiments, Mortar or Artillery Company.

This lonely Manchukoan sentry is wearing civilian dress and would be indistinguishable from the bandits he is on the lookout for. Poorly equipped and trained Manchukuoan units were easy prey for the anti-Japanese guerrillas during the first years of the new state. As the worst elements were weeded out of the army by the Japanese the performance of the Manchukuoan Army did improve. The only insignia worn by some of these early Manchukuoan anti-bandit forces was a yellow armband while the 'bandits' usually wore red coloured ones.

Philip Jowett Collection

Cavalry Brigade (B) Version:
1,075 men – 1,077 horses, Headquarters, 2 Cavalry Regiments, Mortar or Artillery Company.

Infantry Regiment:
899 men – 117 horses, Headquarters, 2 Infantry Battalions with 3 Infantry Companies and 1 Machine gun Company and 1 Mortar Company each.

Cavalry Regiment:
458 men – 484 horses, Headquarters, 3 Cavalry Companies, 1 Machine gun Company.

Teaching Unit:
1,614 men – 717 horses, Headquarters, Teaching Section, Infantry Regiment, Cavalry Regiment, Artillery Regiment, Cadet Company.

Manchukuoan Military Training

The Japanese were determined to build up the Manchukuoan Army in the late 1930s and to improve its reliability and efficiency. Military Training Schools were opened in Mukden and Hsinking with mixed success with both opening in 1938.

Manchukuoan Central Training School – Mukden

The main training academy for Manchukuoan officers was opened sometime in 1938 in Mukden under the command of Lieutenant-General Kuo En-Lin. On 19 November 1938 the first 200 officer cadets graduated from the Academy. In January 1939, 48 Infantry and 24 Cavalry Cadets graduated from the Central Training School and

A mixed force of Japanese and Manchukoan soldiers set out on an anti-bandit operation from their base. The Manchukuoan Cavalry contingent of the force are wearing grey cotton uniforms with straw sun hats. Insignia on the Manchukuoan Cavalry collars would be in the green colour of that branch of the army.

Philip Jowett Collection

This mortar crew of the Manchukuoan Army in the early 1930s are wearing the grey uniform in general service until the mid 1930s. Mortars were often used in China as a substitute for the lack of field artillery and were relatively easily manufactured in local warlords' arsenals.

Masuo Fujita

after 3 months probation they became 2nd Lieutenants. This number was increased in January 1940 when 97 Cadets graduated with 90 of the Cadets being Manchukuoans and 7 being Koreans. After this class the number of willing native recruits seemed to have dried up and this led in the same year to the induction of a number of Japanese cadets with 174 successful applicants from an initial application of 2,000. The successful recruits were to receive the same training as the Manchukuoans and after completion of the course they were to become 2nd Lieutenants in the Army as well as in the Japanese Reserves.

Information on the Hsingking Military Academy is not really available but we do know that its first graduation ceremony took place on 1 July 1938, when 34 graduates passed out. Plans were also put in place in December 1939 for a programme of military training to take place in selected elementary schools by Manchukoan officers to begin in Spring 1940. The Manchukuoans were to be supervised by Japanese 'Military Inspecting Officers' who were to keep an eye on their allies. Other training schools set up by the Japanese in an attempt to improve the standard of the Manchukoan Army included:

Army Signal School (Commanding Officer: Lieutenant-General Wang Chih Yu)
Army Medical School (Commanding Officer: Colonel Chou Nai P'eng)
Gendarmarie Training School (Commanding Officer: Lieutenant-General Ying Chen Fu)

Mongol Military Academy

The ethnic Mongolian population of Manchukuo provided a large number of recruits to the Manchukuoan Army and made up the majority of the Cavalry force. In an attempt to foster the martial spirit of the Mongolians in Manchukuo it was decided to open a Mongol Military Officers' Academy in the South of Hsingian Province. The Academy was opened in 1934 at the small town of Wang Yeh-Miao, which was garrisoned by Japanese troops. When first opened in March 1934 the academy was sited in existing buildings in the town before suitable new barracks could be constructed. The two year course was to include a great deal of religious and other classes which aimed to create 'Good Mongols' who were proud of their history. Japanese Reserve Officers acted as instructors at the Academy and were told foster the cadets Mongolian Martial spirit. Japanese cadets who were to go on to serve in the Mongol units of the Manchukuoan Army were also accepted into the Academy. The first years course began with 100 cadets, with 64 graduating in June 1936, and although we do not know how many completed the course in 1937, in 1938 only 34 graduated.

Japanese Advisors in the Manchukuoan Army

The Manchukuoan Army, Navy and Air Force were trained and supported by a system of Japanese Advisors who dominated every aspect of the 'puppet' state's Armed Forces.

As soon as the decision to raise a Manchukuoan Army was taken by the Japanese they set up a team of advisors. The first 22-strong group of Japanese Army and Navy advisors was sent to help in the organisation of the new army. A more formal structure for the training group was introduced in July 1932 with the setting up of a

A motley looking unit of Manchukoan Army soldiers are pictured at night preparing to take part in the invasion of Jehol Province under Japanese command. None of the men appear to be wearing the same combination of uniforms although all are wearing the early pattern fur hat. The flag with single five-pointed star is somewhat of a mystery on it and bears no relation to the Manchukuoan national flag.

Illustrated London News

Military Adviser Department under the jurisdiction of the Manchukuo Ministry of Defence. The Military Adviser Department allocated advisers to each garrison area under the existing system and each military district after the reorganisation of the Manchukuoan Army. One of the main problems in the early days of this system was the shortage of advisers, who were a little thin on the ground. The advisers were also not usually of high enough rank to give them the authority they needed to control the officers of the Manchukoan Army.

This problem of lack of authority led to difficulties with the Manchukuoan Army officers, who were largely former officers of the Nationalist Young Marshal's Army. All other Chinese 'puppet' armies were recruited using a few ex-Nationalist officers but not on the scale of the Manchukuoan Army. The large number of former Nationalist Army officers in the Manchkuoan Army were able to resist the changes introduced by the Japanese. They were particularly obstructive when they felt that changes affected the power and influence they had previously enjoyed. Not surprisingly the Japanese were determined to assert their control over the Manchukuoan Army and introduced a three tier system to achieve this. This new system would they hoped create enough Japanese advisers to control all Manchukuoan units from the highest down to smallest level. The first tier consisted of serving officers of the Kwangtung Army who served in the Manchkuoan Army Headquarters. These higher-ranking officers held all the power in the Army and were helped in this by having the only access to the ammunition stores. Although officially having a mainly advisory role they were in fact in complete control and this was even more so when the higher ranks of the Manchukuoan Army were filled with more pliable and 'loyal' officers. A second tier consisted of retired or reserve officers from Japan who had been officially invited over to Manchukuo. In time every regiment in the army had a Japanese Training Officer and every battalion, company or squadron had an adviser. At first these advisers were allowed to wear their old Japanese uniforms but they were subordinate to active serving Japanese officers. These reserve officers were given a rank one grade higher than their former rank in the Japanese Army. The third tier consisted of Japanese officers who were former NCO's who had been released by the Japanese Army. These men were borderline officer material who had just missed out on promotion and were willing to become officers in the Manchukuoan Army. This grade of officer were seen as a vanguard for the hoped-for the immigration of Japanese to Manchukuo. Although these men were part of the Manchukuoan Army and wore the 'puppet' army's uniform their loyalty was still to the Japanese Emperor. After taking training courses alongside Manchukuoan officers the Japanese were to be posted as platoon commanders. The more senior or able of these officers then went on to take an advanced course and then took up the role of company or battalion commander.

Mongolians in the Manchukuoan Army

The ethnic Mongolian population of Manchukuo was 1,112,000 and lived mainly in Hsingan Province with smaller numbers in Lungkiang Province. Mongols came from the Khalkhas, Buriat, Daghor, Olot and Barga tribes with all having a reputation as good cavalrymen. Mongolians made up a substantial part of the Manchukuoan Army and provided the vast majority of its cavalry. As with their illustrious ancestors who had conquered a vast empire in the Middle Ages they were renowned for their horsemanship and were mounted on small and sturdy Mongolian ponies. They were armed in the early days of Manchukuo with lances and sabres and various models of carbine and rifles left over from the Young Marshal's Army. With the standard-isation of the weaponry in use with the Manchukuoan Army they were then equipped with the Japanese Type 44 carbine. According to Manchukuoan publications of the period the most prestigious unit of the Manchukuoan cavalry was the 'Hsingan Brigade'. The Japanese employed the Manchukuoan cavalry mainly in scouting and reconnaissance roles and to provide flank guards. During the Nomonhan Incident between the Soviet Union and the Japanese in 1939 Manchukuoan Cavalry were employed in this role.

According to a British Intelligence report of 1947 the Mongolian region was divided up into 2 defence zones in 1935, which doubled to 4 zones in 1936. In 1937 they were again reduced to 2 zones and given the designation of the 9th and 10th Military Headquarters with a Mongol General in command in each. According to the same report the number of ethnic Mongolian troops in each Defence zone was 3,000 men. If the figure is to be believed, the fact that by 1945 over 1,200 Mongol Officers and 60,000 other ranks had been trained for service in the Manchukuoan Army meant that there was a very large turnover of men. Whether this high turnover was due to a high rate of desertion or another factor is not known.

Manchukuoan Army Equipment

In the early days of the Manchukuoan Army small arms came mainly from 'war booty' taken from the former Nationalist Garrison of Manchuria. There were a wide number of different types of rifle in use with the Nationalists in Manchuria and the Manchukuoan Army inherited these. There were 26 different types of rifle in use with the Manchukoan Army and 20 kinds of pistol, which of course led to problems with logistics. Various types of Chinese produced copies of the Mauser rifle were in service as well as versions of the Austrian Mannlicher and Steyr rifles.

Obviously there were great problems created by the large number of types of rifle in service and plans were put underway to introduce the Japanese Arisaka 38 rifle and carbines as the standard models. The first step towards this was taken in 1935 with the issue of 50,000 Type 38 carbines to the Manchukoan cavalry. Over the next 2 to 3 years the infantry were gradually issued with the Type 38 rifle and by the early 1940s this was just about complete. By 1945 the Manchukuoan Army was certainly issued with the same weaponry as their Japanese allies, even if they were often the older pattern. Second line and Local Defence Guard units were probably issued with the cast-off Chinese rifles as they were no longer needed by the Manchukuoan Regular Army. The Local Defence Guard were issued with obsolete Japanese, rifles such as the Murata 1880 model and even the 1877 Snider breechloading musket, similar to the type used by the Union and Confederate Armies in the American Civil War of 1861–65!

Machine guns were again of various makes previously in service with the Nationalist Armies in Manchuria pre-1931. The Czech ZB30 light machine gun was the most popular model of light machine gun but as with all other Chinese weaponry just about every model produced in the world saw service in the Nationalist Army and therefore found its way into Manchukoan service. Heavy machine guns, for instance, could have been Chinese-made copies of the German Maxim 08 water-cooled models or imported French Hotchkiss air-cooled models. In 1936 the ZB30s were replaced with Japanese Type 11 light machine guns and 4 were issued to each company with plans to increase this number to 6 or even 8, but these were never completed. Japanese heavy machine guns were introduced into service with the Manchukuoan Army and these were the elderly Type 3 (1914) model. A Machine Gun Company had 4 Type 3s and plans were laid to replace this model with the 7.7mm Type 92 heavy machine gun, but again this was not fulfilled before the end of the war.

In 1933 the number of rifles and machine guns in service was 77,268 rifles, 441 light machine guns and 329 heavy machine guns.

This Manchukuoan gun crew are serving a 75mm field piece which was probably from the artillery park of the former ruler of Manchuria, the Young Marshal. Although the early Manchukuoan Army was fairly large in numbers heavier equipment such as this was in short supply. Some more modern weaponry was supplied by Japan but never in the quantities needed to make the Manchukuoan Army more than a policing and anti-guerrilla force.

Masuo Fujita

A battery of Manchukuoan mountain guns prepares to fire during a training exercise in the early 1930s. Most artillery in service with all Chinese armies of the period were of this light and easily manoeuvred variety. As with most other equipment used by the early Manchukuoan Army these guns were formerly in use with the Nationalist North Eastern Armies of the Young Marshal.

Masuo Fujita

Firing from behind an earth shelter a Manchukuoan Infantryman in the early 1930s is taking part in an exercise. We can clearly see the five-coloured enamel star cap badge on the front of his peaked cap. He is armed with an Arisaka rifle which were supplied to the Chinese War-lords in Manchuria before the Japanese invasion.

Masuo Fujita

In an attempt to improve the supply of arms to the Manchukuoan Army, the Fengtien Arsenal was enlarged so that it could manufacture and repair rifles, machine guns and artillery for service in the Army. Rifles and ammunition were produced in a number of private factories under the control of the Japanese. The Mukden Arsenal produced a unique rifle with characteristics of both the Japanese Arisaka and the German Mauser. This rifle was made for the Manchukuoan Army in 7.92 mm calibre and was also reported in use with the Japanese Army.

Heavy Equipment of the Manchukuoan Army

As with the small arms in service with the Manchukuoan Army the heavier equipment came initially from captured Chinese sources. The Chinese Nationalist Army was short of heavy field guns and most of the artillery in use with them in Manchuria in 1931 would have been light infantry and mountain guns. These guns were the Austro-Hungarian produced 75mm M13 and German 75mm M14 mountain guns and a handful of Austro-Hungarian 75mm M11 and 104mm M14 field guns. The number of artillery pieces in service in 1933 was 281 infantry guns, 88 mountain guns and 70 field guns. As with the small arms it was soon decided to standardise the Manchukuoan artillery with Japanese equipment. The two main types of Japanese artillery which were issued to the Manchukuoan Army were the Model 38 (1905) 75mm field gun and the Model 41 (1908) mountain gun. A number of the Type 11, 37mm flat trajectory infantry guns were also in service and these were usually used in the anti-tank role.

Anti-aircraft artillery in use with the Manchukuoan Army was all of Japanese makes with the main type being the Type 88 75mm model. A strong emphasis was put on the anti-aircraft defences of Manchukuo due to the fear of possible Soviet bombing from the base in Vladivostock. Because of this fear a fair number of anti-aircraft guns must have been in service but no exact numbers are available. What is known is that ten 12cm high-elevation guns were removed from the vessels of the Manchukuo Navy in 1944 to be used as anti-aircraft guns in defence of An-shan Iron Foundry. The Foundry was at that time coming under heavy air attack not from Soviet bombers but from US B–29 bombers based in China.

Manchukuo Armoured Forces

Armour used by the Manchukuo Army included a handful of British-made Wolseley armoured cars as well as French Renault armoured cars of unknown types. About 30 Japanese Type 92 heavy armoured cars were in service as well as a number of improvised models built on Japanese truck chassis. The improvised or 'homemade' armoured cars were large ungainly vehicles with small 37mm cannon mounted in a rotating turret. Most of the armoured cars were operated by the armoured branch of the military academy. The Manchukuo River Defence Fleet also operated armoured patrol cars on the frozen Sungari River in winter, when it was impassable to their gunboats. These large home-made cars were able to carry up to 15 or 16 men and were also built on truck chassis.

Tracked armoured vehicles used by the Manchukuo Army included 8 Renault NC27 light tanks, 20 British made Carden-Lloyd MK VI tankettes and possibly a handful of Renault FT–17 light tanks left over from the Army of the Young Marshal Chang Hsueh-liang who controlled the province of Manchuria until thrown out by the Japanese in 1931. The Manchukuoan Army received little in the way of new tanks from the Japanese until the last few years of its existence. In 1943 the Japanese Army did condescend to 'loan' the Manchukuo Army 10 obsolete Type 94 tankettes which were used to form an Armoured Company.

The Automobile Corps

In an attempt to train drivers for the motorised units of the Manchukuo Army a 1st Independent Fengtien Motorcar Unit was organised in 1935. The unit had 8 passenger cars, 22 trucks, 8 armoured cars and 5 motorcycles. Another 6 Motorcar Units were formed before the end of the war and were located in the following headquarters: 1st Motorcar Unit 'Fengtien', 2nd Motorcar Unit 'Mudanjiang', 3rd Motorcar Unit 'Quiquihar', 4th Motorcar Unit 'Harbin', 5th Motorcar Unit 'Xinjing', 6th Motorcar Unit 'Dongjingcheng' and 7th Motorcar Unit 'Chengde'.

According to Manchukuoan Government sources the Automobile Corps performed well during the various anti-bandit operations, transporting forces. The reports stated that the Corps was used to transport troops, supplies and ammunition during the Tungpientao and Sankiang anti-bandit operations and during the fighting during the invasion of Jehol and the Nomonhan Incident in 1939. Photographs of the Corps in the late 1930s show trucks transporting light artillery into battle on their backs.

The Bandit Problem in Manchukuo 1931–38

The early years of the Manchukuoan Empire were plagued by largescale resistance to the new regime from anti-Japanese guerrillas. As the remnants of the Nationalist armies of the Young Marshal Chang Hsueh-liang in Manchuria retreated south ahead of the Japanese invaders large numbers of soldiers were left behind. These men were faced with a few choices: firstly, to surrender to the Japanese and become 'puppet' soldiers in the new state of Manchukuo's Army, secondly to return quietly to their homes, often thousands of miles away, or lastly, to continue to resist. The forces under arms in Manchuria had been ordered by the Nationalist government to cease fighting as the province had been given up as lost. Large numbers of patriotic soldiers chose to ignore this order and to continue to fight the Japanese and soldiers of the new state of Manchukuo. They were also joined by large numbers of civilian volunteers who wanted to resist the Japanese occupation.

The Manchukuoan Chief Executive Henry Pu-Yi is pictured shortly before his coronation as 'Puppet' Emperor of Manchukuo. He is wearing a Manchukuoan Officer's uniform with the five-coloured star cap badge on the front. Unfortunately for the propagandists, Pu-Yi never really carried off the role of a military leader even when dressed for the part.

Philip Jowett Collection

Several former commanders of the Young Marshal's armies chose to lead these anti-Japanese forces and soon became national heroes in China. The foremost of these resistance leaders was General Ma Chan-shan whose men had fought heroically against the Japanese invading forces. His army had fought a series of rearguard actions against the Japanese on the Chinese Eastern Line and Tsitsihar, but eventually being totally outgunned, they had been forced over the Soviet Border. General Ma's heroics had not gone unnoticed by his enemies and the Japanese decided to try and recruit him to fight for them. Colonel Doihara Kenji, the chief Japanese intriguer in Manchuria, made contact with General Ma and offered him a fantastic sum of money to join the Manchukuoan Army. Ma accepted and offered to make a tour of the North of Manchuria on behalf of the Japanese to try and placate the local population and convince them to accept the rule of Manchukuo. No sooner had he escaped the control of the Japanese then General Ma went back on his word and used their money to recruit a new army to fight them. During his short period of service with the Japanese

Ma ordered his men to wear yellow armbands to show their allegiance to Manchukuo. After a while, and having replenished his stocks of ammunition and re-gathered his forces strength, he revealed his true loyalties and returned to fighting the Japanese. He then distributed red armbands to his men but advised those who were stationed near Japanese lines to continue to wear the yellow armband to fool them into not attacking.

As part of the re-armament programme for the Man-chukoan Army the Japanese supplied them with the elderly Type 3 medium machine gun. Although this type was being replaced in Japanese service some were still in use in 1945 and the Manchukuoans would have been grateful for any machine guns they could get their hands on. Not surpris-ingly the Japanese equipped their allies with the weaponry that was being phased out of service in their army.

Masuo Fujita

Anti-Japanese Armies in Manchukuo

According to Japanese sources the strength of the Manchurian guerrillas increased greatly during the course of 1932. At the start of the year there were 130,000 but by the summer this had increased to 200,000. A large influx of new recruits to the anti-Japanese resistance came from the former soldiers of the Young Marshal's North-Eastern Army. This large increase in numbers took the total to approaching 360,000 men. This huge problem had to be addressed by the Japanese and they therefore launched a series of anti-guerrilla operations throughout the early to mid 1930s. These operations were launched using large numbers of Manchukoan troops in support and were largely successful. So much so that by 1935 the numbers of resistance fighters had been reduced to 20–25,000. By 1938, according to Japanese figures, the resistance had been mainly confined to the north-east of Manchukuo and only numbered about 7,300 men. The large resistance armies of 30,000 men or so in 1932 had also been reduced to small guerrilla bands of 30 or so men by 1938.

Manchukuoan Anti-Bandit Operations 1932–33

Subjugation of Anti-Kirin Army – March to June 1932
This operation, which lasted from March to June 1932, was to clear the 20,000 Nationalist troops of the so called 'Anti-Kirin' Army. The campaign was launched with Japanese forces, and the Manchukuoan units involved were 'Kirin' Army – 7th and 8th Infantry Brigades, 2nd and 3rd Cavalry Brigades, with a total of 7,000 men. Some of the ships of the River Defence Fleet were also involved – the *Lisui, Litsai, Kiangping, Kiangching* and *Kiangtung*. The campaign pushed the Nationalist forces into the north of the province and secured the control of the Sungari River.

First Tungpientao Clearance – May to June 1932
Tang Chu-wu a Manchukuoan commander who revolted and surrounded the Japanese consulate at Tungho. Immediately a Japanese force of police was sent to relieve the siege with a force of Manchukuoan troops in sup-port. These were the 1st and 2nd Detachments of the 'Fengtien' Army and totalled 4,000 men. Although the revolting forces were quoted as 20,000 strong this is almost certainly an exaggeration, but after heavy fighting the anti-Japanese forces retreated undefeated. The Manchukoan contingent were quite badly mauled and their performance was far from convincing.

Ma Chan-shan Subjugation – April to July 1932
This campaign was launched against the Headquarters of Ma Chan-shan, the most famous of the anti-Japanese Commanders. Manchukuoan forces totalled 5,000 and were the 1st and 2nd Detachments of the 'Heilungkiang'

A unit of ethnic Mongolian Cavalry are pictured in the early years of the Manchukuoan Army armed with roughly made lances. The lances have pennants in the colours of the new Manchukuoan flag with a yellow field and red, blue, black and white vertical stripes. Cavalry units made up a substantial and important part of the Manchukuoan Army throughout its thirteen-year history.

Army. This, as usual, was a mixed Japanese Manchukoan operation and was opposed by approximately 6,000 guerrillas. The poor performance of the Manchukuoan soldiers led to Ma Chan-shan's force escaping to fight another day.

Li Hai-ching Subjugation – May 1932
An attack against a strong guerrilla force of 10,000 men in the southern region of Heilungkiang province was launched by a 6,000-strong Manchukuoan force of the 'Heilungkiang','Kirin' and 'Taoliao' Armies. The Manchukuoan Army was made up of the 1st Infantry Brigade and 1st Cavalry Brigade of the 'Heilungkiang' Army, the 1st Cavalry Brigade of the 'Kirin' Army and 1st, 4th and 7th Detachments of the 'Taoliao' Army. The joint Japanese and Manchukuoan force attacked from three directions, dispersed the guerrillas and took control of the region.

Feng Chan-hai Subjugation – 20–25 June 1932
This operation was really just a series of skirmishes between units of the 'Kirin' Army of the Manchukuoan Army and guerrillas of the anti-Kirin forces. The Manchukuoan units were the 'Kirin' Railways Guard, Cavalry Corps and 1st Infantry Brigade totalling 1,600 men. The Manchukoans suffered 150 men killed while the Japanese claimed to have killed 1,000 guerrillas.

First Feng Chang-hai Subjugation – June to July 1932
An operation to clear the districts of Shuangcheng, Acheng, Yushu, Wuchang and Shulan of anti-Japanese Forces. The Manchukuoan contingent of the force was made up of the 4th, 5th and 8th Detachments of the 'Taoliao' Army and the 'Liu' Brigade of the 'Kirin' Army. The 7,000-man Manchukoan force along with the Japanese completely cleared the districts of the 15,000 'bandits'.

Mongolian Bandit Subjugation Operation – 20–31 August 1932
Mongolian bandit forces attacked the Ssutao railway line and took the small town of Tanyuhsien-cheng. The Manchukuoan relieving force was made up of the 7th and part of the 1st Detachment of the 'Taoliao' Army totalling 2,500 men. After a short battle Tanyuhsien-cheng was retaken and the Mongolians retreated.

Second Feng Chang-hai Subjugation –2 September 1932
A 7,000 strong Manchukuoan force of the 'Kirin' Army attacked a 10,000 strong force of 'Feng Chang-hai' bandits who were retreating after their defeat in July. The guerrillas were moving towards the Chinese held province of Jehol and the Japanese command wanted to stop this. Although surrounded the majority of the guerrillas managed to make good their escape into Jehol.

Su Ping-wei Subjugation 'Machouli Incident' – September to December 1932

A unit of the Manchukuoan Army under the command of Su Ping-wei revolted against Japanese rule. Loyal units of the 'Hsingan' Army totalling 4,500 attacked the rebels with Japanese forces and after heavy fighting the rebels were defeated on 5 December and Sung Ping-wei and remnants of his force retreated into Soviet territory.

Second Tungpientao Subjugation – October 1932

The 'Fengtien' Army cleared the Tungpientao district of guerrillas and took the surrender of 1,000 men and killed 270 more. As usual the 8,000 Manchukuoan troops acted as support troops to the much smaller Japanese forces that made up the vanguard of the force.

Li Hai-ching Subjugation – October 1932

The Li Hai-ching guerilla force of 3,000 men tried to attack the Manchukuoan and Japanese forces in South Heilungkiang Province. When confronted by the 3,500 man Manchukuoan-Japanese force the guerrillas retreated into Nationalist-controlled Jehol Province.

Ki Feng-Lung District Subjugation – 6–20 November 1932

An operation to clear the Ki Feng-lung district of guerrillas, a 5,000 strong force of Manchukuoan soldiers consisting of a Battalion of 'Chinganyuchitui' Guard Corps and the 2nd Regiment of Cavalry of the 'Fengtien' Army and a Cavalry Detachment of the 'Kirin' Army.

Third Tungpientao Subjugation – 22 November–5 December 1932

This operation was launched to finally clear the remnants of the guerrilla forces that had regrouped after the Second Tungpientao Subjugation Campaign. The Manchukuoan force was made up of a unit of 'Chinganyuchitui' Guard Corps as well as locally-raised forces from Yalu, Central and Shenghai districts totalling 5,000. The operation was a success and led to the capture of 1,800 bandits, some of who may have been recruited into the Manchukuoan Army.

Kirin Province Subjugation – October and November 1933

A large-scale operation involving 35,000 men of the Manchukuoan Army to clear the Province of Kirin entirely free of guerrillas. The Manchukuoan force included the whole of the 'Kirin' Army as well as the 1st Cavalry Brigade and the 3rd Detachment of the 'Heiungkiang' Army. Also involved were the 'Chingan' Army Artillery Corps and the Hsinching Independent Cavalry Detachment. The operation was a success and led to the capture or death of a number of prominent anti -Japanese guerrilla commanders.

Manchukoan Army Anti-Bandit Operations

During the early 1930s the Manchukuoan Army conducted a large number of anti-bandit operations in an attempt to destroy the various guerrilla groups in the country. These were usually in the form of sweeps to try

A rather archaic looking signals unit of the Manchukuoan Army is pictured with a pony to carry the reels of cable which were the favoured form of communication in the Imperial Japanese Army. The signal flags mounted on the saddle were also a short-range method of communication between Manchukuoan units.

Masuo Fujita

A line of Manchukoan soldiers on parade wear the fur hat with the five-pointed star cap badge on the front. The men are all armed with Japanese weaponry, with some having Arisaka rifles and others being armed with 6.5mm special training machine guns.

Robert Hunt Library

and locate and destroy the elusive guerrilla bands. One such operation was witnessed by Englishman Peter Fleming and described in his 1934 book *One's Company*. He was allowed to accompany a unit of 175 Japanese and 400 Manchukuoan soldiers with a single mountain gun. The operation was conducted in the countryside around the city of Fushun and involved a great deal of marching and no fighting. The nearest that the operation got to seeing any bandits was a claim by some of the Manchukuoan soldiers that they fired at a group of guerrillas in the distance. It was obvious to Peter Fleming that if it came to a fight the Japanese troops would be in the forefront with the Manchukuoan soldiers playing a purely support role.

The average Manchukuoan soldier of the early 1930s had no great dislike of the 'bandits' he was sent to fight. In fact, a few years before, many of the men would have been in the pay of the same master when serving in the North East Army of the Young Marshal. Soldiers who now found themselves in the pay of the new government of Manchukuo always changed sides again if necessary. This was made easier by the fact that both the early Manchukuoan Army and the anti-Japanese fighters wore the same basic uniform in the early 1930s.

A. R. Lindt, in his 1933 book *With Bandit and General in Manchuria* recounts the story of when he visited one of the local warlords in Manchuria and saw that the guards on the city gates wore the yellow armband of Manchukuo. He was then informed that they could quite easily change these for the red armband of the rebels when ordered to do so by their commander. Manchukuoan soldiers often came to an arrangement with the 'bandits' that the latter should retire when the former were on patrol. The Manchukoan soldiers even arranged special signals of rifle shots which warned the 'bandits' of their approach. As Owen Lattimore wrote in his book *Manchuria: Cradle of Conflict* "He will have one signal by groups of rifle shots which means "We are on patrol, but nothing serious," and another which means "Look out! We'll fight you if we find you!". This is not to say that some Manchukoan soldiers were not willing to fight for the new regime, as Chinese soldiers were used to changing employers, and if they didn't fight they wouldn't get paid.

The fate of bandits or guerrillas that fell into the hands of the Japanese and Manchukuoan forces was grim, with few escaping death. Under a law enacted in Manchukuo in September 1932 a law for the 'Provisional punishment of bandits' allowed for the disposal of any captured bandits. This law gave *carte blanche* to the Manchukuoan Army and the Japanese to kill anyone suspected of being a bandit or aiding and abetting them. During the anti-bandit operations conducted by the Japanese and their Manchukuoan allies any captured guerrilla was quickly despatched. Under the same law, whole villages would be destroyed and its inhabitants put to the sword if suspected of helping the guerrillas in any way. Rewards were offered for each bandit killed and figures for the number killed were sent by the commanding officer to the Manchukuo War Ministry who issued the money.

Doubts over the truth of the 'kill' ratio were expressed by officials of the War Ministry and so the notorious 'Order No. 213' was issued. This order demanded that when the Manchukuoan soldiers killed a bandit they should remove his left ear and then send it to the War Ministry. The order was quoted as saying "During the manoeuvres against the 'Hunhuzi' bandits, commanders of sections send reports containing figures of those alleged to have been captured and shot and they demand the reward offered, but it is impossible to verify these reports. Henceforth, in the case of shooting it will be necessary to cut off the left ear of every enemy shot and deliver it to staff headquarters as proof. If the weather is hot and preservation of these ears is thereby rendered difficult, they should be fried thoroughly in oil and then delivered to headquarters as proof in order to receive the reward".

The Manchukuo Army suffered heavy casualties during the Anti-Bandit operations and in the period from May 1932 to May 1935, according to Japanese sources, its losses were: Officers – 313 killed, 111 wounded, Non-commissioned Officers – 216 killed, 167 wounded and Enlisted Men – 933 killed, 964 wounded. With a few other casualties included, the total for this period was 1,470 killed and 1,261 wounded.

Table 1 – Bandit activities in Manchukuo 1935

	Jan	May	Sep	Total
Number of bandit raids	2,325	3,835	4,628	39,151
Number of bandits involved	93,880	193,737	205,405	1,783,880
Number of suppression expeditions	1,502	2,284	2,820	24,150
Bandit Losses				
Killed	763	1,600	1,155	13,338
Wounded	847	1,113	1,214	11,815
Captured	274	204	164	2,703
Arms lost	406	466	634	6,265
Rounds of ammunition lost	2,457	9,258	5,134	91,780
Horses killed	696	453	681	7,248
Horses captured	262	357	731	3,810
Suppression Troop Losses				
Killed	61	136	143	1,361
Wounded	107	150	275	2,276
Held captive	31	66	82	753
Arms lost	34	228	170	2,404
Rounds of ammunition lost	36,737	23,295	5,503	218,644
Horses killed	33	23	12	571

Table 2 – Size of bandit groups and raids 1935

	Raids	Size of bandit groups		
		1–30 men	51–100 men	301–500 men
January	2,325	1,743	131	12
February	1,617	1,102	142	7
March	2,632	1,958	188	19

An anti-bandit operation was launched against the 1st Route Army of the Communist guerrilla forces in the region of North Tungpientao. This operation, which lasted from October 1936 to March 1937, was to be the first time that Manchukuoan units had operated without the support of Japanese units. The operation was to be a test of the effectiveness of the 'new' Manchukuo Army and 16,000 men were used in the campaign. Manchukuoan units engaged in 528 'battles' or skirmishes during the campaign and killed or captured 2,030 guerrillas including a number of their high-ranking leaders. The Manchukuo Army suffered quite heavy casualties during the fighting and was found to be particularly vulnerable to night attacks by the guerrillas. Manchukuoan soldiers presumably had not received much in the way of night fighting training.

Another anti-bandit operation was launched in the region of the three rivers Amur, Ussuri and Sungari, where most of the anti-Japanese guerillas were gathered. This long-term Extermination Campaign lasted from November 1937 to March 1939 with 25,000 Manchukuoan troops involved. Western eyewitness accounts of anti-bandit operations are few and far between, and after the outbreak of war in Europe in 1939 few westerners would have

Smartly turned out Manchukoan Cavalry wear the new type of field cap introduced in the late 1930s and are armed with the modern Model 44 cavalry carbines with folding bayonets attached. This unit obviously comes from one of the better formations of the Manchukuoan Army as evidenced by both their smartness and their up to date rifles.

Robert Hunt Library

ventured into Manchukuo. One who did witness the aftermath of an anti-bandit operation was Willard Price, who visited the country in 1941. He recalls the large number of bandit attacks on the roads around the town of Yi Tung Hsien 30 miles from the capital Hisinking where he was staying. He was present when a Manchukuoan Army unit returned from dealing with a group of bandits who had been making these attacks. He reported:

During the afternoon the Manchukuoan troops came back. They brought 18 severed heads – gruesome and pitiable objects. I was in the city hall talking to the Chinese Mayor and his Japanese 'Policy Determiner' when the soldiers entered and laid out the 18 heads on the long table. I squeamishly removed my teacup from the table. The Mayor asked "These are the heads of the Hung hu-tzu?" "They are" replied the captain in charge. The Mayor turned to his official thorn in the flesh, the Japanese policy determiner, who had been sent to the town to reorganise its affairs according to Japanese ideas. "You see" he said, "our brave men have killed all these and put the rest to flight". But the Japanese was suspicious. "Are you sure" he asked the captain "that these are not the heads of the village men who were killed by the bandits?" The captain was indignant "No, no! these are the bandits". "I have been in that village" the Japanese persisted. "I think I recognise some of these faces". "Your pardon, but you are mistaken." "How many of your men were killed in the fight?" The captain squirmed a little. "Well, we were lucky. No one was killed." "I don't see that any of you were even wounded. And yet you killed 18 men. That was a great feat." The captain mumbled assent "You had ten rounds of ammunition. How much have you left?" "None left. It was a very hard fight." "It must have been. Where are your guns?" "After we had used up all our ammunition, we had to throw our guns aside and fight with our knives." "So you still have your knives?" "It is a great pity. I know, but in our haste we forgot our knives, and they were left behind." The Japanese slowly rose to his feet and his manner became menacing. "You fought no bandits! Instead you gave them your arms and ammunition so they could continue to make difficult our administration of Wangtao, the Kingly Way, with which we seek to restore peace and happiness in this country. You will go to your barracks. You will await trial by military court.

Military Campaigns Of The Manchukuoan Army

The Invasion of Jehol, 23 February–28 March 1933

After the conquest of Manchuria and the setting up of the state of Manchukuo the Kwangtung Army decided to push further into China by seizing the Inner Mongolian Province of Jehol. They first ordered the Chinese Nationalist forces to withdraw behind the Great Wall of China, which they demanded should become the border between China and Manchukuo. When the Chinese refused to obey the Japanese demands the Kwangtung Army invaded on 23 February 1933 with a force of 2 Infantry Divisions, 2 Independent Mixed Brigades, 1 Cavalry Brigade and a Tank Regiment. About 42,000 Manchukuoan soldiers were involved in the invasion and this force was made up of 7 Detachments of the Taoliao Army, 3 Detachments of the National Foundation Army, the National Protection Army, National Salvation Army and the 1st Brigade of the Guard Corps. Manchukuoan commanders in charge of the 'puppet' contingent were Generals Li Chi-chun and Chang Hai-peng. The campaign lasted just over a month and at the end the Chinese had been pushed completely out of Jehol before the fighting ended on 28 March. Jehol fell relatively easily to the Kwangtung Army, with much of the blame for the Chinese defeat going to the Governor of the Province General Tang Yu-lin, who was executed for his incompetence. Western news reports of the time claimed that the Manchukoan contingent in the invasion fought particularly well, with one detachment disarming and capturing 5,000 Chinese soldiers.

Soviet-Japanese Border Disputes 1931–45

During the 1920s and 1930s a large number of disputes broke out between the Soviet Union and Japan along the poorly-defined borders between Mongolia and the newly-created Empire of Manchukuo. The People's Republic of Mongolia was a client state of the Soviet Union in much the same way as Manchukuo was a 'puppet' state of Japan.

Soldiers of the 3rd Sub Unit of the Manchukoan Army Military Academy undergo drill in their barracks in the 'puppet' Empire of Manchukuo in the early 1940s. They are wearing full kit made up of Japanese equipment and are all armed with Arisaka Type 38 rifles. This unit is obviously a 'model' one and it is doubtful whether all Manchukuoan troops were this well turned out. The soldier in the foreground is a Private 1st Class as is shown by the two gold stars on his maroon coloured shoulder boards.

Robert Hunt Library

These border disputes had their origin in the Russo-Japanese War of 1904–05 when the Imperial Russian Army and Navy had suffered a heavy defeat, and Tsarist Russia had been forced to give in to many of the Japanese demands for territory in Manchuria. Under the terms of the Treaty of Portsmouth signed on 6 September 1905, Russia withdrew her forces from Manchuria as part of these demands and this allowed the Japanese to increase their influence in that region. The Japanese were to pressure the Chinese government into giving them concessions in their country including the rights to operate the South Manchuria Railway. The Japanese-owned South Manchuria Railway Company was allowed to police the line using Japanese troops without referring to the Chinese Government.

From the establishment of Manchukuo in 1931 until its demise in August 1945 there were constant minor border disputes and clashes between Japanese and Manchukuoan troops and their Soviet and Mongolian adversaries. The Japanese were convinced that the resistance forces in Manchukuo were receiving aid from the Soviets. These suspicions were confirmed on a number of occasions when captured guerrillas were found to be carrying Soviet ammunition. Kwangtung Army officers were also annoyed that guerrilla units which retreated over the border into the Soviet Union were given shelter. Despite repeated calls by the Japanese for the guerrillas to be returned to them for punishment the Soviets usually refused to co-operate.

The Changkufeng Incident July-August 1938

The fighting during the Changkufeng Incident centred around the hill of the same name near the mouth of the Tumen River on the eastern border of Mongolia with Manchukuo. This strategic position had been seized by the Soviets and fortified at first with 12 men who were reinforced to 40 men and by 20 July up to 250 men with heavy weapons. Fighting had broken out on 11 July and it soon escalated from a mere skirmish into a small but fierce encounter. Initial Japanese forces reached 3,200 men of the 19th Division and these were reinforced to an eventual strength of 7,000 by the end of the fighting. Soviet forces were heavily reinforced and by the time the fighting ended were reported at 21,000 men with up to 200 tanks, 120 artillery pieces and an air element of 100–220 planes. With the odds stacked so highly in favour of the Soviets all Japanese efforts at pushing them back were bound to fail. When an armistice was signed on 10 August, the Soviets were still in control of the hill and its surrounding area and the Japanese had suffered a humiliating defeat. Both sides suffered heavy casualties in the fierce fighting with the Soviet losses estimated at 3,000 and the Japanese at 1,439. The Manchukuoan Army involved in the Changkufeng Region were less than enthusiastic and although the Japanese wanted to use them in the front line they saw little fighting. One veteran of the Manchukuoan Army who fought in the campaign said that "At the first sound of shooting we just lay crouched in the trench or on the ground and refused to pull a trigger". Even worse for the Japanese were Manchukuoan units which changed sides during the Changkufeng fighting and on one such occasion 3 regiments of 'puppet' troops mutinied and turned 'rebels' as soon as the firing began.

Smartly turned out recruits of the Manchukuoan Army present arms for the Japanese propaganda cameras. They are wearing the field cap which was modelled on the Japanese type but had a flatter crown. The Colour Sergeant in the foreground has three gold stars on a single gold stripe on his maroon coloured shoulder boards.

Robert Hunt Library

The Manchukuoan Emperor Pu-Yi in the grounds of his palace with officers of senior officers of his army and staff. On the far right of the photograph and second from left are soldiers of the Emperor's Bodyguard. Pu-Yi's chest is emblazoned with numerous awards and decorations, some left over from his previous incarnation as Emperor of all of China up to 1911, while the rest are either Japanese or Manchukuoan awards created since the birth of his Empire in 1934.

Robert Hunt Library

The Nomonhan Incident, May-September 1939

Following the Changkufeng Incident in 1938 a ceasefire was agreed between the Soviets and the Japanese. Any peace between the two powers was bound to be a temporary one however with their mutual territorial ambitions in the region. Japanese encroachments on the borders of Mongolia and with their client state surrounded on two sides the pressure was on the Soviets to act. The fighting began on 11 May 1939 when a small Mongolian Cavalry detachment attacked a Manchukuoan Army observation post. A Manchukoan Regiment then intervened and fighting broke out between them and Mongolian reinforcements. Soviet troops then came to the aid of their Mongolian allies and reinforcements were rushed up to the border area including armour and aircraft. With a similar build up on the Japanese side up to a strength of 75,000 men and 500 field guns the fighting soon spread and accelerated into large scale battles. The Japanese were overwhelmed by the superior numbers and quality of both Soviet armour and artillery. Soviet forces inflicted a heavy defeat over the Japanese Imperial Army and Air Force during the campaign, who learnt some hard lessons about the inferiority of much of their weaponry.

Manchukuoan and Mongolian troops were involved in the fighting in a mainly supporting role, although manpower shortages on the Japanese side led to them deploying some Manchukoan units in the frontline. In total some 18,000 Manchukoan troops were employed during the Nomonhan Incident, mainly cavalry. At the start of the campaign in May the 7th and 8th Manchukoan Cavalry Regiments were held in reserve. These units were then reinforced up to Divisional strength as the fighting progressed before finally being sent to the frontline at the end of July. The 7th and 8th Regiments were used as a flank guard on the left of the Kwangtung Army as it advanced towards the River Halha. The 1st Cavalry Regiment was then committed to the fighting in the Northern sector in late August as the situation became increasingly desperate for the Japanese. Although given a frontline role during the fighting in August their performance in general left a lot to be desired. The 'Hsingan' Detachment of the Manchukuoan Army had been heavily defeated in the intense fighting at the beginning of the month and a 3,000 strong mixed Infantry-Cavalry reinforcement, the 'Shihlan' Detachment had been brought up to the line to replace it. After the new force came under heavy attack on 19 August the Manchukoans mutinied and 300 of them escaped across the Halha River into Mongolia. Even though eventually the Japanese officers in command of the Detachment managed to the form the remaining Manchukuoans back into an *ad-hoc* unit the Kwangtung Army command had lost faith in their satellite troops. The Japanese continued to employ their Manchukoan troops in the frontline only because of their chronic shortage of manpower.

The Manchukuoan Army suffered quite heavily during the Nomonhan Incident with 2,895 casualties. In assessing the performance of their Manchukuoan 'allies' after the war some Japanese sources did say that they performed creditably and that they were prepared to expand the army further.

Manchukuoan Army Conscription

The expansion of the Manchukoan Army after 1939 depended on the introduction of conscription, which was duly promulgated in April 1940. It took a year for the so-called 'Army Law' to be fully introduced in April 1941,

The caption to this hotograph reads "Manchukuoan, Mongolian and Japanese officers look for danger zones at the frontier". Presumably therefore they are a mixed group of Manchukuoan and Inner Mongolian officers under the watchful eye of their Japanese advisors. All wear very similar uniforms so it is impossible from this photo to distinguish their individual nationalities. The Inner Mongolian officers would be from units of that nationality within the Manchukuoan Army.

Robert Hunt Library

which called for every able-bodied and sound-minded man between the ages of eighteen to forty to be called up for military service. All youths on reaching nineteen years were to be registered and examined for their suitability for service and then 10% were selected. Selection took place on the basis of the physical fitness and education attainment and the loyalty of their families to the regime.

When this procedure proved unworkable on occasion the Japanese combed the country from county to county filling up the ranks with conscripted men. One example of this conscription took place in the county of Tailai in Heilungkiang with a population of 100,000, where 1,000 men were conscripted or 10% of the whole population. This figure obviously produced a much higher rate of conscription of the male population than the 10% proscribed by the Army Law. Pay in the early 1940s was 12 Japanese Yen a month for Privates and 65 Japanese Yen a month for Lieutenants.

Attempts to foster a patriotic and loyal spirit in the Manchukuoan Army were almost constantly undertaken throughout the period of Japanese control. The 'Hsieh-ho Hui' or Concordia Association was set up by the Japanese as the one political party of the state along the lines of the Nazi Party in Germany. All members of government institutions and state employees were obliged to be members and particular emphasis was placed on recruiting the youth of Manchukuo. Amongst the various youth groups set up under the umbrella of the Concordia Association were the Youth Protection Corps. This Corps was given the role of railway protection along with other paramilitary sections of the 'Hsieh-ho Hui'. All Manchukoan youth organisations were constantly imbued with patriotism and its members were being prepared for future service with the Manchukuoan Army. Propaganda publications issued by the Manchukuoan Government emphasise that military training undertaken by the Hsieh-ho Hui youth groups were to develop the boys 'mind & spirit' not to prepare them for the Army. According to reports this constant pro-Japanese propaganda 'from the cradle to the grave' did, over the fourteen year period of the Manchukoan Empire, manage to create a certain level of martial spirit amongst its youth.

White Russian Units in the Manchukuo Army

The first attempts to 'tap into' the potential manpower available in the large émigré White Russian population in Manchuria began in 1932 soon after the Japanese takeover. Large numbers of White Russians had escaped to Manchuria during the Russian Revolution and the Civil War which followed it. They provided a ready made source of highly motivated anti-Soviet volunteers who were willing to fight their old enemy. White Russians were first used from July 1932 onwards to guard the Manchukuo railways and two units of 250 men each were formed. They were enlisted, armed and equipped in Harbin and were reportedly joined by a third infantry detachment and a small cavalry unit. The success of these small White Russian units led the Japanese to think that they might be worth recruiting on a larger scale. A request from the White Russian residents of Harbin to the Manchukuoan Chief Executive, Pu Yi to be allowed to raise a 10,000 man 'Defence Force for Self Protection' does not seem to have been granted. Obviously the Japanese wanted any White Russian forces that were raised to be firmly under their control and this would have been too much like an independent army. The Japanese officer in charge of the 'Tokumu Kikan' or Special Service organ in Manchukuo did, however, approach General Kosmin, the Chairman of the Russian Fascist Party in the state, to raise White Russian units. He promised Kosmin that although the units raised would be small they would be the nucleus of a 'White' Army that would fight side by side with the Japanese eventually in the proposed attack on the Soviet Union. The first White Russian units formed by Kosmin were only 200 strong in total, although other small units were raised on a local basis by the Japanese. These units appear to have been mainly formed from amongst the Émigré Cossacks and would have been used as scouting cavalry.

By the mid 1930s there were about 4,000 'Russian White Guards' in Manchukuo and these were employed in protecting the railways, important roads and gold fields. Many of the White Russians were recruited by the so-called 'Refugees Bureau' a Japanese-controlled organisation supposedly led by Russians. The Bureau recruited White Russians to perform these military tasks and promised them 60 Dollars a month plus a free uniform, lodgings and 'European' food. In practice most White Russian Guards found that they were posted in isolate posts miles away from anywhere. They were given Chinese food and their quarters were described as 'unfit for animals', they were treated like virtual slaves and never saw any of the money they had been promised. This treatment, not surprisingly, led to mutinies amongst the White Russian units including, in August 1933, an incident at Tungpei Station. The 21-strong unit mutinied and killed 2 Japanese officers and 5 soldiers, took 5 machine guns, set fire to the station and fled. Although the White Russians could be unreliable they were still regarded by the Japanese as worth employing. In 1936 the Japanese decided to bring all White Russians willing to fight for them into the Manchukuoan Army and to this end the Asano Brigade was formed.

The 'Asano' Brigade

It was suggested in 1936 by a Japanese Kwantung Army staff officer Colonel Kawabe Tosahiro that it would be a good idea to form one unit to incorporate all White Russian volunteers. Despite various efforts it took until 1938 to raise the unit, which was called the 'Asano Brigade' after its Japanese military advisor Colonel Asano

Mongol horsemen of the Manchukuoan Army go out on an anti-bandit operation on their sturdy Mongolian ponies. Ethnic Mongols made up the vast majority of the Manchukuoan Cavalry and earned a good reputation as hard fighters. They are all wearing the fur hat and winter version of the Japanese khaki tunic while the officer at the front seems to be wearing a darker coloured type.

Robert Hunt Library

Takashi. The unit was stationed at Erchan, a village on the Sungari River known as 'Second Station' which was 60 miles from Harbin. At first it numbered only 200 men but was soon expanded into a 5 company force of 700 men. The Asano Brigade was officially part of the Manchukuoan Army and was sent to fight in the Nomonhan Incident as part of the Japanese 23rd Infantry Division. The 23rd Division was commanded by an ex-head of the Tokumu Kikan in Harbin who realised that the Asano Brigade would be useful to act as infiltrators and scouts. Japanese forces were totally outgunned and outmanoeuvred in the campaign and suffered heavy losses with the Asano Brigade being almost totally destroyed. After its destruction in 1939 the Brigade was reformed, but this time only to perform sabotage and other covert operations in Soviet territory.

During the period of 1940–41, 2,000 White Russians were trained in covert warfare to go behind Soviet lines in captured uniforms to perform sabotage operations. The high losses suffered by the Brigade during these operations and the general attitude of the Japanese towards them led to a great deal of disillusion amongst the men. In fact the White Russian population in general in Manchukuo had lost faith in the Japanese by the early 1940s and realised that they would never be part of an anti-Soviet Crusade. By the end of the war in 1945 there were reported to be 4,000 in the Brigade including Cossack units. The Asano Brigade was caught up in the *blitzkrieg* invasion of the 'puppet' state of Manchukuo by the Soviet Army in August 1945. Little is known of the fate of the White Russians during this time but any captured brigadiers would have received short shrift from the Soviets.

Manchukuoan Army 1937

When the fighting between Japan and China broke out on 7 July 1937 the Nationalist Chinese 84th Division invaded Manchukuo. The Manchukuoan Army was ordered to be partially mobilized and this took until the end of July. Manchukuoan units were sent to the border region to confront the invaders. In an action on 17 August a 1,200 strong Chinese unit attacked a Manchukuoan unit which suffered a number of casualties, including a Major General Chuchiahsun who was killed. The 5th Cavalry unit of the Manchukuoan Army was attacked on the 20th in thick fog and was surrounded and suffered heavy casualties. Another senior Japanese officer in service with the Manchukuoan Army, Major General Fuji was also killed in action during a battle in the region of Heitayingtzu. In various actions during August the Manchukuoan Army had a number of clashes with Chinese units and came off worse in most of them. The arrival of a Colonel Misaki to take over command of the Manchukoan units in the area improved matters somewhat. Although their performance improved throughout the campaign they did suffer quite heavy losses. In the 19 battles or skirmishes that took place during the fighting the Manchukuoan forces lost 60 killed and 143 missing in action.

A march-past of Manchukoan Local Defence Guards armed with the Japanese copy of the 'archaic' 1877 Snider rifle. The men are wearing a simple khaki uniform with peaked cap, tunic and breeches tucked into puttees, their uniforms are completed with the wearing of white parade gloves.

Philip Jowett Collection

The Japanese formed Defence units to defend Manchukuo from amongst the Japanese immigrant farmers who had settled there. This small unit of Defence Guards are armed with two types of captured Chinese Nationalist rifles , the Mauser 98k and the Hanyang 88. These men would have been considered Manchukuoan citizens and could have been recruited into the regular Manchukuoan Army.

Imperial War Museum HU73377

Elite & Special Units of the Manchukuoan Army 1932–45

Capital Guard Units

In the first few years of the existence of Manchukuo, while Pu -Yi still had the rather incongruous title of Chief Executive, special units were formed to guard both his person and his capital, Hsinking. These units were the Guard Corps for the office of the Chief Executive, which was recruited exclusively from men of Manchu decent and were responsible for guarding Pu-Yi's offices. The 'Iweichuntuan' or Chief Executives Bodyguard, which was Pu -Yi's personal guard, also formed guards of honour at state occasions. Garrison troops of Hsinking were the Kirin Railway Corps and the 'Independent Cavalry Corps for Guarding the Capital'. The Independent Cavalry Corps was formally the 4th Cavalry Brigade which had taken part in the invasion of Jehol and were transferred to Hsinking in March 1933.

The 'Chinganyuchitui' – Special Guard Corps

A Special Guard Corps was formed first in Fengtien Province, eventually extending to being raised in all the provinces of Manchukuo. This Guard Corps or 'Chinganyuchitui' performed well in combat, as during the early anti-bandit operations it was often in the forefront of the fighting.

'Eastern Jewels' Anti-Bandit Force

The most exotic force raised to fight on the side of the Manchukuo Empire was the force of bandits raised in 1932 by the Manchu Princess, Yoshiko Kawashima, who was popularly known as 'Eastern Jewel'. She was the daughter of Prince Su, a famous Manchu Prince who had sent her to Japan to be educated. She soon learned to love Japan and developed a hatred for all things Chinese, which led her to offer her services to the Japanese Secret Services when she was old enough. There is not unfortunately room here to recount her numerous adventures in the service of the Japanese. She was however a relative of the Manchukuoan Emperor Pu-Yi and tried to use any influence she had over him to get him to co-operate fully with the Japanese. Eastern Jewel suggested to the Japanese commander in Manchukuo that she should recruit a force of bandits to act as an anti-bandit force, the idea being that a unit made up of bandits would be more effective in fighting their former comrades, based on the old adage "It takes a thief to catch a thief". Eastern Jewel's anti-bandit force was supposed to have been between 3 –5,000 men and to have operated in this role for a few years. By 1933 the force had reached a strength of 5,000 men and when the Japanese invaded the Chinese province of Jehol in February of that year she offered them the services of her force. The chauvinistic Japanese officers in charge of the operation were appalled to be offered help by a woman and refused. Even so her force was allowed to continue its activities while the problem of bandits in Manchukuo continued and a Chinese newspaper report of early 1936 said that they were still in existence with the 'Mysterious Miss Kawashima' in command of them. Eastern Jewel was to lose much of her influence with the Japanese in the late 1930s but remained loyal to them until the end of the war. When she fell into Nationalist hands in 1945 she could expect little mercy and she was swiftly shot by a firing squad.

The 'Hsing an Chun' – Mongolian Independence Army

(This force should not be confused with the Inner Mongolian Army under Prince Teh Wang which fought for independence for the region from the mid 1930s – see below)

The 'Hsing An Chun' or Mongolian Independence/Autonomous Army was an army formed from amongst the ethnic Mongolian population of Manchukuo. In fact efforts by the Japanese to exploit the Mongolians wish for some form of autonomy in the parts of the Manchukuoan state where they lived predated their support of the forces of Prince Teh Wang by a few years. The Japanese were constantly mischief making in the region and would support any group which they thought might create problems for the Chinese Nationalist government. In 1931, before their invasion of Manchuria and their creation of the 'new' state of Manchukuo, the Japanese gave 3,000 Fengtien Arsenal 7.9mm Mauser rifles to a group of disenchanted Mongolians. They then set up a 'puppet' organisation with the aim of recruiting any Mongolian willing to fight for independence. The recruits were a mixed bunch with the best and most reliable of them coming from the Mongolian School at Heilongjiang

Another photograph of a Defence unit formed from Japanese immigrants to Manchukuo receive rudimentary training from an NCO in the early 1940's. These young recruits would be responsible for protecting their settlements from the increasing Communist guerrilla activity in Manchukuo during later years of the regime.

Philip Jowett Collection

in Manchuria. These young and idealistic Mongols were to form the cadre of the new army while the majority of the recruits came from less promising sources. The vast majority of men for the Mongolian Independence Army were sent by some of the local 'Banner' leaders in Inner Mongolia as their 'contribution' to the fight for independence and were of poor quality. They were made up mainly of ex-bandits and other undesirables who the Inner Mongolians were glad to be rid of. Japanese officers were sent to the headquarters of the Army to act as advisors to the commanders of this new force. In fact there is little doubt that they were the ones who really gave the orders and tried to wield this disparate group of men into an army of sorts.

After a period of training and organisation the Army had a strength of 3 'Chuns' or armies, with each having 7 or 8 regiments. The term Army is misleading as each of these 'Chuns' had a total strength of 2,000 men, giving each so-called regiment a strength of only 250 or so men. Equipment used by the Mongolian Independence Army was the usual mix of old and new with the Fengtien arsenal rifles being supplemented by heavy mortars from the same source and ZB–26 light machine guns imported from Czechoslovakia. The status and purpose of the Mongolian Independence Army changed with the Japanese takeover of the whole of Manchuria and the formation of the Manchukuo state in 1932. Before the Japanese takeover of Manchuria they had allowed the Mongols to hope that they might achieve true independence for the region; this was now shown to be a charade. The army now took the title of 'Hsing An Chun' or 'Army of Hsing An Province' where it was to be based.

When the army was established in its new base area it was reorganised into a mainly cavalry force and attached to

The Manchukuo Army had little armour and these 'homemade' armoured cars made up a large part of its force. They were built on Japanese truck chassis and appear to be armed with light machine guns in their rotating turrets and small cannon with shield at the front.

Tank Museum

the newly organised Manchukuoan Army. The force had a strength of 2 cavalry regiments and 1 independent cavalry 'Tui' (which stood here for a partial regiment). During the Japanese invasion of the province of Jehol in 1933 the 2 cavalry regiments of the 'Hsing An Chun' were employed. It was then allowed to expand further by incorporating many of the defeated former Nationalist garrison of Jehol who were formerly in the service of the defeated Chinese commander General Tang Yu-lin, known as 'Jade Unicorn'. This large scale expansion allowed the 'Hsing An Chun' to take over garrisons all over Hsing An province with the following organisation:

Western Hsing An Garrison – 3rd & 4th Cavalry Regiments.
Eastern Hsing An Garrison – 5th & 6th Cavalry Regiments & 1 Independent Mountain
Gun Battery.
Northern Hsing An Garrison – 7th & 8th Cavalry Regiments & 1 Border Police Battalion
(this later was expanded to form the 9th Cavalry Regiment).

The 'Hsing An Chun' was not at this stage officially part of the Manchukuoan Army but served as a sort of 'free corps' alongside them in the anti-bandit role. It spent the next five or six years fighting against the anti-Japanese resistance fighters with some success. From the end of 1936 to the middle of 1937 the 1st, 2nd and 6th cavalry regiments were formed into the Hsing An Force and were deployed against the anti-Japanese United Army in the 'Three Rivers' Region. A reinforced 5th Cavalry Regiment also saw action in late 1937 in support of the Japanese Army that had invaded Northern China after the outbreak of full scale war between the two countries following the Marco Polo Bridge Incident. The force advanced through the Great Wall and fought for three months in the passes just south of it before returning to their base in Manchukuo.

In 1938 a Hsing An Military District Headquarters was formed to centralise the force, and the Eastern and Western Garrisons were disbanded with their men being combined into one force. The mountain battery of the former Eastern Garrison was expanded to form an artillery regiment and the mortar companies from each cavalry regiment were combined to form a mortar regiment. At the same time all the local irregular forces formed under the Eastern and Western Garrisons were consolidated and an 11th Cavalry Regiment was raised from them. This reorganisation and expansion continued with the Hsing An going from a force of 9 cavalry regiments and 4 mountain gun batteries to a much larger army of 12 cavalry regiments, 1 artillery regiment, 1 mortar regiment, 2 independent mountain batteries and a motorised transport unit. In a further effort to expand and improve the army an officers' military academy was opened in 1934 to supply a steady supply of reliable commanders for the force.

Although the Hsing An was as, we have already said, a supposedly independent Mongol army, it always worked closely with the Manchukuoan Army proper. It was only a matter of time before the Hsing An was forced to become an official part of the Manchukuo Army and this happened in 1940. The so-called Mongol Independence Army was 'absorbed' into the Manchkuoan Army and the Hsing An Military District was replaced by the 9th and 10th Manchukuo Military Districts. For the next few years the Hsing An Chun continued to perform well and would seem to have been trusted by their Japanese masters. This was evident in 1944 when the 3rd, 4th and 11th Cavalry Regiments were reinforced to form the Hsing An contingent of a new anti-guerrilla force sent to fight Communists in the south-western region of Manchukuo directly under the command of the Japanese. This 'Tesseki Butai' or Iron Stone Unit (see below) was to become an elite unit of the Manchukuoan Army.

'Ching An Tui'- Pacification Brigade

A special anti-bandit force was formed in October 1931 by a Japanese businessman who was a retired army officer in Shenyang. Given the title of 'Ching An Tui' or Pacification Brigade it was stationed in the former workers quarters of the Fengtien Military Arsenal. He began by recruiting a number of fellow retired Japanese Army officers and these were joined by former officers of the Young Marshal's Army to act as a cadre. His aim was to raise a special unit that could aid the Japanese Kwangtung Army in its anti-bandit operations. After managing to recruit sufficient officers he then raised the 1st Infantry Guerrilla Brigade which consisted of 2 battalions with a total of 9 infantry companies. According to another source on the subject it possessed only 3 infantry companies, 1 cavalry squadron and a battery of mountain guns. The headquarters of the Brigade had the usual staff including sections for ordinance, medical, veterinarian and a communications unit. The Brigade was expanded with the formation of the 2nd Infantry Guerrilla Brigade, as well as separate cavalry and artillery units. Recruits came at first mainly from the ex-soldiers of the Young Marshal's Army and the local vagrants, thieves and other riff-raff from the region. Although non of these recruits were exactly reliable they were willing to fight for money and their commander made sure that they were paid regularly three times a month. This was in sharp contrast to the rest of the armed forces of Manchukuo, who were very rarely paid on time.

In March 1932 the Brigade was renamed the Pacification Army and had a regular organisation of 2 infantry regiments, 1 cavalry regiment and 1 artillery battalion. Each regiment had 3 battalions, each with 3 companies and a machine gun and a mortar company while the cavalry regiment contained 4 squadrons. As with many other so-called armies in China the force was never much more than a Brigade Group.

March 1932-January 1938: Pacification Army 'Ching An Jun'
February 1938-May 1940: Pacification Division 'Ching An Shi'
June 1940-August 1945: 1st Division

Unit 53 or Unit 868

This special unit was formed in September 1941 with the title of the 2nd Manchukuo Guerrilla Detachment. The unit was under the control of the Kwangtung Army Military Intelligence Section and was formed to perform covert guerrilla operations in Soviet-controlled Siberia. After the German invasion of Russia in 1941 the Japanese felt able again to try and inflict some kind of damage on the Soviet Union. They had been badly beaten by the Russians in the fighting in Nomonhan in 1939 and although they could not spare enough troops or resources for a full-scale war with the Soviets they did want to attack them in some way. The Manchukuoan Army had always been indoctrinated into regarding the Soviet Union as the main enemy and had been trained to support their Japanese masters in this role. Although only small, this new Manchukuoan unit was to at least launch a token war against the Russians. The unit's first 100 recruits came mostly from the Mongolian population of Manchukuo and the best available recruits were chosen. Many of the Mongolians had served in the so-called Mongolian Independence Army and their average age was over 30.

'Chien Tao Tui' – Korean Support Infantry Detachment

A special unit of the Manchukuoan Army was raised in Jiandao Province by a Manchurian businessman of Korean descent in November 1937. He proposed to the Japanese that they should utilise the large number of Koreans living in Manchukuo to help fight the Communist guerrillas. The Japanese were in favour of the idea as they surmised that the Koreans would have no loyalty to the Chinese and could be more trusted than the usual Manchukuoan recruits. They began by appointing a few trusted Koreans and Japanese to hold the main posts in the force. After these key posts were filled the unit was officially formed on 15 December 1938, with the first batch of recruits arriving at the training centre in early 1939. The first two groups of recruits were made to sit entrance exams but this was dispensed with after the introduction of conscription in Manchukuo in 1940. Some non-Koreans were included in the first two batches of recruits but the 3rd to 7th groups of recruits were raised only from the ethnic Koreans of Manchukuo. The first organisation of the Chien Tao Unit was made up of a headquarters, an infantry company and a mortar battery. This initially small force was expanded year on year with a fresh intake of about 700 men per annum. Taking into account the large number of casualties and desertions of about 400 per year then the actual expansion in numbers was about 300 per year. In 1940 the Chien Tao was provided with another infantry company, giving it an official strength of two infantry companies and one mortar battery. The mortar battery was reported to be armed with 'rapid firing' mortars, which may have been the model which had been manufactured in the Fengtien Arsenal for a number of years.

For the first four or so years of its existence the 'Chien Tao Tui' was heavily involved in fighting anti-Japanese guerrillas in Manchukuo. It was given the title by the Japanese of 'Korean Support Infantry Detachment' and was well regarded by them as a ruthless anti-bandit unit. In 1944 the unit was sent over the border into Hopei Province by the Japanese to help fight Communist guerrillas there. It stayed in the region until the end of the war when the fate of its volunteers is not known. During its service in North China the 'Chien Tao Tui' had again earned a reputation for brutality and was reported to have laid waste to large areas which came under its rule. It is safe to assume that any men of the unit who were captured by either the Nationalists or Communists would have received short shrift. The 'Chien Tao Tui' was one of the few 'puppet' units to earn the respect of the Japanese and the whole unit seems to have been indoctrinated with their employer's martial spirit. This is well demonstrated by the words of the units official song:

> For the pride of the age, for Manchukuo's great prosperity,
> We are the vanguard of the gathering army, valiant fellows of Korea,
> Undertake the mission of our forefathers, arise, arise!
> The army has only just been formed, but the indomitable spirit of Yamato drives us on,
> We are following the will of the Emperor,
> Special Service Force, We are the chosen of the Emperor!

'Tesseki Butai' – Iron Stone Unit

As the war drew to a close the Chinese Communist forces infiltrated in larger and larger numbers into Manchukuoan territory. Communist forces were particularly strong in the south-western region of Manchukuo and existing Japanese and Manchukuoan forces in that area were finding it increasingly difficult to contain them. Therefore it was decided in Autumn 1944 to form a special unit of the Manchukuoan Army known as 'Tesseki Butai' which was given the nickname of the 'Iron Stone Unit' to act as an elite anti-guerrilla force. The unit consisted of two brigades, one of cavalry and one of infantry, and was made up of various nationalities. Chinese, Koreans and Japanese formed the Infantry Brigade of approximately 4,750 men while Mongolians made up the Cavalry Brigade of about 5,000 men. The Cavalry Brigade was given the task of guarding the open plains of the region while the Infantry Brigade operated in the mountainous regions. As an elite unit the 'Tesseki Butai' was given priority in weaponry and equipment and its men were armed with the latest Japanese Type 99 rifles and carbines and the Type 93 heavy machine gun. The unit was given anti-Communist indoctrination before being sent to the front in the hope that this would prepare the men for the task ahead of them. Reports of the time indicate that the men did not take this propaganda too seriously and by this stage in the war there was little enthusiasm left in this remote corner of the war. The 'Tesseki Butai' suffered heavily when it did see action and would have been destroyed in the final days of the war.

The Manchukuoan Army 1940–45

The Manchukoan Army spent the last five years of its existence fighting the increasing Communist guerrilla threat in Manchukuo and in Northern China. Most of the active fighting by the Manchukuoan Army would have been undertaken by its elite special units (see above). The majority of the Manchukuoan Army were still seen by the Japanese as unreliable with questionable loyalty. One instance of this disloyalty took place in January 1940 when General Mo Sing-ya went over to the Nationalists with his regiment after killing all their Japanese advisors. The Japanese were happier to leave Manchukuoan units to perform the standard 'puppet' troop's role of guard duties in pacified areas. Information on the role of the Manchukuoan Army during the 1940–45 period is not readily available. By 1940 Manchukuo had fulfilled its propaganda role for the Japanese and as they moved south into the Pacific from December 1941 the Chinese mainland became more or less a sideshow. The Japanese Imperial Army still maintained substantial forces in occupied China and Manchukuo but these were to maintain the 'status quo'. Some attempts were made after 1940 to improve the overall standard of the Manchukuoan Army and small numbers of heavier equipment such as tanks and artillery were issued to them (see above). Apart from its role in operations into Jehol in 1933 and Northern China in 1937 the Manchukuoan Army was kept within its own borders. One interesting report does states however that some Manchukuoan troops were employed during the fighting in Burma in early 1944.

Strength of Manchukuoan Army 1940–45

According to Soviet intelligence sources in 1944 the Manchukuoan Army had a strength of 200,000 to 220,000 men in the following units:

1 Pacification Division (3 infantry regiments, 1 artillery regiment)
1 Guards Brigade
9–10 Infantry Brigades (each with 2 infantry regiments of 2 battalions and 1 mortar company)
21 Mixed Brigades (each of 1 infantry regiment, 1 cavalry regiment and 1 battery of mountain artillery)
2 Independent Brigades
6 Cavalry Brigades (each with 2 cavalry regiments and 1 battery of horse artillery)
1 Cavalry Division (with 2 cavalry brigades, 1 battalion of horse artillery)
7 Independent Cavalry Regiments
11 Heavy Artillery Units (1 per district)
5 Anti-Aircraft Regiments

Soviet Invasion of Manchukuo, August 1945

As the war in Europe ended in April 1945 the Soviet Union gave the Japanese Empire a year's notice that it was renouncing its mutual non-aggression pact with them. They then began to transport large numbers of troops from their victorious army in the West to the Far East. The implications of these troop movements were not of course lost on the Japanese and their Manchukuoan allies and they tried to prepare for the inevitable invasion of Manchukuo. At the time of the Soviet invasion of Manchukuo the 'puppet' state's army had an approximate strength of 200,000 men. The Leavenworth Papers gives the strength of the Army as 8 infantry divisions and

White Russian Cossack Emigrées practice their famous horse riding skills in the Sanho Region of Manchukuo, which they had made their home since the early 1920's. They had formed themselves into self defence units such as this before volunteering to fight in the special White Russian Brigade of the Manchukuoan Army. When fighting with the Manchukoan Army they swapped the classic Cossack clothes for Japanese type uniforms while still retaining their own distinctive insignia

Philip Jowett Collection

A despondent looking group of Manchukuoan soldiers are held prisoner by their Soviet captors after the invasion of Manchuria in August 1945. Many of these former 'puppet' soldiers were allowed to be recruited by the Chinese Communists as a useful source of ready trained troops.

Novosti

7 cavalry divisions. Although reasonably well trained and armed with small arms and small calibre artillery the Manchukuoan Army was in no way capable of resisting the huge and highly mechanised Soviet invading army. There were only a handful of elderly tankettes and armoured cars in the Manchukuoan armoured units. Even then most of the Manchukuoan armoured vehicles had probably been taken from them by the desperate Japanese forces. The Manchukuoan Army's main strength was in its cavalry force and it was this branch which was to see much of the fighting during the invasion.

When the Soviet *blitzkrieg* was launched on 8 August the invasion force was made up of 76 battle-hardened divisions with over 4,500 tanks. This huge force soon swept aside both the remnants of the Japanese Kwangtung Army and the demoralised Manchukuoan forces. During the early stages of the invasion small units of Manchukuoan Cavalry were in action against the Soviets on several fronts. As the Soviet troops advanced towards the city of Hailar they encountered several Manchurian cavalry units which they easily defeated. The Garrison of Hailar was made up of the Japanese 80th Independent Mixed Brigade and the 119th Infantry Division. Units of the Manchukoan Cavalry were part of the garrison which surrendered the city. Soviet advances continued unabated and the city of Fuchin with its garrison of Japanese and Manchukuoan units fell to the Soviet 171st Tank Brigade with forward elements of 361st Rifle Division on 11 August. Japanese and Manchukuoan defenders either surrendered or retreated to the south and east in an attempt to continue the fight. All the remaining Manchukoan and Japanese troops in the Fuchin region held out for two more days before surrendering on the 13th. After the fall of Fuchin the Soviet southwards advance continued with an amphibious assault on the city of Chiamussu on 16 August. The assault was led by the Soviet 632nd Rifle Regiment along with the 171st Tank Brigade, 361st and 388th Rifle Divisions. Japanese resistance was soon broken and the Manchukuoan 7th Infantry Brigade surrendered the city.

Manchukuoan cavalry forces were also in action on the right of the Trans-Baikal Front in Inner Mongolia. A mixed Soviet-Mongolian force under General Pliyev Advanced across the Inner Mongolian desert between the 12–14 August at a pace of 90–100 kilometres per day. This force's targets were the cities of Dolonnor and Kalgan and as they advanced they swept aside local Inner Mongolian Cavalry. On 14 August General Pliyev's left-hand column encountered a small Manchukuoan cavalry force which they easily defeated and then entered Dolonnor.

As the Soviets advanced the Japanese and the Manchukuoans fell out amongst themselves and heavy fighting between them broke out in the capital, Hsinking. This fighting lasted from 13–19 August, just two days before the final capitulation of the Japanese-Manchukuoan forces on 21 August. During the desperate few weeks of Japanese-Manchukuoan resistance some Manchukoan soldiers turned on their Japanese officers. The Japanese officers were usually killed by their mutinous Manchukuoan troops in revenge for the brutal treatment meted out to them over the years. Small numbers of Manchukoan regulars and auxiliaries did continue to fight alongside their Japanese allies until the end but these were in the minority. After the first week or so most Manchukoan units simply melted away unless restrained by their Japanese officers.

During their thirteen-day campaign the Soviets claimed to have captured a total of 30,700 non-Japanese soldiers and killed a further 10,000. The total of captured was made up of 16,100 Chinese, 3,600 Mongolians, 700 Manchurians and 10,300 Koreans. Presumably the Koreans were auxiliaries of the Kwangtung Army while the Chinese, Mongolians and Manchurians were all soldiers of the Manchukuoan Army. Confusion is caused by the Soviet description of 16,100 'Chinese' prisoners who were in fact Manchukuoans, and the listing of 700 Manchurians who were said to include a number of White Russians. Presumably any White Russians who fell into Soviet hands would have received short shrift from their captors. The disbandment of the 200,000 strong Manchukuoan Army meant that a large number of armed men were aimlessly wandering around the Manchurian countryside. Nationalist units dealt harshly with any Manchukoan soldiers who fell into their hands and this led to large numbers of them going over to the Communists, taking their valuable arms with them. This large body of trained and equipped men was taken advantage of by the Communists who were desperately short of manpower. They pragmatically took 75,000 of the ex-Manchukoan soldiers into their ranks while the Nationalist ignored this source of new recruits. It was to take the Communist officers and cadres months to drill these men into a reliable force. Even though the ex-Manchukoan soldiers who served with the Communists continued to be unreliable and still deserted on occasions they did at least allow the Red forces to expand their army. This large influx of new recruits allowed the Communists under the command of Lin Piao to organise 8 new columns, 7 cavalry divisions, 1 artillery division and 3 independent divisions. As well as the new recruits from the former Manchukuoan Army the Communists also gained vast amounts of equipment belonging to the Japanese and Manchukuoan forces. This equipment amounted to 300,000 rifles, 138,000 machine guns and 2,700 field guns.

CHAPTER THREE

Chinese 'Puppet' Governments and Armies 1931–40

Japanese Intrigues in northern & Eastern China 1933–37

Japan's intrigues in the north of China between its invasion of Manchuria in 1931 and the outbreak of full scale war in 1937 were numerous. They constantly plotted and schemed in an attempt to form 'friendly' governments in so-called buffer states in the region. Although outwardly these intrigues were attempts to set up 'puppet' governments, their main aim was to destabilise the Central Government in Nanking. The Japanese were also concerned to secure their northern flank from the remnants of the KMT north Eastern & north Western Armies. They also wanted to create a buffer zone between Manchukuo, Mongolia and the rest of China. In the Japanese scheme of things any 'puppet' state that survived in north China would serve several purposes. Firstly they would stop the recruitment of northern Chinese to fight the Japanese. Secondly they would stop the supplies of arms and other aid to resistance forces that were active in Manchukuo during the early and mid 1930s.

One of the first attempts at forming a mini 'puppet' state took place in April 1933 in the triangle of land between the Great Wall and the Luan River. The Japanese Kwangtung Army organised the setting up of the regime without authority from the government in Tokyo. Their aim was to 'test the water' and see how the Nationalist government reacted before trying to expand the territory the new 'state' controlled. A 'capital' was set up in the town of Chingwangtao and the 'puppets' flew the old Republican five barred flag over its HQ. The Kwangtung Army's hope was that the 'nameless' state would become a catalyst for other local leaders and government bodies in northern China to break away from central government control. It was also an open secret that the Japanese were trying to persuade a number of prominent Chinese leaders to take charge of the new state. These efforts were centred on the retired General Wu Pei-fu, the former leader of the Chihli warlord clique who had gone into retirement after his army's defeat in 1925. Wu Pei-fu was one of the few warlord army leaders to come out of the period with his reputation in tact and had gained a great deal of respect as a learned man. When he retired he went into a monastery to study the Buddhist religion and seemed quite happy to live out his days there. He did however agree to discuss the possibility of joining an anti-Nationalist government as its figurehead. His insistence on the government and its armed force being a purely Chinese affair without Japanese interference made the idea a non-starter in the Kwangtung Army's eyes and he remained in retirement. Support for the new state disappeared as quickly as it had appeared and the Kwangtung Army withdrew its support. This setback did not however dishearten the Japanese who had simply used the state to prove that the Chinese central government would not react to their provocations. The Japanese were always ready to recruit any local military commander in north China who offered them his services. A US intelligence report of 26 March 1935 describes the careers of three of these military commanders, Generals Li Chi-chun, Shih Yu-shan and Liu Kuei-tang.

General Li Chi-chun

General Li Chi-chun was sixty years old in 1935 and was a native of Hopei province, having enjoyed a long if unsuccessful military career. After serving in the Republican Army during the Revolution of 1911–12 he reached the rank of General. His military record for the next twenty years is a little sketchy but he does not seem to have achieved anything of note during this period. Suddenly in early 1933 he appeared at the head of an army of several thousand men in the Luantung region to the south west of Sanhaikwan in the newly created state of Manchukuo. His army was very active in this region during the first half of 1933, fighting anti-Japanese guerrillas. General Li's army called itself the 'National Salvation Army' and its men carried the five barred flag used by the Chinese Republic from 1912 to 1928. The National Salvation Army claimed to be ready to fight the Japanese but this was soon proved to be a charade. Their real intention was to set up an independent government in northern China with support from the Japanese Army. They made a nuisance of themselves in the border area between Manchukuo and the north of China and captured a few small towns in the latter. The signing of the Tangku Truce between China and Japan put paid to Li's activities as it agreed to the setting up of a neutral demilitarised zone in the area he had hoped to use as a base for his new 'government'. Li was called to Dairen in Manchukuo and presumably received orders from his Japanese masters to stop all activity in the region. At the time he claimed to have 10,000 men under his command and was told that 2,000 of them would be recruited into the 'Demilitarised Zone Peace Preservation Corps' while the rest of his force would be disbanded. The Peace Preservation Corps was supposed to be a neutral force recruited from various groups of disbanded and unemployed Chinese soldiers. General Li then disappeared from the scene and reports of the time say that he took up residence in the favourite retirement place of former employees of the Japanese, their concession in the Chinese city of Tientsin. Presumably he had been suitably rewarded for his work for the Japanese and would be kept in reserve in case he was needed later.

General Shih Yu-san

General Shih Yu-san was regarded as a an able and efficient military officer with plenty of experience who had graduated from the Paotingfu Military Academy in Hopei province. His early military career was spent in the service of the famous 'Christian Warlord' Feng Yu-hsiang in the 1920s. He rose rapidly through the officer ranks and went from battalion to division commander in a very short time. General Feng Yu-hsiang's 'Kuominchun' or 'Peoples Army' was at first in opposition to the Nationalist Northern Expedition of 1927–28, and when General Shih Yu-san was captured he was given command of the Nationalist 13th Route Army and then made governor of Anhwei province. In 1930 he joined a revolt led by Generals Feng Yu-hsiang and Yen Hsi-shan against Chiang Kai-shek's Nationalist Government and when it was defeated he fled to Dairen in Manchuria. After Manchuria was taken over by the Japanese in 1931, General Shih Yu-san was said to be in Mukden, where he accepted an appointment to command a military force under the orders of the Japanese. His force operated in the same region of Luantung, south-west of Sanhaikwan, in the same area as General Li Chi-chun. General Shih and his force of several thousand were in action throughout the first few months of 1933 and their operations were again stopped by the signing of the Tangku Truce in May. After the Tangku Agreement, General Shih Yu-san effectively lost control of his army and his force was disbanded, with 1,000 of them joining the Peace Preservation Corps in the demilitarised zone.

General Liu Kuei-tang

General Liu Kuei-tang was basically a bandit leader who also spent periods of his lawless career in the service of various armies and governments. He became a bandit at the age of ten in the mountains in the south of Shangtung province. After rising through the ranks of his bandit band he found himself in command of a large number of men. He then decided to surrender himself and his men to a regular Chinese Army unit, which absorbed them. This recruitment of surrendering bandits was a common practice in China during the first half of the 20th century. The bandits would often be then issued with new arms and equipment and then they would often desert and revert to their old bandit ways. General Shih and his men were to do this at least twice during the next few years and surprisingly were accepted back into the army each time. In 1931 Shih and his men were 'reorganised' yet again into the army and sent by General Han Fu-chu to garrison an area of north Shangtung. After revolting yet again they were sent by the 'Young Marshal' Chang Hsueh-Liang in 1933 to help defend the province of Jehol from the invading Japanese force and their Manchukuoan allies. Not surprisingly General Liu immediately went over to the Japanese and he was made a Manchukuoan commander. Under Japanese orders he then took his force into the south-eastern part of Chahar province, in the Dolonor region. This region was still under the control of the Chinese government and the Japanese were happy for anyone to cause problems for their forces there. He then led his men to the west into Chahar province and advanced as far as Changpei, north of the city of Kalgan. The invasion of Chahar was reported at the time as a Manchukuoan Army operation but it was probably undertaken by General Liu without the permission of his 'new' employers. General Liu then began to talk to the Nationalist commander in Chahar, General Sung Che-yuan who offered him the chance to change sides yet again! This General Liu duly did and he was given the ridiculous title of 'Bandit Suppression Commander of Eastern Chahar'. His force was stationed at Chihcheng and soon came into conflict with the local Chinese Militia when he tried to collect taxes over and above those due. General Liu wasn't happy in his new posting and applied to General Sung to transfer his command to somewhere more prosperous. He was having difficulty feeding his men let alone giving them the other little luxuries such as plunder that they had been used to in the past. After repeated refusals from General Sung to transfer him and his men he led them in yet a further rebellion on Christmas day 1933. They sacked a couple of towns and then moved southwards with their loot loaded onto hundreds of camels and thousands of donkeys which they had commandeered. Both his Chinese and Japanese employers had now finally had enough of General Liu and his men and neither army was willing to risk recruiting him again. His army wandered around the area bordering Chahar and the newly introduced Demilitarised Zone crossing the line between them if threatened by either Chinese or Japanese forces. By New Years day 1934 he was only 15 miles from Peking and attacked a town which alerted the Chinese garrison to his army's presence. Strong Nationalist forces under General Han Fu-chu sallied out to meet him and managed to defeat his army. General Liu was however a survivor and evaded capture, making his way to the Japanese concession in Tientsin where he contacted the Japanese again and offered his services.

Japanese intrigues continued in north China right up until the full scale invasion of the rest of China in 1937. Major General Doihara Kenji planned to set up an autonomous government in Chahar Province in Inner Mongolia in June 1935 under the control of KMT 29th Army commander, Sung Che-yuan. Sung was a former subordinate of Feng Yu-hsiang, the 'Christian Warlord' and was a real maverick. Nationalist commanders like Sung had no real loyalty to Chiang Kai-shek or the central government and were always prone to collaboration with the Japanese. If this plan had been successful he would then have fostered other similar mini-governments in north China before unifying them into one larger 'puppet' regime. This north China 'puppet' state was reported to have been given the provisional name of 'Huapeikuo' or 'North China' and would have consisted of the provinces of Hopei, Chahar, Suiyuan, Shantung and Shansi. The planning for this northern Chinese 'puppet' state was cancelled when the East Hopei regime was declared. During this confusing period of intrigue by the Japanese secret service in north China 'puppet' governments could be formed and dissolved in a period of a few days. If a 'puppet' government failed to achieve the aims set it by its Japanese masters then the regime would be dissolved and Dohihara would move onto his next project. They also were willing to encourage any other groups in other areas of China who were ready to rebel against Chiang Kai-shek's Nationalist government. Intelligence reports of 1936 claim that one such group was planning to try and set up an independent government in Fukien province on the south eastern coast of China. This group supposedly had the backing of two prominent former Nationalist generals, Ch'en Ming-su and the hero of the battle from Shanghai in 1932, Ts'ai T'ing-kai. The real leader of the planned revolt however was General Kao Cheng-hsueh, who formed the 'Chinese Peoples Revolutionary Alliance'. He bought arms in Japanese-ruled Formosa, which was just across the straits from Fukien, and some so-called 'bandit activity' was reported in the province at the time. Another Fukien group organised in Formosa with presumably backing from the Japanese garrison there called itself the 'Fukien Provincial Autonomous Commission' and planned to set up a regime along the lines of the East Hopei government created by Yin Ju-keng. Nothing came of the plans of either of these groups, although they do illustrate the Japanese willingness to support any group who they believed might weaken the Chinese government's hold on even a tiny piece of territory. Of course. all these plots and schemes would be made unnecessary by the outbreak of open war between China and Japan.

East Hopei 1935–37

Following clashes between Chinese and Japanese forces south of the Great Wall a truce was signed which led to the Demilitarising of the region. The 'Tangku Truce' signed on 31 May 1933 led to the withdrawal of all Chinese troops in the Demilitarised Zone and their replacement by a Chinese Peace Preservation Corps or 'Pao-an-tui'. This Peace Preservation Corps was to police the Demilitarised Zone as a 'neutral' force and although they were armed, they were limited to small arms. The Demilitarised Zone became an area of intrigues and plots by the Japanese as they tried to influence the Chinese in the region. Their intention was to try and set up a small 'puppet' state which could become the catalyst for a new pro-Japanese government in north China. To achieve this they needed to persuade one of the high-ranking Nationalist officials to come over to them. They found that the Nationalist Commissioner of the Luantung De-militarised Zone in Eastern Hopei, Yin Ju-keng was open to persuasion and he became head of their 'puppet' regime. Yin Ju-keng had ambitions to lead an anti-Nationalist and anti-Communist government in north China. He proclaimed the 'Autonomous Government of Eastern Hopei' on 25 November 1935 with its 'capital' or headquarters at Tungchow with himself as self-proclaimed leader of the new state. The governing body of the East Hopei Government consisted of 9 men of which 5 were commanders of Peace Preservation Corps units under Japanese control.

Yin Ju-keng, the leader of the East Hopei Government reviews a parade of his 'puppet' army from a podium. Yin is dressed in a Japanese khaki uniform as is the officer to his right and they have a five-coloured enamel star on their peaked caps. East Hopei only adopted the five barred pre-1928 Republican flag and its star insignia after a year of the regime's existence.

The state of East Hopei comprised the northern 25% of Hopei province and covered 10,000 square miles with a population of 4,000,000. Although the new government claimed to control a large area and population its real power hardly extended outside the confines of its squalid 'capital' Tungchow. In fact the Japanese, who had of course sponsored the regime, did not even extend official recognition to it themselves. For the first year of its existence East Hopei did not even have its own flag and continued to fly the Nationalist flag. To celebrate its first anniversary the flag of East Hopei was unveiled, but in a typical unimaginative move by the 'puppets' they adopted an old and redundant banner. They chose as the symbol for their new state the old five barred flag as used by the Chinese Republican Government between 1912 and 1928. The use of the flag of the Republic was quite apt as the various governments that flew it from 1912 until 1928 had only a little more credibility than the East Hopei regime. East Hopei was financed largely from revenue taken from smuggling of Japanese goods through its territory. In the strange situation that existed in north China at the time the state also continued to receive subsidies from some Chinese companies. For instance the Peking-Liaoning Railway Company paid the East Hopei government $100,000 and the Chang Lo Salt Company $250,000, to be allowed to continue their respective businesses. Much of East Hopei funds were spent on the military with a large part of the budget going to pay for the Japanese military advisors. Yin Ju-keng reportedly also donated the huge amount of $2,000,000 to Prince Teh Wang's Inner Mongolian forces fighting in the Suiyuan Campaign in 1936. Whether this money came directly from the East Hopei treasury or whether it came from Japanese sources is not known. The fascist nature of the regime was demonstrated by the $200,000 which was spent on huge celebrations to mark the first anniversary of the government in 1936.

The East Hopei Army 1935–37

The East Hopei Army was raised from the former Peace Preservation Corps soldiers who were raised as a so-called neutral force for policing the Demilitarised Zone in the area south of the Great Wall.

The Japanese officers of the Kwangtung Army tried to create an anti-Communist army from the unreliable East Hopei forces. Japanese advisors who were attached to the army drilled the men by day and then gave them anti-Communist lectures by night. The Japanese advisors had a great deal of influence within the Army – in fact they had the final say in all matters. This intensive training went on for a year and by the end the Japanese hoped that they had created a reliable and well-trained force. The East Hopei Army was, however, only intended to be a local policing force and the heaviest weaponry that they were allowed to carry were rifles and side arms. As far as is known the Japanese did not even allow them to have a single machine gun and they certainly never had any artillery of any kind.

Yin Ju-keng had grand plans for his state and his army and claimed that his 'anti-Red' army had a strength of 20–30,000 and would deal with the Red Army in northern Shensi. He also planned to raise the grandly titled 'Sino-Japanese-Manchukuo-Mongolian Army' with which he would take on his enemies, the Communists and Nationalist Government in Nanking. The East Hopei army operated on a very limited and local basis and its main military operation during its short life took place in December 1935. This operation was undertaken by the 4th Detachment of the East Hopei Army and was an attack on the Nationalist town of Taku and the port of Tangku. The forces defending the two towns were from the 32nd Nationalist Army and initially put up a fierce resistance. In the attack 2 'puppet' soldiers were killed and the East Hopei force withdrew, 'licking their wounds'. Threats were then made to the defenders by the Japanese and to avoid provoking them the units of the 32nd Army were ordered to retreat. The East Hopei Army then advanced into the two towns and extended Yin Ju-keng's rule over them without having to fire a shot. The only other military operation by an East Hopei Army unit was a revolt against the rule of Yin Ju-keng led by Chao Lei in September 1936. Chao was the commander of the Peace Preservation Corps in the towns of Tangshan, Fengyun and Tangku and had been implicated in a plot against Yin. When he was dismissed from his post he led 400 of his men in a mutiny and kidnapped two Japanese officials including his unit's military advisor. Chao's men escaped into the countryside taking their hostages with them but were pursued by Japanese military forces. The mutineers released the Japanese and then shook off their pursuers and disappeared into the countryside.

Although Yin had ambitions to spread his anti-communist message over the whole of northern China, in reality there was little that he could do to affect the situation outside the confines of his 'mini state'. His attempts to woo the population of northern China were limited to a few propaganda campaigns. In February 1937 he did get his Japanese masters to drop propaganda leaflets from their planes over the northern Chinese cities of Tsangchow and Shihciachuang. These leaflets called for the rest of northern China to join with East Hopei to form an anti-Nationalist government and he demanded that north China adopt the old Republican five barred flag. These demands from Yin Ju-keng fell on deaf ears and East Hopei never became the catalyst for further expansion of pro-Japanese regimes in north China until the outbreak of full-scale war in 1937.

The East Hopei Army had 4 corps divided into 3 brigades each, with each brigade divided into 3 sub-brigades, each one possessing a Japanese Advisor. In an attempt to make the Army appear more substantial the brigades were also described as divisions, although the organisation stayed the same.

Table 3 – East Hopei Army, May 1937	
1st Corps 'Tungchow'	4,000 men (Commander: Chang ching-yu)
2nd Corps 'Tsunhwa'	4,000 men (Commander: Chang Yen-tien)
3rd Corps 'Iwanchow'	4,000 men (Commander: Li Yun-sheng)
4th Corps 'Tangshan'	4,000 men (Commander: Han Tze-his)
Training Corps 'Tungchow'	2,000 men (Commander: Yin Ju-keng)

The Tungchow Mutiny

The East Hopei Government went out of existence following events which occurred in the state's 'capital' of Tungchow on the morning of 29 July 1937. In the strange situation which existed in Tungchow there was a unit of 800 Nationalist soldiers of the 29th Army under the command of General Sung Che-yuan camped outside the town's walls. These Nationalist troops were allowed by Yin Ju-keng and his East Hopei Government to stay encamped outside the city walls despite Japanese attempts to remove them. It may seem strange that a large unit of the Nationalist Army should be camped outside the walls of the 'capital' of a state which had been set up in opposition to their government, but such was the bizarre status of East Hopei. The trouble in Tungchow began when the Japanese troops tried to disarm the Nationalist soldiers on 27 July and they resisted. According to witnesses at the time the Japanese overcame this resistance and killed some 500 of Sun's men when they cornered them against the city walls. In the early hours of 29 July, remnants of the Nationalist troops and rebellious East Hopei Army units attacked the Japanese garrison. Several thousand men of the 1st and 2nd Corps of the East Hopei Army were reported to be involved in the mutiny. A massacre of the Japanese population of Tungchow then took place with over 250 civilians being killed. Only about 60 of the Japanese civilians involved in the running of the East Hopei Government survived the massacre. The Chinese vented their years of frustration on the luckless Japanese and according to reports of the time a number of atrocities took place. About 20 Japanese soldiers were killed including Lieutenant Colonel Hosoki, the head of the Special Service Mission, and a further 13 were wounded. The attacking forces were claimed to total over 5,000 men including all the trainee officers from the East Hopei military academy. Yin Ju-keng's headquarters situated in a Confucian temple was destroyed along with a large part of the 'capital'. Japanese reinforcements were sent to put down the rebellion and soon restored order but this uprising spelled the end of East Hopei as a separate state. Yin Ju-keng was rescued from the hands of the mutineers when they came to hand him over to what they thought was the victorious 29th Army. Yin was set free and taken to the safety of the Japanese Embassy. Yin was now seen as incompetent by his Japanese sponsors and an embarrassment to them and was removed from power in East Hopei but was not, contrary to popular reports of the time executed. He did, in fact, go on to serve the Japanese in other capacities until 1945, when he was captured by the Nationalist authorities. His continued employment by the Japanese after his failure in East Hopei does show how hard it was for them to find Chinese high-ranking officers who were willing to serve in their 'puppet' administrations.

The East Hopei Army did see service on the Japanese side during the early days of the Japanese invasion of northern China in 1937. According to *The History of the Sino-Japanese War 1937–1945* by Hsu Long-hsuen & Chang Ming-hai, the bulk of the East Hopei Army was part of the Japanese force in the Peking-Tientsin area. This Japanese force made up of the 5th Division, 20th Division and 3 independent brigades, and was supported by "the main force of the puppet East Hopei Army".

Provisional Government Army 1938–40

The Provisional Government of China was formed on 14 December 1937 in Peking with Wang Ke-min as President. At first the Provisional Government was allowed no army of its own and relied for security on a lightly-armed 5,000-strong Police force. In May 1938 the first steps were taken to the forming of a regular army by the opening of a Military Academy for officer training at Tungchow. The Academy had an initial intake of 100 cadets, who received a one-year training course to prepare them to become the officers of a new and 'untainted' Army for the Provisional Government. The President of the Provisional Government, Wang Ke-min made a 'morale boosting' speech to cadets at the Military School at Tungchow in which he said "When you enter the army you must remember that the army is now a national one, and not as in the past a personal one. You must distinguish between friend and foe, Japan is our friend, Communism our foe".

A parade of Provisional Government troops takes place in Peking in 1938 with a 'puppet' Police band playing in the foreground. In the distance we can make out the marching columns of the 'puppet' army who are armed with spears. Other poorer quality photographs of the same parade which show the soldiers closer up show more details. They are wearing armbands and marching behind their unit flag, which has the five barred flag in the fly and three red stars on a white field.

Philip Jowett Collection

Soldiers of the Provisional Government Army doing early morning exercises as part of their training in Peking. The Provisional Government Army provided a very basic uniform to its soldiers and it should be noted that some of the men are wearing civilian trousers.

Philip Jowett Collection

This new Army was to be raised in so-called 'Sound Parts of the Country' where the population did not have a particular loyalty to the Nationalist Government or the Communists. Until the cadets at the Tungchow Academy were ready to take up their commands in the Provisional Government Army former Nationalist officers were recruited as a temporary measure. On 10 February 1939 a Training School was opened for non-commissioned officers with 1,000 cadets undergoing a six month training course. The Provisional Government Army had a target strength of 13,200 men and was divided into 8 infantry regiments of 1,650 men each. Six of the regiments were formed into 3 brigades, with each brigade being under the command of a Chinese Major-General and a Japanese advisor:

Table 4 – Order of Battle – Provisional Government Army, September 1939

1st Brigade 'Peking' (Major General Liu Feng-chih)
1st Regiment – Peking, 2nd Regiment – Tungchow

2nd Brigade 'Paotingfu' (Major General Huang Nan-peng)
3rd Regiment – Paotingfu, 4th Regiment – Chengtingfu

3rd Brigade 'Kaiping' (Major General Lu Cheng-sheng)
5th Regiment – Kaiping, 6th Regiment – Tangshan

7th Independent Regiment 'Tientsin' (Colonel Sun Chi-chang)

8th Independent Regiment 'Tsinanfu' (Colonel Ma Wen-chi)

In the streets of Peking in 1938 a truck full of Provisional Government soldiers pose for the camera while on patrol. They are all wearing peaked caps with cotton tunics, trousers and puttees, all in a mid brown colour. The badges on the peaked caps are eight-pointed stars, which was one of the two types of insignia used by the Provisional Government Army. This unit has a mixture of armament with the man on the right having a Taisho-11 1922 light machine gun and the officer in the centre carrying a Japanese 'Shin-Gunto' sword.

Philip Goody

Two 'puppet' soldiers in Northern China pose for a snap with a Japanese officer of the Imperial Army. It is fairly rare to find a Japanese officer willing to be in the same photograph as his 'racially inferior' allies. Both of the 'puppet' soldiers are wearing the grey cotton peaked cap worn mostly in the north of China and grey heavy cotton tunic and breeches. The man on the right has some kind of rank on his left sleeve and both men have large metal cap badges.

Philip Jowett Collection

Men of a hastily formed pro-Japanese militia ZB-26 machine gun crew in the city of Kukiang pose for the camera a few days after its fall. In every city that the Japanese captured they attempted to raise local forces to help them police them. The men are dressed in civilian clothes and only have their headbands to identify them as a military force.

Robert Hunt Library

In addition to these forces a 400 strong bodyguard unit was formed to protect the 'puppet' government officials after all of Wang Ke-min's Japanese bodyguards were killed in the course of their duties.

Provisional Government Army

The age of recruits for the new army was from eighteen to twenty-five, and former soldiers of the Nationalist Army were not allowed to join. Former officers of the Nationalist and pre-1928 warlords' armies were encouraged to join, however, and a 'Mutual Society for the Chinese Republic' was set up to try and reassure them that they would be welcome. Lower ranking officers were to be aged between twenty five and thirty-five years and had to have served for at least a year in their previous military careers. On entry to the Provisional Army they had to undergo a three month training course. The senior officers had also to have served for at least a year and were to be aged between thirty and forty years, and upon joining the Army they were to attend a six month training course.

Pupils from the Tungchow Military Academy were given the rank of either Lieutenant or 2nd Lieutenant when they graduated. The first group to leave the Academy were made up of 41 Lieutenants and 257 2nd Lieutenants. With 191 ex-Nationalist officers who joined the Provisional Government Army and had received the six month course, this brought the number of junior officers up to 448.

Conditions of Service

The conditions of service for new recruits in the Provisional Government Army were published in the press in northern China in September 1939, and were as follows. Recruits had to be between seventeen and twenty-five years of age, over 4ft 8ins tall and had to bring certificates from the village headman and head of the family. Pay started off for a 3rd Class Private at 15 Dollars a month rising to 16.50 Dollars for a Private 2nd Class and 18 for a 1st Class Private. A 3rd Class Private would become a 2nd or 1st Class Private after one year's service and if a Private received a favourable report he may be promoted to Corporal or Sergeant. The Provisional Government also promised to provide every recruit with a new uniform, shoes and blankets.

Reformed Government Army 1938–40

When the Japanese Central China Area Army captured the Nationalist capital of Nanking it decided to form a 'puppet' government there in an effort to rival the Provisional Government in Peking which had been formed by the North China Area Army. The Government was formed on 28 March 1938 under the leadership of Liang Hung-chih, a former official of the pre-1928 warlord governments. Few men of any status could be found to serve in the government, especially after the excesses committed by the Japanese troops when they took the city a few months previously. Another weakness of the Reformed Government from the Japanese point of view was that the officers of the Central Area Army had little or no experience of organising 'puppet' governments. The North Area Army officers on the other hand were well practised in the art after years of setting up small and short-lived regimes in that region. The poorly organised nature of the Reformed Government was reflected in

A 'rag-tag' unit of the Reformed Government Army on parade in 1939 are wearing a real mixture of uniforms. They are all wearing khaki cotton uniforms with some having German M35 steel helmets and the others Japanese models. The officer has a Japanese 'Shin-Gunto' sword as issued to many 'puppet' officers as a mark of their authority. This poorly turned out group illustrates the ad-hoc nature of the Reformed Government's forces.

Philip Jowett Collection

Huang Ch'i-hsing, the Vice Minister of Pacification, and commanding officer of the Reformed Government Army. He is wearing a Japanese officer's field cap and tunic, with the badge of the Reformed Government on his cap. On the collar of his tunic he has his rank of Major General indicated by a gold eight-pointed star on a gold-coloured patch. We can just see the handle of this 'Shin-Gunto' Japanese officer's sword presented to him by his Japanese masters.

Philip Jowett Collection

This group of Reformed Government soldiers from the Pacification Department of the 'puppet' regime's army are having rifle practice under the supervision of the Japanese instructor with the armband. They are armed with captured Chinese Mauser Hanyang 88 rifles which was one of the most common types in use with the Nationalists.

Philip Jowett Collection

The same unit of Pacification troops of the Reformed Government take aim during rifle drill at anti-guerrilla training school. All the men are dressed in the simple light khaki cotton uniforms with Japanese field caps of the other ranks type. On their caps they would have the five-petalled flower badge used by the Reformed Government Army.

Philip Jowett Collection

the poor state of the Army raised by the regime. Early units of the Army seem to have been formed in a hurry and photographic evidence indicates that the first units were of very poor quality. When the threat of 'bandit' activities in the region of Nanking became apparent the government formed Pacification Units to try and counter these guerrilla forces. These units were stationed in various districts:

1st Pacification District – Chekiang & Kiangsi Provinces
2nd, 3rd, 4th Pacification Districts – regions south of Yangtze River
5th Pacification District – regions north of Yangtze River

In December 1938 the Pacification Minister, Jen Yuan-tao announced that the Army of the Reformed Government stood at about 10,000 men. He also announced that a Military Academy had been opened in November to train officers in preparation for the expansion of the Army. The Academy had 320 cadets aged eighteen to twenty-five who it was hoped would not be 'tainted' by previous service with the Nationalist Army. Most of the rank and file of the Reformed Army were ex-Nationalist soldiers and the aim was to create a new 'class' of loyal officer to lead these unreliable men. The year-long training course given by 20 Japanese instructors ended in November 1939 and was to be followed by a further six month period. Officers, however, were needed to command the expanded Army which by November 1939 had a strength of 30,000 men in 10 regiments of 3,000 men each. It is doubtful if the six month course was completed, as by March 1940 the regime ceased to exist with its absorption into the new Reorganised Government in Nanking under Wang Ching-wei. The performance of the Reformed Government Army during its short life was not exactly inspiring, with news reports stating that the 'puppet' soldiers fled from guerrillas whenever they came into contact with them. The morale of the higher-ranking Reformed Government officers may also have been affected not only by their men's poor performance but also by the uncertainty of their future. This insecurity came from the knowledge that their regime and its army was always intended by the Japanese as a temporary measure until a unified 'puppet' government for all of occupied China could be organised.

An additional force was formed in June 1939 to police the coastline and inland waterways under the control of the Reformed Government. The so called 'Water Patrol Corps' was to serve as an independent force under the command of Vice-Admiral Hsu Chien-ting, who was formerly in command of the Nationalist Chinese Yangtze Squadron. A 'Water Police Training School' was set up with an initial enrolment of 150 cadets, who were to be trained by 30 Japanese and 30 Chinese instructors during the six month course. The Corps was to guard the coast and patrol the Yangtze River and Lake Tai, although there were few vessels available for this role.

There were also plans to create an Air Force of the Reformed Government and although these did not progress very far a number of Japanese training gliders were purchased.

Inner Mongolia 1935–40

The situation in Inner Mongolia during the period covered by this book is one of the most complicated and intricate stories of the history of 'puppet' governments and their armies in China. Inner Mongolia was part of China and was ruled from afar by the new Nationalist Government of Chiang Kai-shek. It was a vast region of open plains and desert inhabited by hardy nomads who were the ancestors of the Mongol herdsmen who became the warriors who had conquered one of the largest empires in history under the command of the brilliant general Genghis Khan and his successors. The region is divided into four provinces of Jehol in the East, Chahar, Suiyuan and in the far west, Ningsia. Inner Mongolia had already been the scene of conflict with the Japanese invasion of Jehol in 1933 and its incorporation into the 'puppet' state of Manchukuo. What was left of Inner Mongolia seemed, to the Japanese, to be up for grabs and they hoped to bring it under their sphere of influence.

The Mongols of Inner Mongolia were organised in tribes or 'Meng' which were further subdivided into Banners or 'Ch'i' – a practice left over from the time when the Mongols were a warrior people. Although officially under the rule of the central government in Nanking, the Inner Mongolians were allowed a certain amount of autonomy. This limited power was not enough for some of the Inner Mongolian leadership and they began to press for full independence from Nanking. The Inner Mongolians had several grievances against Nanking, with the most important one being the Chinese policy of allowing unlimited migration of Han Chinese to their lands. Inner Mongolians worried that their small Mongol population would soon be swamped

王　德
蒙古聯合自治政府主席

Prince Teh Wang, the most prominent Mongolian leader of the 1930s and 40s, is pictured here on a propaganda postcard issued by he new 'puppet' government of Inner Mongolia in 1937. The Inner Mongolia regime was allowed all the trappings of an independent government by its Japanese sponsors.

Philip Jowett Collection

by the large number of Chinese farmers moving into the region. Teh also resented the Central Government for failing to defend Jehol against the Japanese and allowing it to be taken over by them. Several of the young Princes of Inner Mongolia began to agitate for greater freedom from the central government and called for an end to Chinese migration. The most prominent of these leaders was Prince Teh Wang, leader of the West Sunid Banner, who had been active in Mongolian politics since the mid-1920s. Chang Hsueh-liang, the 'Young Marshal' who in late 1928 had been appointed as commander-in-chief of the North-East Border Region called a meeting of all the Inner Mongolian princes and nobles. Teh Wang recieved a warm welcome and was given a personal tour of the main Manchurian arsenal and was presented with a number of rifles with ammunition along with a couple of mountain guns. He was also promised military advisers to train his personal army but at the same time a similar amount of arms and training was offered to the other Inner Mongolian princes in effort to keep the delicate balance of power in the region. In a further attempt to keep the Prince in the government camp he was given the honourary command of the Nationalist 1st Anti-Japanese United Army in Chahar Province. However, after this force failed to stop Japanese incursions and raids in the Province, he was dismissed and his army disbanded. Teh Wang continued meantime to try and gain some kind of autonomy from the Nanking Government and did manage to get the Nationalists to recognise the so-called Mongolian

Local Autonomous Political Council. This Council soon turned out to have little influence and was largely ignored by the Nationalist Government.

While negotiations between the Inner Mongolian Princes and the Nanking Government continued the Japanese stepped up their intrigues in the region in an effort to destabilise the situation. Japan's constant meddling in Inner Mongolia had begun soon after their invasion of the province of Jehol. They were plotting with local warlords and bandits to try and form small regions under their control. The intention was that if the Chinese Government did not resist these incursions into their territory the Japanese could gradually expand them. In June 1935 in the Dolonnor region the Japanese set up an independent 'Hsien' or district, with its own military force wearing their own insignia and who were trained by 'foreign' advisors. A month later the Japanese also set up a so-called Peace Preservation Corps in Chahar, northern Inner Mongolia, under the leadership of General Chang Yun-jung, with a strength of 3,000. The force was armed and equipped by the Japanese and were issued with 150 rounds of ammunition each.

The Japanese realised, however, that their best chance of taking control of Inner Mongolia without a full-scale invasion was through Prince Teh Wang. The Prince had become disillusioned with the Nationalists and tired of trying to gain autonomy for Inner Mongolia through negotiation and began to toy with the idea of throwing in his lot with the Japanese. In October 1935 Japanese Major General Doihara finally persuaded the Prince to join the Japanese and to trust them to support his aim of creating an independent Inner Mongolian State. After a few months delay Teh Wang made his formal break with the Nationalists in February 1936 by announcing the convening of a Mongolian Military Government conference at his Headquarters. As well as most of the other

Inner Mongolian soldiers of Prince Teh Wang's Army gather at their headquarters in Pailingmiao in 1936. They are dressed in a paramilitary uniform of sorts with the native tunic or 'deel' and turbans. Prince Teh Wang's men were sometimes well armed and this group has Czech ZB-26 light machine guns of the latest type.

Philip Jowett Collection

Banner chiefs one important guest was the Chief of Staff of the Japanese Kwangtung Army. At the meeting Teh Wang formally announced the formation of the Mongolian 'puppet' regime. He deigned that the calendar followed by the new government would start from the date that Genghis Khan ascended the Mongol throne, So 1936 became Ch'eng Ch' 731 or 731 years since the event. The Japanese attending the meeting gave their heartiest congratulations to Teh Wang and his new government and ominously offered him their help to 'Restore Mongolia'. Nationalist government reaction to Prince Teh Wang's announcement was rather surprising. Instead of condemning him as a traitor they decided that there was nothing they could do to remove him for the moment so they legitimised his role by making him head of the Chahar Political Council. Prince Teh Wang's new 'state' only controlled the north of Chahar province but he soon developed plans with his Japanese masters to launch an invasion of Suiyuan province.

The Inner Mongolian Army 1929–36

Prince Teh Wang's first armed force was made up of his own personal retinue known as the 'Pao An Tui' or

'Security Force' and his bodyguard, and numbered about 900 men. He had been given a number of Model 13 or Mukden Mauser rifles with a supply of ammunition and a couple of mountain field guns by the Young Marshal Chiang Hsueh-liang in 1929. These arms were given to the Prince during a tour of the Mukden Arsenal in Manchuria while he was attending a conference of all the Inner Mongolian princes at the invitation of the Young Marshal. Rifles had been given as a token of friendship by Chiang to all the attending Princes but Teh Wang was to use his in future fighting with the Nationalist authorities who had donated them to him. Teh Wang's personal force was small but in comparison to other Inner Mongolian army's was quite efficient. This was partly achieved with the help of a a small number of unofficial Japanese advisors. The Prince had two Japanese officers on his staff for a number of years, who acted as his close advisors. Arms were also given to Teh Wang from Japanese stocks which they held in Manchukuo. The Inner Mongolian Army which fought in the Suiyuan campaigns in 1936 and in the fighting in 1937 was a polyglot force. It was made up of Inner Mongolian tribesmen, Chinese deserters and seconded Manchukuoan regulars. Bandits of various races also made up a large part of the army with some having been in the pay of the Japanese for a number of years. The men of the Security Force did owe allegiance to Prince Teh Wang but many fought for his army for purely monetary reasons.

An officer of Prince Teh Wang's personal bodyguard salutes during a parade near his headquarters in 1935. He is dressed in a typical Mongolian fur hat with metal pommel and a heavy sheepskin coat. The ammunition pouches around his waist are for the Mauser 1896 automatic pistol, which was in widespread use in all of China. This elite unit of the early Inner Mongolian Army would have received the best uniforms and equipment that the Prince could supply.

Illustrated London News

A cavalry unit of Prince Teh Wang's own private army rides past on their sturdy Mongolian ponies in April 1935. Note the standard bearer with the early Inner Mongolia banner and a bugler in the front of the main body of cavalry. This unit is quite smartly turned out and would have formed the nucleus of the later and much larger Inner Mongolian Army which fought in the Suiyuan Campaign of 1936.

Illustrated London News

Li Shou-hsin's Invasion of Northern Chahar 1935

Li Shou-hsin, former Colonel in the Nationalist Governments Jehol Provincial Army, led a group of Manchukuoan irregulars in an invasion of north Chahar on 24 December 1935. The six 'Hsiens' of north Chahar, comprising Kuyuan, Paochang, Kangpo, Huateh, Shangtu and Changpei, were only lightly defended by several thousand Nationalist Peace Preservation Corps. Li's force soon overran the region and began preparations for the invasion of Suiyuan Province which began a year later. The attack had been supported by a squadron of Japanese planes and a handful of Japanese tanks.

Preparations for Suiyuan Campaign 1936

The Japanese and her Inner Mongolian Allies were intent on expanding their rule from northern Chahar into the Nationalist-controlled Suiyuan Province. Japanese intelligence agents had been laying the ground work for the invasion for quite a while and had set up a network of radio operators disguised as Buddhist priests. In the shadowy war that was taking place in this remote region Japanese troops were reported at various places, and were obviously up to no good. The Japanese officer responsible for conducting this secret war was Captain Takayoshi Tanaka, head of the Special Service Agency for Inner Mongolia. He decided that this war would be run his way and refused to listen to advice from the Inner Mongolian leaders. The majority of the Inner Mongolian force was poorly armed, with only about 50% of them having rifles. Li Shou-hsin's 'Manchukoan' contingent were, however, well armed and relatively well trained. Nevertheless, many of the force were basically untrained levies or poorly disciplined bandits who had been hastily recruited. Disunity amongst the various and exotic groups that made up the Suiyuan invading force did not bode well for their morale when they went into action. This disunity was shown by the disagreement over the choosing of a slogan for the invasion. Prince Teh Wang favoured the slogan "Independence for Inner Mongolia" but it was pointed out that the Manchukuoan contingent in the Army would not appreciate this. Tanaka suggested the slogan "Overthrow

This Inner Mongolian dignitary receives a salute from an Inner Mongolian soldier at the headquarters of the puppet army. The soldier is dressed in a civilian deel tunic with probably a Japanese Army fur hat with the flaps worn down.

Masuo Fujita

Chiang Kai-shek" as a unifying slogan but this displeased the Inner Mongolians, so a compromise led to both being adopted. The defence of Suiyuan was in the hands of General Fu Tso-yi, the Nationalist Military Governor of the province. He had at his disposal his own local forces as well as a number of 'elite' units such as anti-aircraft troops sent to reinforce him from Nanking.

Extensive plans for the invasion involved the Japanese spending 6 million Yen on arms and ammunition. Much of the arms and equipment came from the defeated Chinese North-East Army. The Japanese did admit to selling some arms to the Inner Mongolians, and Major General Kita was quoted as saying, "In order to off-set Outer Mongolia's highly mechanised army, which is equipped by Russia, we have assisted Inner Mongolia by selling them airplanes". When asked where the Inner Mongolians got the money to pay for these arms he said "Reports that these Mongols are too poor to buy tanks, armoured cars and munitions are untrue, for they have assets such as a vast opium harvest. We have been paid in kind." The 'Secret' War being conducted in Suiyuan was an undeclared conflict, with the Japanese fighting a war by proxy. Chinese press reports talk of Japanese aircraft as coming from a "Certain Quarter" and unexploded bombs dropped by these planes were said to bear the markings of "A Certain Foreign Country"! There were also constant references to advisors who came from some unknown nation.

Preparations for the invasion also included the setting up of an air arm to help the Inner Mongolians with air support. This 'Inner Mongolian' Air Force was an entirely Japanese affair with Japanese planes, Japanese aircrews and Japanese insignia. The Japanese did not even bother to try and disguise the origin of the aircraft by

A patrol of the Inner Mongolian Army is pictured during the later years of the life of the 'puppet' government. By this time a uniform was being worn by the Army of Prince Teh Wang and these men wear Japanese khaki ones Shoulder insignia on the officer would have been a mid-blue cloth background with yellow metal stars, using the same rank system as the Manchukoan Army.

Masuo Fujita

applying some kind of Inner Mongolian insignia to at least create the illusion of an independent force. Reports suggest that the force totalled 28 planes with 3 bombers, 8 fighters and 5 scout planes stationed at Changpei, 40 miles north of Kalgan. Changpei was the main airbase for the force and had a store of 8,000 tins of aviation fuel. Other smaller groups of aircraft were stationed at Pailingmiao (5 planes), and Shangtu (5 planes). The Inner Mongolian Air Force flew a number of missions in support of the ground forces and bombed a number of Suiyuan towns. One major attack was on the city of Taolin, undertaken by a force of 7 planes which dropped a total of 100 bombs on the Nationalist outpost. The bombing, instead of having the desired effect of softening-up the defences, only seems to have stiffened the defenders resolve. The 'mercenary' Inner Mongolian Air Force suffered relatively heavy losses to special 'elite' anti-aircraft units sent from Nanking and by December 4 planes had been shot down.

Ground support for the attack came from a few pieces of field artillery and a few Japanese armoured cars, all reported to be crewed by Japanese 'advisors'. Aid for the Inner Mongolians came from other sources, with 150 motor vehicles being supplied by the South Manchukuo Railway. Other help from Manchukuo came in the form of communications equipment provided by the state's Telegraph and Telephone Company.

Reportedly, a total of 30 Japanese tanks or tankettes were sent to support the fighting, presumably with Japanese crewmen. In keeping with the exotic mix of the most modern with the medieval in this campaign the invading Inner Mongolian force also commandeered all available camels and mule carts to help with their transport needs.

The Suiyuan Campaign 1936

The invasion to conquer Suiyuan finally began in October 1936, with the attacking force initially advancing in good order, with Prince Teh Wang, Pao Yeu-ching and Wang Ying's force at the head of the attack, whilst General Li Shou hsin's force remained in support. Japanese staff officers were in command of the attack and small Japanese units of 20 to 30 men were included in the attacking forces to add some experience.

The first fighting began when contact was made between the Inner Mongolians and the defending Chinese KMT force at the town of Hongor on 14 November. A major attack by the Mongolians began next day but they were poorly deployed and had to retreat. Several attacks were launched against the city's walls and each time these were repulsed with heavy losses amongst the 'irregular' Inner Mongolian troops. The Inner Mongolians were not lacking in courage but were not adequately trained for this kind of assault. What made the world sit up and take notice was the performance of the Chinese Nationalist defenders. Ever since the first clashes between the Chinese and the Japanese in the invasion of Manchuria in 1931 the Chinese had felt inferior. In fact you could trace this feeling of military inferiority back to the Sino-Japanese War of 1894 in which the Chinese were soundly beaten. Now for once they were beating a Japanese-led force and the world's press reported on their performance. A final Inner Mongolian attack was launched on 16 November in a snow storm and was broken up by a sustained hail of heavy machine gun fire. They were then taken by surprise by a Nationalist counter- attack on the 17th, which led to a disorganised retreat of most of the force. A disorderly retreat by the Inner Mongolians and their Japanese advisors then followed and continued until their reached their Headquarters in the city of Pailingmiao. They then began to regroup and re-equip for another offensive with the help of their Japanese advisors who tried to train them again.

General Fu Tso -yi received intelligence from within the city of Pailingmiao that the Inner Mongolians were in disarray and decided that if he attacked quickly he might be able to take advantage to capture it. Fu sent a mixed infantry and cavalry force on a flanking movement far to the west of Pailingmiao, and attacked the city from that direction. A series of suicidal attacks were launched against the city and were finally successful when three Nationalist trucks drove straight at the gate and broke through them. The defending forces were reported to mainly comprise the 7th Inner Mongolian Division. Inner Mongolian losses during the taking of Pailingmiao were 300 killed, 600 wounded and 300 captured, which, for such a small force, were heavy. A great deal of equipment and supplies were also left behind in the city and were gratefully received by the Chinese victors. This 'booty' included 10,000 bags of flour, 500 tins of 'precious' petrol, 400 rifles and 10 machine guns. Heavier equipment captured was put on display to the world's press to prove Japanese involvement in the fighting and included Chevrolet trucks and several field guns of unknown origin. 'Secret' Japanese plans for the region were also captured in Pailingmiao and these outlined their grand plan to set up a 'puppet' empire. The plans were for a 'Ta-Yuan Ti-kuo' or 'Great Yuan Empire' which was to incorporate the whole of Inner Mongolia with the Chinese north Western province of Sinkiang.

Order of Battle of Inner Mongolian Army, Suiyuan August 1936

Li Shou-hsin's Command	3,000 'Jehol' Mongols
	1,000 ' Chahar' Mongols
Pao Yueh-ching's Command	2,000 8th Mongol Division
	2–3,000 Mixed Mongol Irregulars and Bandits
Te Wang's Personal Troops	1,000 men
Total	9–10,000 men

This disparate army was supposed to be formed into divisions of about 1,500 men, with each of these being made up of 3 regiments of 500 men each. Each regiment was made up of 4 cavalry squadrons plus a machine gun company, with an official strength of 120 men. Of course, this organisation would have been hard to achieve with the forces at the disposal of the Inner Mongolians.

Inner Mongolian Equipment 1936

The Army was armed with the usual wide variety of rifles, most of which had been bought by Prince Teh Wang or acquired from the Japanese. 10,000 Model 13 Mauser rifles manufactured in the Mukden Arsenal were given to the Inner Mongolians. Other more exotic types of firearms found their way to Inner Mongolia and included the Swiss Sig. Model 1930 sub-machine gun, used in small numbers by bodyguard troops. How this modern model of sub-machine gun which didn't see service with any of the other armies in China found its way to Inner Mongolia is not known. Machine guns used by the Inner Mongolians totalled 200, with some of them being the Czech ZB–26 light machine gun. This type had been in service with the Young Marshal Chang Hsueh- liang's forces and were captured by the Japanese in 1931–32 and handed on to the Inner Mongolians. Artillery pieces in service with the Inner Mongolians totalled 70 and these were made up of mortars as well as a few mountain and field guns. Again these would have come from captured Nationalist sources and would have been a variety of types, with the replenishing of ammunition being a problem. Reportedly, a handful of tanks and armoured cars were in service with the Inner Mongolians. These would have mostly likely been vehicles captured by the Japanese during their takeover of Manchuria and crewed by Japanese.

A Japanese advisor salutes a couple of child soldiers of the Inner Mongolian Army of Prince Teh Wang. The small population of Inner Mongolia meant that any able-bodied man with a few exceptions could be recruited into the Army. This photograph suggests that the lack of recruits was made up to some degree by the use of very young boys hardly able to hold their rifles.

Masuo Fujita

Inner Mongolia 1937–40

Even though the Inner Mongolians had been defeated in their first attempt to invade the provinces of Suiyuan under Nationalist Chinese control their Japanese 'masters' had no intention of giving up. For the next eight months a series of small scale battles and skirmishes took place over the vast empty territory of Suiyuan. The fighting was low key, and even in the larger scale battles only involved a few hundred horsemen on each side. Japanese intrigues continued throughout this period with Western newspapers reporting in April 1937 the setting up of a new Mongol state in the north of Chahar province with the name of 'Mongokuo'. At the same time there was reported military activity in the east of Suiyuan with Inner Mongolian irregulars clashing with Nationalist regulars. The Inner Mongolians fortunes were to change with the escalation of the low-key war into full scale fighting in the rest of China following the Marco Polo Bridge incident, during which their forces became far more heavily involved.

These 'rough' looking infantry in Teh Wang's Inner Mongolian Army were probably recruited from amongst the 'Han' Chinese population. All the cavalry in the army would have been drawn specifically from pure born Mongols, often leaving the role of foot soldier to non-Mongols. They are all dressed in unkempt uniforms of wadded cotton and have been issued with Japanese Army fur hats complete with yellow star. The only equipment that they seem to have been issued with are canvas bandoliers to hold their ammunition in.

Masuo Fujita

On 25 August, units of Prince Teh Wang's Army were involved in heavy fighting with 3 KMT Divisions supported by Japanese airpower and inflicted 2,000 casualties. The KMT force was made up of the 7th Division and 2 divisions of poor quality Shansi Provincial troops. The action began with a Chinese attack on the Inner Mongolians, who were occupying good defensive positions; the Nationalists were beaten back. Japanese air attacks were said to be largely responsible for the successful defeat of the Chinese offensive. On 3 October Inner Mongolian troops, reportedly led by students from the 'Youth Military Training School', recaptured Pailingmiao from its KMT garrison a year after it fell to them.

Over 20,000 Inner Mongolians, nearly all cavalry in 6 or 7 small divisions (some sources state 9 divisions) advanced at the same time to take all the provinces of the country still held by the Nationalists apart from the far western province of Ninghsia. The Inner Mongolians had the support of a number of Japanese tanks and planes and were divided into 2 forces, with one under the command of Pao Yueh-ching and the other under Teh Wang himself. Inner Mongolian forces were also involved in the Battle of Taiyuan, which lasted from early September until 9 November.

Inner Mongolian Military School

The Japanese set up a Military Training School at Changpei in 1936 with an intake of 500 Cadets. Although promised an all-round education the cadets soon became disillusioned when the training was purely military. Nearly half the cadets left the School and the remaining 300 constantly complained about the conditions in general and the poor quality of food in particular. The Japanese instructors wrily commented that, "The Great Genghis Khan had conquered Europe with far worse supplies of food".

Wang Ying and the Great Han Righteous Army

Wang Ying was another of those 'maverick' military leaders in the confused situation in China and its outlying provinces who offered their services to the Japanese in the 1930s. He persuaded the Japanese Kwangtung Army that he could recruit an army from amongst the military stragglers in the South of Chahar Province which was still under Nationalist control. The Japanese were agreeable to his plan and also agreed to bribe the Nationalist Chairman of the Chahar Political Committee with a 'gift' of 2,000 rifles to let Wang enter the region on a recruiting drive. He was successful with his campaign and managed to recruit enough men to form 2 divisions. These recruits were then sent north of the Great Wall and received training from Japanese advisors. They were equipped with the captured weapons of the former Nationalist East Chahar Garrison. The Japanese intention was to use his 'mercenary' force to launch another attack into Eastern Suiyuan Province after its first attack failed in the Summer of 1936. The attack was launched in January 1937 and was a disaster for the 'Self Righteous Army' as it suffered heavy losses.

The 'Great Way' Government Army 1937–40

The 'puppet' municipal government of Greater Shanghai was formed on 5 December 1937 to control the Japanese occupied sectors and the outlying areas of the city. Other 'puppet' local municipal governments, usually given the designation of 'committee' or 'commission', had been set up in newly conquered Chinese cities by the Japanese. These local governments were strictly temporary measures however and were soon disbanded after a few weeks or months and their officials absorbed into the larger 'puppet' regimes. Shanghai was a special case because of its importance as a trading and international centre which had always held a unique status in pre-war China. For this reason it was decided that Shanghai or 'Greater Shanghai' should have its own government largely independent of the Reformed Government in Nanking.

Although Greater Shanghai came within the territory of the Reformed Government the relationship between the two regimes was always rather ambiguous. During the short life of the two regimes the relationship between them was never really settled and the firm Japanese control over both meant that it was never open to debate. The 'Great Way' or 'Ta-Tao' Government did not control the whole of the city and had no jurisdiction over the French Concession or the International Settlements in Shanghai. These International Settlements were policed by a multi-national force, the Shanghai Municipal Police Force or SMP. Finding a leader or 'Mayor' for the Ta-Tao Government was not easy as the job was seen as a 'poisoned chalice' by most candidates. Eventually a candidate was found by the Japanese, a shadowy figure called Su His-wen, who was originally from Formosa and proved to be a totally unsuitable man for the job. He was replaced in October 1938 by Fu Hsiao-an, a former administrator in a local warlord government, which was overthrown by the KMT Northern Expedition in the late 1920s. Fu Hsiao-an led the Ta-Tao Government under heavy Japanese guard for two years before his assassination in October 1940.

The 'Ta-Tao' Paramilitary Police

Although the Great Way or Ta-Tao Government had no army of its own it did have a Sizeable paramilitary police force which acted as such. The Ta-Tao Police were given the task of policing the occupied region of Shanghai and also contested control of the roads and districts of those areas of the city policed by the International Settlement's Shanghai Municipal Police (SMP). This force was truly international, mainly British, but including amongst others a unit of White Russian Émigrés. For the three years of the Great Way Government's life the Ta-Tao Police constantly applied pressure on the SMP as it tried to protect the borders of the International Settlements. On several occasions the Ta-Tao Police erected illegal roadblocks and set up cordons on roads that were officially under the control of the International Settlements. Although the Ta-Tao Government could not openly infringe on the areas under international control they used their 'puppet' police force to constantly exert subtle, and not so subtle pressure on the SMP.

The police started off as a tiny force of 64 men in January 1939 and due to this lack of manpower it could not impose its rule over the areas of Shanghai it was responsible for. An expansion of the force was undertaken and it reached a strength of 230 in February, and an impressive 5,155 men by April. By June 1939 the Ta-Tao had 11 branch bureaus, 5 police stations and 8 other units which included a training depot, river police corps and a hospital and had a total strength of 5,662 men. A further increase in the numbers took place in July 1939, by which time the force now had a strength of 6,125 men and women. This hastily recruited and trained force was of poor quality and its men were almost totally unreliable. They were issued with old Chinese rifles and 50 rounds of ammunition each, which was a very generous allocation of bullets for a 'puppet' force to receive.

Finding recruits for the Ta-Tao Police was difficult and anyone, no matter how unsuitable, was usually taken into the force. One group of recruits came in a roundabout route from the prisons of Shanghai via the Nationalist Army. When the final battles between the Nationalist Army and the Japanese for Shanghai were underway the gates of a few large prisons were opened by the Chinese and the inmates were given rudimentary rifle training and sent into battle. Surprisingly the men fought well and a group of 1,000 were massacred after finally laying down their weapons. Another unit of ex-prisoners decided to offer their services to the Japanese and were allowed to surrender. They eventually found their way into service with the Ta-Tao, and soon went back to their old criminal ways, although this time in uniform. The Ta-Tao Police were provided with uniforms, but not much else, as their wages were at starvation level. They were expected to make up their wages by extorting money in 'phoney' taxes such as a 'protection tax' from the poor civilians who came under their control. Most of the robberies that took place in the area were also reportedly down to Ta-Tao Police in civilian clothes. The Ta-Tao also often looked the other way when others were committing the crime and presumably taking a 'kickback' for not intervening. A small number of women were also recruited into the Ta-Tao Police to help with body searches on women at the various customs posts which were set up around the city.

In an effort to improve the performance of the Ta-Tao, a cadet course was set up at the Civic Centre and about 300 cadets were enrolled on the course. On the occasion of the celebrations to mark the first anniversary of the founding of the Great Way Government the Ta-Tao put on a major show of force. In a march past in front of the Mayor of the city in front of the Shanghai town hall, 5 companies of the Ta-Tao Police totalling 900 men were on display.

Another more heavily armed force known as the 'Military Armed Police' was recruited from former Nationalist guerrillas who had surrendered to the Japanese. These men came over to the Japanese with their weapons in exchange for a payment of $10 and a monthly payment of $20. This force was established in the Western district of Shanghai under the command of a former Brigadier General of a warlord army. The Japanese planned to increase the force to 15,000 men eventually, but this figure was never reached. A 700 strong former Nationalist guerrilla force was also formed into a regular police unit, which added to the manpower available to the Ta-Tao regime.

The Ta-Tao Police were ordered to patrol the extra-territorial roads of the SMP and to gradually force them out. This led to rival groups of police patrolling the same area and to clashes which sometimes ended in bloodshed. Gun battles between the Ta-Tao Police and guerrilla forces took place at times as the latter infiltrated into Shanghai. Armed clashes also took place between the Ta-Tao and the SMP at regular intervals, with both sides suffering quite heavy casualties. Mayor Fu Siao-en, head of the 'puppet' government, would disclaim any responsibility for attacks by his Ta-Tao Police by issuing statements such as "Only loafers and bandits would resort to such dastardly acts and the Shanghai City Government strongly disapproves of such action". A less deadly type of conflict also occurred between the SMP and the Ta-Tao when both forces had constables giving conflicting traffic signals on the same road or junction. This could, of course, have led to numerous traffic accidents if it wasn't for the fact that most motorists completely ignored the Ta-Tao officer's directions.

Although the Ta-Tao Police Force seems to have been largely ineffective it continued to perform its role up to establishment of the Wang Ching-wei government in March 1940. The Great Way Government then came under the control of the new government in Nanking, but as with other small 'puppet' regimes it retained some autonomy. One sign of this semi–independence from Nanking was that the Ta-Tao Police was expanded to a strength of 7,501 men in January 1941.

White Russians and 'Semi-puppets' 1932–40

White Russians in China

Ever since the Russian Revolution of 1917 there had been a substantial number of Russian Émigré refugees in northern China and Manchuria. Thousands of former Russian Imperial officers and their families had escaped across the frontier into Chinese territory at the end of the Russian Civil War during the early 1920s. These Royalist or White Russians had found employment in various fields including, of course, the military. Many White Russians fought in the armies of Chinese warlords in the 1920s, where they provided an elite force in several of these armies. In the 1930s most of the White Russians had lost their roles, as the northern Warlords were defeated by the Nationalist Northern Expedition. The Émigré communities in China and Manchuria were a readymade source of well motivated anti-Communists who were often willing to co-operate with the Japanese occupying powers. Ex-Russian Imperial Army officers and their sons were often ready to volunteer for military tasks as long as they were promised to be fighting 'Reds', whether they be Soviet or Chinese communists. Some of the first White Russians to be employed in a military role did so on behalf of the Provisional 'puppet' Government in Peking. White Russian units were deployed along important military roads and railways in the region of Peking and were under the control of the Provisional Government. The units involved were described as 'regiments' but eyewitnesses stated that there could not have been more than a few hundred in total.

Ataman Semenov

One of the most colourful characters involved in the shady politics of Manchukuo and other occupied areas of China during the 1930s and 40s was Ataman Semenov. The Ataman was the leader of the White Russians in the later stages of the Russian Civil War, in the remote region of Trans-Baikal on the border between Siberia and Mongolia.

In the early 1920s the Ataman led a mixed force of Japanese-sponsored Trans-Baikal Cossacks and Mongols in an extremely vicious guerrilla campaign against the Soviets in the area. After the defeat of the Ataman's Army by overwhelming Soviet forces in September 1921 he made a narrow escape to Japanese-held Kwangtung territory by aeroplane. He then installed himself in the Manchurian city of Darien and was a resident there when the Japanese created the state of Manchukuo in 1932. Almost at once he offered his services as a leader of the White Russians in Manchukuo to the Japanese. Although the Japanese regarded him as a potential 'tool' in any future war with the Soviet Union he was seen as too much of a hothead to become the overall leader of all White Russians. His main support came from amongst the survivors of his own Trans-Baikal Army and he was too 'unstable' for most White Russians.

One of the most fantastic schemes proposed by Ataman Semenov was that put forward to his Japanese masters in 1939. Ataman Semenov took his plans to the highest ranking officers of the Kwangtung Army in Hsinking the capital of Manchukuo on 19 September. His plan was for nothing short of the Japanese conquest of the northern half of East Asia. The first part of the plan involved forcing the Soviets out of Outer Mongolia, which was a Communist state under Russian control, and then combining it with Inner Mongolia to create one Mongolian state. Next, Chinese Turkestan or 'Sinkiang', the north-western province of China would be incorporated into the state, as it had a Mongolian population of 1,000,000. The proposed state would have had an area of 2,492,495 square miles and a population of 10,555,000 people. This Mongolian 'superstate' would then have been purged of all Soviet and Nationalist Chinese influence and would have created a buffer against the Russians to the north. Of course to achieve this scheme the Japanese would have had to go to war with the Soviet Union as well as continuing their war with China. If successful, the new Mongolian Empire would be integrated with Japanese-ruled Korea and Manchukuo to create an Asiatic Empire of 700 million people with an area 30% larger than the United States.

The Ataman's timing could not have been worse, as the Japanese Army was suffering a heavy defeat at the time of his suggestions at the hands of the Soviets in the Nomonhan Incident. If the Japanese had been successful in their campaign they may well have been willing to attempt the scheme, but as it was, it was quietly forgotten. The Japanese had not finished with Semenov's services completely however, and according to some reports he was utilised in 1940. In March of that year he was told by the Kwangtung Army to raise White Russian units to serve in the Nanking Army of Wang Ching-wei's regime. According to this report he formed 3 regiments of 1,000 men each, who were sent to Nanking to form a well-disciplined force to bolster the poorly trained 'puppet' army.

Local Governments of Central China 1937–40

As the Japanese advanced southwards through Central China, city after city fell to them as the Nationalist force retreated westwards. Often the first act of the Japanese when entering a city was to set up a municipal government from amongst any local Chinese officials who were willing to serve them. These so-called committees, commissions and associations were usually led by elderly local officials with many of having formerly served in the various warlord governments in the 1920s. The city of Wuhan Peace Maintenance Association, for instance, contained five main officials, all of whom were over sixty years of age. Two of the Wuhan officials were former Generals of the Warlord era, Yang Chan-shu and Wu Chi-tse, and both were former pupils of Japanese military schools, and were described as being very pro-Japanese. To protect these 'puppet' bodies the Japanese also often recruited local militias to patrol the cities until more permanent forces could be raised. These militias were recruited from amongst the youths of the newly conquered cities and were given rudimentary training by Japanese officers. They were then armed with captured Chinese weaponry and sent on patrol to replace the Japanese soldiery. The *ad hoc* nature of these forces is illustrated by the city of Kukiang Militia, who were dressed in civilian clothes, with a simple white headband which had their title written in Chinese characters in black ink on the front.

Local Militia & Police

In most Chinese towns and cities conquered by the Japanese local 'puppet' organisations were set up, such as Peace Maintenance Commissions, Committees and Governments. These were set up immediately to try and give legitimacy to their claims that they were liberators, not conquerors. These locally-raised militias were recruited by the Japanese from any of the local population who were willing to serve them.

Missed Opportunities

Attempts to recruit new 'puppet' leaders

The Japanese and their Chinese allies were constantly attempting to persuade some of the less pro-Chiang Kai-shek Nationalist Generals to support them. In December 1938, for instance, Wang Ching-wei tried to persuade the independently-minded Warlord of Kunming Province, Lung Yun to support him. Many of the military governors of the outlying provinces of China owed little real allegiance to the Chiang Kai-shek regime.

These provincial governors were often former warlords of the pre-1928 period, and although officially part of the Nationalist government, would not have taken very much persuasion at all to change sides. The Japanese were to lose out on a great opportunity to recruit many of the more important Chinese military leaders by their attitude towards the Chinese in general. Their high-handed approach to the Chinese and their brutal treatment of both prisoners of war and civilians alike did nothing to tempt them to throw in their lot with the Japanese. Most Nationalist generals were passionately anti-communist and in this they were in total agreement with the Japanese Army. If the Japanese had exploited this mutual hatred of the Communists while at the same time being more generous in their treatment of the Chinese population things might have been a little different. A prime example of the Japanese failure to exploit the potential recruits to their side were that of General Yen His-shan.

Yen Hsi-shan of Shansi Province

Nationalist General Yen Hsi-shan had ruled Shansi province from 1911 as a local 'Tuan' or Warlord and was the great survivor of that turbulent period in Chinese history. Yen was fiercely independent, vehemently anti-communist, and was no lover of the Nationalist government of Chiang Kai-shek. He had reluctantly joined the Nationalist side after realising that they were going to succeed with their Northern Expedition of 1926–28 and its aim to destroy or subdue all the warlord cliques as well as independent Tuans like himself. Some warlords, like Yen, made peace with the Nationalists and put their armies under their banner while trying to retain as much power for themselves as they could. Yen's attitude throughout the 1930s had been that as long as the central government left him more or less alone to rule his province, he was willing to officially support Chiang Kai-shek. In reality he had little time for the Nationalists and largely ignored any directives that were sent from them.

All these factors went to make him a possible supporter of the Nanking regime of Wang Ching-wei, and for this reason he was courted in 1940 by the Japanese in an attempt to persuade him to join them. The secret negotiations, code-named 'Taihaku kosaku' or 'Yen Hsi-shan Operation', made progress in 1941 and led to an agreement. A 'Basic Agreement' and 'Truce Agreement' were signed by Yen and he agreed to join the Nanking Government on his own terms. These were that he would have an army of 300,000 men and was to receive 100,000 new Japanese rifles and a certain amount of heavier equipment including some precious artillery pieces. He was also to receive a monthly payment of 12,000,000 Yuan with a one-off payment of 50,000,000 Yuan to prop up the locally issued currency. The whole agreement fell apart when the Japanese were found by Yen to be less than 100% honest in their dealings with him. Yen was a very astute politician and kept his options open with the Japanese and kept very much on the fence. The Japanese attack on Pearl Harbour was a decisive factor in his decision to remain loyal to the Nationalist Government. He thought that the entry of the United States into the war would eventually mean the defeat of Japan and he did not want to be allied to a future loser. The Japanese tried more drastic means to persuade Yen to join them by launching a small punitive campaign against him in the spring of 1942. He decided that his best policy was to sign a 'secret' agreement with the Japanese for a 'live and let live' policy. Under this agreement the Japanese would leave him alone in his province so that he could concentrate on attacking their common enemy, the Communists. Even though this agreement between Yen and the Japanese held he never came out openly in support of them or the Nanking regime. The Japanese lost a great opportunity of recruiting Yen Hsi-shan as a 'puppet' leader who could have given the Nanking Government a dynamic figurehead to work alongside Wang Ching-wei.

Many Chinese military leaders were strongly anti-communist and if the Japanese had been more pragmatic and allowed them more independence many more would have gone over to them.

General Sung Che-yuan

General Sung Che-yuan was another example of the kind of high-ranking KMT officer who the Japanese attempted to bring over to their camp. He was a former commander in the 'Kuominchun' Army of the 'Christian Warlord', Feng Yu-hsiang. Because of his former allegiance to Feng, who had rebelled against Chiang Kai-shek in 1930, he had little loyalty to the Nanking Government. As commander of the KMT 29th Army in north China in1935 he held a powerful position and was an ideal candidate for the persuasions of the Japanese. Major-General Doihara Kenji, the architect of Pu-Yi's establishment as the Manchukuoan Emperor, was behind intrigues to establish a northern Chinese Government with Sung as head. These intrigues failed, although Sung had shown himself to be a possible future defector to the Japanese if the circumstances were right. In July 1937 Sung and his 29th Army were stationed in the vicinity of the Marco Polo Bridge when the incident occurred which began the Sino-Japanese War. Sung Che-yuan and his officers attempted to settle the dispute with the Japanese by negotiation, and indeed a local treaty was reached. However the Japanese Government had a different agenda and quashed any further attempts at settling the dispute. Sung and his 29th Army were then defeated in the fighting for Peking and he lost his position within the Nationalist Army. If the local treaty had held there is little doubt that Sung Che-yuan and a substantial part of his 29th Army would have crossed over to the Japanese and formed a major 'puppet' force.

CHAPTER FOUR

Chinese 'Puppet' Governments and Armies 1940–45

The Nanking Army 1940–45

The Formation of the Nanking Government

By early 1939 occupied China had been divided up into various regions controlled by several 'puppet' governments which competed with each other for influence. Northern China was controlled by the Provisional Government in Peking formed by the Japanese North China Army in December 1937 while Central China was under the rule of the Reformed Government in Nanking created by the Japanese Central China Army in March 1938. Inner Mongolia was more or less independent of both these governments under Prince Teh Wang. Japan had at first been happy with this situation and had no intention of forming a national government for all of occupied China. When Chiang Kai-shek's Nationalist Government refused to negotiate with the Japanese from its new capital at Chungking a change of policy was called for. Japan had expected that after the disastrous defeats suffered by the Nationalists Chiang would be forced to come to an accommodation with them. His continued resistance now led the Japanese to believe that the only way to defeat him was to create a unified government in occupied China to rival his. Any new government would have to be seen as a realistic rival to Chiang's regime and would have to have a leader with enough status to match his. A dynamic leader to head this proposed government was needed and the Japanese had been approaching prospective candidates without success. Eventually a potential leader was found in the shape of Wang Ching-wei – a former Kuomintang leader who had rivalled Chiang Kai-shek in the Nationalist power struggle of the 1930s and had fallen foul of him. Wang had been a young revolutionary who had gained notoriety by his attempt on the life of the Chinese Imperial Crown Prince in 1910 during the days of the Ch'ing Dynasty. After narrowly escaping the death penalty he had served a period in prison before becoming one of the early disciples of the KMT founder Sun Yat-sen. He then rose to become high profile politician in the Chinese Nationalist Party and was the loser in a power struggle with Chiang Kai-shek. Wang escaped China with a price on his head and a determination to

New recruits to the Nanking Army are drilled by Japanese instructors in front of their barrack buildings. Many of the Nanking Army's soldiers were former Nationalist soldiers who came over to the Wang Ching wei government with their commander. This group are obviously raw recruits and have been raised from amongst the civilian population

**Imperial War Museum
HU55367**

return as the 'true' leader of the KMT. He began to try and undermine the KMT Government by negotiating with regional commanders and warlords who had no real loyalty to Chiang. If he was successful in forming an anti-Chiang alliance he then planned to negotiate peace with the Japanese and co-operate with them against the Chinese Communists. Lengthy discussions took place between Wang and Japanese negotiators throughout 1939 with a final agreement at the end of the year.

The formation of the so-called 'Reorganised Government of China' on 30 March 1940 duly took place in its new capital Nanking. Wang Ching-wei's government officially absorbed the Provisional and Reformed regimes although the Peking-based regime continued to be largely independent as the 'North China Political Council' with Wang Ke-min at its head. In reality Wang Ching-wei's authority only extended to his capital and the area close to the city. Wang was adamant that his was not a new government but was in fact a continuation of the Nationalist Government and was the legitimate one rather than Chiang Kai-shek's Chungking regime. The Chungking government was in Wang's eyes a renegade government Wang said that the new peace between his government and the Japanese allowed him to transfer power back to Nanking where it belonged. He also insisted on retaining all the symbols, flags and insignia of the Nationalist Government to underline this continuation. In addition, he wanted to carry on the 'three principles of the people' of Sun Yat-sen as the official doctrine. The government was to be run along the same lines as the Nationalist regime with Wang at the head of A 5 'Yuan' or department cabinet with Executive, Legislative, Control, Judicial and Examination bodies. Because of factionalism within this new government, Wang had to head more of these largely symbolic committees to avoid conflict.

The Reorganised Government had a strained relationship with the Japanese from the beginning. Wang's insistence on his regime being the true Nationalist government of China and in replicating all the symbols of the KMT led to conflict with the Japanese over the issue of the regime's flag. In fact, the problem of identity faced by the Nanking regime is quite succinctly summed up by the argument between Wang and the Japanese authorities over the flag flown by the regime. Wang insisted that his government was the true Nationalist government of China and that he and his followers were the true disciples of Sun Yat-sen, the founder of the Kuomintang Party. It therefore followed that Wang's government should use the Kuomintang flag of a blue sky and white sun adopted by Sun Yat-sen's party in the 1920s. This flag had been put in a canton on a red field and became the National flag of China after the Kuomintang or Nationalists victory over the warlord forces in 1928. 'How could Wang's new government use the same flag as the government they sought to defeat?' argued the Japanese. Wang's answer to this was that Chiang Kai-shek and his party had hijacked the flag and that their use of it

A 'puppet' soldier undergoes training in grenade throwing with the aid of a wooden dummy grenade. His cap insignia is obscured here but will probably be the white sun on blue sky enamel circular badge as worn by the Nationalists with the addition of the red outer ring which distinguishes it as a Nanking Army type. He is armed with a Arisaka Type 38 rifle issued to him by his Japanese advisors.

Robert Hunt Library

should not prevent its legitimate use by his government. The Japanese also argued that the use by the Nanking Army of the same flag as their enemy, the Nationalists, would lead to confusion on the battlefield. Japanese units would be prone to fire on friendly Nanking Army units flying the flag whom they might mistake for Nationalist troops. The Japanese pressed for the Nanking government to use the five barred flag which had been used by the various 'puppet' governments pre-1940. This was seen as an insult by Wang, who viewed himself as being above the kind of traitors who had served the Japanese before him. Wang Ching-wei's officials continued to fly the white sun on blue sky flag over the public buildings and official residences in defiance of the Japanese. The Japanese realised that Wang would not back down over this issue and proposed a compromise which involved adding a long triangular pennant to the top of the flag. This yellow-coloured pennant which ran the whole length of the flag had the black Chinese characters on it which read ' Peace and National Reconstruction' (ho'p'ing, chien- kuo). A little later the words ' Anti-communism' (fan-kung) were added giving the full phrase of 'Anti-communism, Peace and National Reconstruction'. This phrase would, said the Japanese, distinguish the new government from the 'hated' Nationalists, and at the same time declare the anti-Communist nature of the state. Wang Ching-wei and his government hated the use of this pennant, which they described as a 'pigs tail' and it was often removed when no Japanese officials were about. Japanese officials got their revenge by allowing official bodies in the north of China to continue to fly the five barred flag they had used before 1940. Arguments continued over this issue until in 1943 the Japanese dropped their insistence on the use of the pennant and it was no longer flown.

The Nanking Army 1940–45

No politician in China could hope to retain power without the backing of a substantial military force which owed loyalty to him personally. So as Wang conducted his lengthy negotiations with the Japanese he began to plan for a military force that he could rely on. In late 1938 he sent an envoy to speak to the Japanese and received an agreement from them that if he joined them, they would assist him. The Japanese made promises to help Wang to raise an army of five to ten divisions of troops and that they would provide the instructors. In January 1939 Wang sent two of his associates to Hong Kong to investigate the feasibility of raising such a force. From March of 1939 Wang began to actively look for Japanese support in his scheme to unite all the anti-Chiang militarists in China. This plan called for the formation of a twelve division 'Anti-Communist National Salvation United Army' under the personal command of Wang. The Japanese realised that this plan was far too ambitious and tried to tone down Wang's scheme while still keeping him on their side. Wang had planned at first to raise an independent army by requesting that 50% of the new force's foreign instructors should be German and Italian with the other 50% being Japanese. Wang wanted to use his army for fighting only the Communists, and tried to avoid them being

A line-up of Type 94 tankettes of the Nanking Army on parade are identified by the white sun emblem on the side of the vehicle. Only a handful of these tankettes were given to the Nanking Army to provide a token armoured force for the regime. The crewman is wearing a German M35 steel helmet as worn by the Nationalist Chinese Army and probably taken from the war booty of the Japanese.

Philip Jowett Collection

The commander of one of the small number of Japanese made Type 94 tankettes of the Nanking Army's armoured force signals to the other vehicles in his unit with a flag. These light tanks, which were obsolete by Western standards, were still in service at the time with the Japanese Army.

Philip Jowett Collection

A small unit of 'puppet' soldiers snatch a meal while on patrol and have stacked their Arisaka Type 38 rifles against the wall behind them. The men are all shabbily dressed, with at least one of them being barefooted and their uniforms quite ragged looking. Two of the men have large chevrons above their cuffs with a white or yellow star on them. The other two men have red armbands with a black stripe and a Chinese character on, which would indicate a role such as military policeman.

Philip Jowett Collection

deployed against the Allies. Wang wanted to create a truly politically motivated army that would fight side by side with the Japanese against both the 'illegitimate' Nationalist Government now installed in Chungking and the Communist forces. Because he regarded himself and his government as the true disciples of Sun Yat-sen and his revolutionary spirit he hoped that his army would become the true Nationalist Army. Of course he was to be totally disappointed and even though the Nanking Army had most of the trappings of the Nationalist Army and used the same insignia and such like, it was never going to be a well motivated military force.

The fastest way for Wang to raise an army was by persuading some of the existing KMT army commanders to bring their units over to him. Throughout 1939 Wang Ching-wei tried to convince several KMT commanders in outlying provinces, who had less personal loyalty to Chiang Kai-shek, to join him. He came close to bringing a few of these powerful warlords into his alliance but the increasing anti-Japanese feeling in China stopped them. Amongst the KMT commanders he had tried to woo were Li Ts'ung-jen and Pai Ch'ung-his, who had led an anti-Chiang revolt in Kwangsi in the early 1930s. After his failure to form any alliances and raise a military force that way, Wang turned to the remnant KMT troops who had been left behind when Chiang Kai-shek's Government retreated west to its new capital in Chungking. The KMT forces left behind in Japanese occupied China were made up of regular units, militia and semi-bandit elements. Wang set up the grandly titled 'Peace and National Construction Army General Command' with Wang Tien-mu as commander. In January 1940 Wang called a special conference in Shanghai to try and organise the taking over of all remnant KMT units in the area. Several of the most influential KMT commanders in North China, such as Lee Chang-chiang and Sun Liang-ch'eng, sent secret envoys to discuss coming over to Wang's side. Wang used a combination of monetary bribes and the offer of promotions to persuade these commanders to join him. In a further step towards the creation of his new army Wang set up a military academy in Shanghai in December 1939 (see below).

With the birth of the Reorganised Government in Nanking in March 1940, Wang inherited a number of existing 'puppet' military forces which then came under his nominal control. These included the North China Pacification Command 'Hua-Pei Sui Chung Chun Pu' under General Ch'i Hsieh-yuan. This force had been the main military element of the Provisional Government in Peking. Another major force was the Kiangsu, Chekiang and Anhwei Provinces Pacification Army Command 'Su-Che-An' under Jen Yuan-tao. This force was the former army of the Reformed Government which had controlled Nanking from 1938 and had a strength of about 20,000. These two military forces, with the addition of the minor units of local Pacification Bureaux from cities like Kaifeng and Wuhan, made up the available military resources for Wang. The Su-Chen-An Pacification Army divided into seven military districts became the 1st Front Army, with each military district becoming a division, as well as 2 independent brigades and 2 independent regiments. In addition, Wang reorganised the Loyal and Righteous National Salvation Army temporarily into the 10th, 13th and 19th Divisions.

Under the terms of the 'Japan-China Military Affairs Agreement' between Japan and the Wang Ching-wei Government, the Japanese agreed to help the Nanking regime establish, train and equip an unspecified number of divisions. In January 1941 they firmed this agreement up by stating that they would provide the Nanking Army with some of the large stock of war booty captured from the Nationalists since 1937. The Japanese also provided limited amounts of armaments to the Nanking Army during its life but these were strictly limited. Because the Nanking Army was seen by the Japanese as a strictly infantry force, any heavy arms issued to it were kept to a minimum. In most cases the only type of artillery in use with the Nanking Army were a few medium mortars. Wang Ching-wei had rather grandiose plans to create within the space of five years a well trained and equipped army of fifteen divisions, including all supporting units. The plan also called for the building of arsenals and repair shops to keep this large force in the field. Japanese plans for the Nanking Army were far less ambitious and they were only committed to providing ammunition for the three Nanking Capital Garrison divisions. The Japanese were also loath to allow the Nanking Government to build its own arms factories. One of the best controls they had over the 'puppet' government was the fact that they kept a tight rein on ammunition supply. After lengthy negotiations the Japanese did eventually agree to the setting up of one small arsenal to repair small arms. Sources say that the arsenal also had a very small manufacturing facility which could produce 10 rifles per day. Obviously with an army of a few hundred thousand men this factory would have made little impact on the shortage of small arms. In reality the Nanking Army was always going to be a basic infantry force with small amounts of artillery and armour and with very limited support branches e.g. transport, medical.

The worsening war situation for Japan in the Pacific from 1942 onwards meant that the Nanking Army was to be given a more substantial role in the defence of China than the Japanese had initially envisaged. This increased responsibility was matched by a rapid expansion in numbers of Nanking troops. Unfortunately this increase in numbers of men was not matched by an increase in quality of recruits. The growth of the Nanking Army between 1941 and 1942 was rapid largely due to the defection of large units of KMT troops who were brought over by their commanders. These commanders often played hard to get with Wang and tried to negotiate the best terms for their defection to him. One example of the tangled negotiations between a defecting KMT commander and Wang's negotiating team was that of Lee Chang-chiang. Lee was the Deputy Commander of all KMT guerrilla forces in the Shangtung- Kiangsu-Anhwei Border Region. He had already decided that he wanted to switch sides and it was only a matter of what he could gain from his defection. In March 1940, Lee sent envoys to speak to Wang and his negotiator Chou Fou-hai to agree the terms for his surrender. Lee was promised by Chou that he would become a corps commander and that his force would become a group army. He also asked for a large amount of weapons and ammunition, which the Japanese vetoed as they did not fully trust him. This refusal annoyed Lee, who threatened to change his mind until Wang sent a special envoy in October 1940 to speak to him in his headquarters. The special envoy was in fact Lee's former superior in the Kiangsu military, Miao Pin, who had been one of the first defectors to Wang. Negotiations continued for three months and finally Lee agreed to join Wang, his decision aided by the Japanese gesture of a gift of 250,000

Soldiers of the Nanking Army's Capital Garrison forces celebrate the Wang Ching-wei's Governments declaration of war against the Allied Powers in 1943. They are performing their version of the Japanese 'Banzai' in imitation of Imperial Army soldiers. The men are uniformly dressed with M35 steel helmets and are armed with Chinese produced Mauser rifles

Philip Jowett Collection

From their base in Nanking a unit of 'puppet' soldiers of the Nanking Army climb aboard barges in preparation to set out on an anti-guerrilla operation on 10 January 1941. The flag of the Reorganised Government complete with yellow anti-Communist pennant flies over the barge and the soldiers are dressed in a mixture of light khaki uniforms. Most of the Nanking Army's anti-guerrilla sweeps were undertaken in support of the Japanese Army.

Popperfoto

rounds of ammunition. Lee finally switched sides in March 1941 and brought with him 30,000 men, which was a much needed boost to the Nanking Army's strength. In June Lee's troops were reorganised into the 24th, 25th, 26th and 27th divisions and the 10th and 11th independent brigades. This strong force was almost continuously employed against the Communist New Fourth Army.

Sun Liang-Ch'eng was another key defector who was persuaded by some of his former officers who had already defected to join Wang in April 1942. He brought 25,000 troops and a number of key officers with him, his forces being renamed as the 2nd Front Army, made up of the IV and V corps of five divisions.

The vast majority of Nanking commanders who had defected from the Nationalists were from the regional and provincial armies known as 'Tsa-p'ai. These armies had little personal loyalty to Chiang Kai -shek and had always been suspect to the Nationalist government in Chung king. Most of these officers had served in one of two 'cliques' within the Nationalist Army. Some had commanded units in the former 'North West Army' under the leadership of the Christian warlord, Feng Yu-hsiang who had rebelled against Chiang Kai-shek in 1930. The other group were made of former high-ranking officers of the North-east Army or 'Tung-Pei Chun' Manchurian Army of Chang Hseuh-liang, who had been pushed out of the region by the Japanese invasion of 1931. These former NE Army commanders had been part of the Sian Incident, in which Chiang Kai-shek had been held to ransom by Chang Hseuh-liang in an attempt to get him to concentrate KMT efforts on resisting the Japanese rather than crushing the Chinese Communists. Many of the commanders brought their armies over to the Nanking Regime *en-masse*, as was the case with General Sun Liang-cheng, who defected in April 1942, taking with him his whole force of several divisions. In November of the same year General Pi Chieh-yu, commander of the Nationalist 69th Army, and General Wen Ta-ko, commander of the Training Division of the XIX Army Corps went over to the Nanking Army. Both officers took the majority of their men with them, who were quickly formed into Nanking Army divisions.

The Japanese had at first looked to the retired generation of former high-ranking Chinese military officers to try and persuade them to join the various 'puppet' armies. These former warlord officers of the 1911–28 period were usually in their fifties or sixties by the 1930s. In many cases, they had been thrown out of military service when their armies were defeated by the Nationalists in 1928. Because of the resentment that many of these former officers felt for the Nationalists, they were regarded by the Japanese as potentially reliable recruits. The main problem with ex-warlord officers was that most had not served in a military capacity for nearly twenty years and were out of touch with the latest military thinking. Warlord armies were not known for their military efficiency during the 1920s and this was often reflected by the poor quality of many of the officers. Regardless of these weaknesses the shortage of trained Chinese officers available to the Japanese meant that any source of potential recruits had to be at least considered. The brutal Japanese treatment of the Chinese population however meant that few reputable officers were willing to serve them. Most former warlord officers were fervently anti-Communist and would, in most cases, have fought for the Japanese if they had not treated the ordinary people of China so dreadfully.

'Puppet' commanders, whether from the older or younger generation, had considerable power over the region they controlled. As long as they 'towed the line' with the Japanese they were often allowed to rule their area as petty fiefdoms. Because of the history of the Chinese soldier's personal loyalty to his commanding officer the 'puppet' officers were quite secure in their position under the Japanese. Not wanting to jeopardise this loyalty the 'puppet' commanders had to do something pretty serious for the Japanese to dismiss them from their command. Not surprisingly some 'puppet' commanders abused their power over the local population and when they first came to power were able to acquire large sums of money through extortion of various types. One example of the wealth acquired by 'puppet' army officers is that of Li Fu-chun, who commanded the 30th 'puppet' Division in Kwangtung Province in 1944. In a War Office report of 27 November 1944, Li is described as a former sailor with little education who had jumped at the chance to serve the Japanese and make himself rich at the same time. With the money he had gathered by "looting and plundering" the province, he had acquired a very large area of land and had planted a crop of rice from which he is supposed to have earned the amazing sum of $120,000. He also became the largest sugar cane grower in the region and opened 18 sugar factories each costing $800,000 in capital set up costs. In addition he owned 10 rice mills, 10 ships and had opened 5–6 small munitions factories to produce light arms and ammunition for his army. All this he was able to achieve with about 3,000 men under his command, and of course the backing of his Japanese employers. It is not therefore difficult to see why some Chinese were tempted to turn traitor and serve the occupiers.

To understand what made so many of the KMT units go over to the Japanese side one must first understand the nature of the Nationalist Army of the period. After the victory of the KMT Northern Expedition in 1928 many local warlords decided to throw in their lot with Chiang Kai-shek's Nationalists. Although in theory these ex–warlord commanders were loyal to the Nationalist Government in Nanking their loyalty was often 'paper' thin. Chiang Kai-shek was fully aware of their lack of loyalty and this led to him keeping their armies and divisions short of valuable equipment, especially artillery. At the same time, divisions which owed personal loyalty

In a joint operation by Japanese and Nanking soldiers a Type 89 Medium tank is followed by a mixed group of soldiers. The Nanking soldier behind the tank is carrying the flag of the Nanking Government, which is the same as the Nationalist one but with the addition of a long yellow pennant. This obviously posed propaganda photograph was meant to show that the Nanking Army was fighting side by side with their Japanese allies.

Tank Museum

to him or his closest allies were built up to the highest standard possible. Chiang also used the untrustworthy Nationalist divisions to bear the brunt of the fighting against the Japanese as they were in his view, expendable. This in turn led to resentment amongst these units and often destroyed any remaining loyalty to the central government. These factors meant that when one of these untrustworthy units was surrounded or cut off by the Japanese they were often easily recruited as 'puppet' troops. On many occasions whole regiments, divisions or even armies went over lock, stock and barrel to the Japanese and were soon given new 'puppet' designations. Another explanation for the large number of defections of KMT commanders to the Nanking Army was put forward constantly by the Communists during the war. This accusation was regarding the suspicion that most of the former Nationalist commanders who had defected to Nanking had done so at the orders of Chiang Kai-shek. The rather ambiguous nature of the soldiers position vis-à-vis their relationship with both the Japanese and the government in Chungking fuelled these suspicions. Communist sources claimed that the vast majority of the Nanking commanders were anti-Communist rather than pro-Japanese. The fact that 90–95% of Nanking soldiers were employed either in fighting the Communists or in protecting railways and other lines of communication from their attacks might support this theory. It was claimed that 62% of all Nationalist forces defecting to the Nanking did so on the orders of Chungking. In this way it was said the Japanese would feed these men while the war as on and then at the end of the war they would be armed and ready to deal with the Communists, as part of the Nationalist forces again. Some Nationalist sources supported this theory with the head of the KMT Secret Service, Tai Li, claiming that up to 500,000 of the Nanking soldiers were secretly pro-Nationalist.

The suspect loyalty of most 'puppet' troops and their units created an increasing dilemma for the Japanese as the war progressed. On the one hand they would have liked to employ more and larger 'puppet' units but

This patrol of Nanking Army soldiers marches through a hamlet while on an anti-guerrilla operation. The men are dressed in the same basic uniform as their Nationalist enemies and carry no insignia apart from their armbands. Their uniforms are made from blue cotton faded to a blue grey and would be padded for winter wear. The caption which accompanied this photograph states that the function of the Nanking Army was "To stop riots, hold down the populace and to keep the Nanking Government in power".

Imperial War Museum HU73371

A light machine gun team of the Nanking Army are pictured in this photograph, dated 19 February 1943. All the men are dressed in grey cotton uniforms with the new cap badge of the Nanking Army on the front of their 'ski' caps. The machine gun is a Czechoslovakian ZB-26, which was one of the main types in service with the Chinese Nationalist Army. The two riflemen are armed with Czech versions of the Mauser rifle, again taken from captured Nationalist stocks.

The Mainichi Newspapers

on the other they could not trust them. The Japanese were loath to create effective 'puppet' units as they were worried that they would simply go over to the guerrillas *en-masse*. Any 'puppet' unit was not allowed to exceed 3,000 men and the number of machine guns issued to them was severely restricted. Little, if any, artillery was given to 'puppet' formations and most sources indicate that the heaviest ordinance of these units was one or two light mortars. As a safeguard against mutiny by the 'puppet' soldiers the Japanese had to know that they could destroy quickly any unit that tried to fight against them. The start of the Pacific War and the extra constraints put on the Japanese by the need to send their troops from mainland China to this new theatre led to a change of policy. 'Puppet' units were increased in size, up to 6,000 men and were allowed to possess heavy machine guns and a few pieces of light artillery. The Japanese still kept 'puppet' units weak by only allowing a few of these heavier weapons per unit. Neithertheless the fighting capability of Nanking units was increased by this new weaponry and compared to the Communist and Nationalist guerrillas they faced, they were well equipped. The new Nanking Divisional organisation was:

HQ company
3 infantry regiments (each of 3 battalions, of 3 companies each)
1 mountain artillery battery
1 engineer company
1 signal unit

These Nanking Army organisation changes were rarely, if ever, adhered to, and there was a great disparity in the size of units. The designations used by 'puppet' units lead to a great deal of confusion with some so-called armies having 2,000 or less men, while some divisions had 6,000 or more men. Only the best units of the Capital

Garrison divisions would have had anything like a standard organisation. Measures were taken to try and improve the efficiency of the Nanking Army, including the opening of an ordinance repair workshop in May 1942. Factories were also reportedly established to manufacture rifles although heavier weaponry does not seem to have been produced. A central wireless station was also established in Nanking with relay stations in various parts of occupied China in an attempt to try and improve communications between the army command and outlying garrisons. Any small improvements were however mainly cosmetic and the overall efficiency of the Nanking Army remained unchanged.

When it comes to the morale of the average 'puppet' soldier in the Nanking Army a distinction is usually made between those who came under the direct control of the Nanking Government and those in the outlying regions of occupied China. Intelligence reports of 1944, for instance, stated that 'puppet' units which had been trained by and took orders from the authorities in Nanking were of a much higher standard than those that were outside their immediate control. The same reports stated that the ordinary 'puppet' unit raised by a local 'puppet' official on an *ad-hoc* basis could often be defeated by a much smaller guerrilla unit. In fact the report said that Communist guerrillas had been able on occasion to defeat 'puppet' units ten times their number. Although the Nanking trained 'puppet' units were of a much higher calibre than the locally raised units, they were not up to the standard of the Japanese troops they usually fought beside. Nanking-trained troops were, according to these reports, as well armed as their Japanese allies, and were often recruited from amongst the farmers of the region, who had been dispossessed by the fighting. They presumably blamed the guerrillas for their loss of livelihood and saw service in the 'puppet' army as their only option other than starvation.

Organisation of the Nanking Army 1940–45

In January 1943 it was reported that the units in and around Nanking were reorganised into a 'Metropolitan Defence Army'. The Army had a strength of 30,000 men in two divisions and were directly under the command of the Military Council. These divisions were to be responsible for the defence of Nanking and its government and were to be reinforced by another division, which was under formation. Reports from 'puppet' sources in Peking claimed that the strength of the military forces under the Nanking Government in central and south China in October 1943 was 42 divisions, 5 independent brigades and 15 independent regiments. General Jen Yuan -tao's Army which was stationed in the Nanking and Shanghai area and had 9 divisions, 2 independent brigades and 2 independent regiments. In the capital itself was the Nanking Garrison Army or 'Metropolitan Defence Army' of 3 divisions, which formed Wang Ching-wei's most loyal force. Presumably the 3rd Division had been formed between January and October (see above). In Northern Kiangsu Province was the 1st Group Army under the command of General Li Chang-chiang, which had 4 divisions, 2 independent brigades and 1 independent regiment. General Yang Kuei-yi, Chief of Staff of the Wuhan Provisional Headquarters, had 3 divisions, while in Shantung and Hopei Provinces, General Sun Liang-cheng, who commanded the 2nd War Zone, had about 20,000 men in an undesignated number of divisions. General Chen Yao-tsu had 2 divisions in Kwangtung Province; the other 21 divisions were presumably spread out over the rest of occupied China. As with other reports from intelligence sources the above list is frustratingly incomplete and makes it impossible to get the complete picture of 'puppet' unit organisation and distribution.

In February 1944 British intelligence sources estimated that the total of 'puppet' troops and militia were 627,200 men. These were divided into 327,400 regulars and 299,800 irregulars and local militia. Nationalist sources quoted the number of 'puppet' troops as 683,569, while Communist authorities reckoned that in 1945 there were 900,000 'puppet' soldiers, these being split into 410,000 regular troops and 490,000 local armed units.

The number of General Officers who defected to the Nanking Government was quoted by Nationalist sources as 12 in 1941, 15 in 1942 and 42 in 1943. Communist sources reckoned that between 1941 and 1943, 67 General Officers defected to the Nanking Army, taking with them 500,000 of their men.

British intelligence sources claimed that in March 1943, Wang Ching-wei agreed to the proposal by Japanese Prime Minister Tojo that he should conscript 4,000,000 youths in North China. These young men were to receive three months' training before being sent to the front. Due to the constraints of the Japanese war effort and shortages of equipment, grand schemes like this never materialised.

Even though by 1944- 45 the writing was on the wall for the Japanese in the Pacific, they remained dominant in China. 'Puppet' troops were still fighting for the Japanese right until the end of the war, and during the Battle of Western Hunan in March 1945 the Japanese offensive force included the 2nd 'Puppet' Division. In fact some Nationalist soldiers were still defecting to the Japanese as late as April 1945. Although the Japanese may have

In June 1942, President Wang Ching-wei reviews a unit of his Reorganised Government's so-called 'Nanking' Army in Kwangtung Province. The men are all well turned out, as befits a honour guard, and have all been issued with captured Nationalist M35 German steel helmets. These unit flags are almost identical to those used by the Nationalist Army and follow the pattern of the Nanking Army's use of their political enemies' insignia. Perhaps the best indication of the identity of these troops apart from the presence of Wang Ching -wei is the Japanese supplied Taisho-11 1922 light machine gun carried by the man on the right of the photograph.

The Mainichi Newspapers

been heavily defeated in the Pacific the situation was different on the Chinese mainland. In occupied China the Japanese still held sway and the 'puppet' soldiers were not to know how suddenly the war would end in August.

As the 'puppet' armies grew in size some conscription took place to fill the ranks, even though voluntary recruitment was usually sufficient. The Wang Ching-wei Government continued the same conscription policies as the Nationalist regime. In most cases though, there were enough ex-bandits, local hoodlums and above all starving peasants to make conscription unnecessary. On occasion though, the Nanking Army and the Japanese did resort to forcible conscription and had press gangs round up local youths. This method of 'recruiting' soldiers for the 'puppet' army was never an official policy of the Wang Ching-wei Government, however. A survey of 1940 stated that the make up of the 'puppet' army in Anhwei Province was made of roughly 50% peasants and 50% former military men. These ex-military men were either ex-KMT soldiers or bandits.

The Nanking Government 1940–45

Even from the early days of the Nanking Government it became obvious to all, including Wang Ching-wei himself, that he had no real power. The main role for the Nanking regime was to act as a propaganda tool for the Japanese. As part of this propaganda role the Japanese had been applying pressure on Wang and his government to declare war on the Allied powers. Although Wang resisted all the Japanese efforts to try and get him to make this move he could not refuse forever. So finally, on 9 January 1943, he formally declared war on

Great Britain and the United States. This declaration of war did not apply to the Soviet Union, with whom Japan still had a mutual non-aggression pact. Wang Ching-wei continued to be the dominant force behind the Nanking Government but his health was failing and complications caused by the bullet from an assassination attempt led to him travelling to Japan for treatment. He died in a Tokyo clinic on 10 November 1944 and was succeeded by his deputy Ch'en Kung-po. Ch'en had little real influence and the real power behind the regime was Chou Fou-hai, the mayor of Shanghai. Apart from a few 'fanatics', the majority of 'puppet' officials had long ago lost any faith in the Japanese and were looking for a way to co-operate with the Nationalist Government. Chou Fou-hai had been secretly negotiating with Chiang Kai-shek since 1942 and had been supplying information to the government in Chungking. After the death of Wang Ching-wei the Nanking Government had lost what little legitimacy it previously had. It stuttered on for another year and continued the display and show of a fascist regime, which included a state funeral for their former leader. The Nanking Government would only survive as long as the Japanese Empire could maintain its war effort. Although the Japanese Imperial Army still continued to launch offensives against the Chinese Communists and Nationalists into 1945, these were more or less holding exercises. In August, with the collapse of Japan and its surrender on 2 September, the end of the Nanking regime was swift.

Few military forces remained loyal to the Nanking Government and one of the few units to do so was formed from the cadets of the Nanking Military School. The cadets began to set up barricades and dig trenches in the centre of Nanking and fighting broke out between the pro-Ch'en Kung-po and pro-Chiang Kai-shek factions. Any resistance was, of course, only token, and in most cases the Nanking forces handed over their arms and bases peacefully to the Nationalists. All over China 'puppet' units decided to declare their allegiance to Chiang Kai-shek and his government and fought to stop Communist forces taking over their areas. In north China, six former Nationalist Generals who had turned traitor rejoined the Nationalists with their armies and were ordered by Chiang Kai-shek to resist Communist attempts to fill the vacuum left by the Japanese surrender.

A unit of Nanking Army troops march out of the ruined walls of a city under the control of the Wang Ching-wei government. They are wearing khaki peaked caps, which were no longer in common use with Chinese armies after the 1930s. The flag is a version of the Nationalist Army's flag with a white sun on a blue field, a yellow fringe and a yellow border down the pole side. The yellow pennant proclaiming the anti-Communist nature of the Nanking government is attached to the top of the flag.

The Mainichi Newspapers

It was the civilian 'puppet' leaders who were to suffer most after their defeat and some of the most prominent were put through show trials before facing execution. Wang Ching -wei had escaped any punishment, of course, by his death in 1944, as he would certainly have faced a firing squad. His successor to the leadership of the Nanking Government, Ch'en Kung -po did not escape that fate, and was tried and executed on 5 April 1946. Liang Hung-chih, the former head of the Reformed Government in Nanking from 1938 to 1940, was found in hiding and after a trial, he too was executed. Wang Ke-min, the former head of the Provisional Government before 1940 and head of the North China Political Council from 1940 to 1945, died in prison in Peking awaiting trial in December 1945. The Nationalists had long memories and when the leader of the state of East Hopei, Yin Ju-keng, fell into their hands, he was put on trial and shot in 1946. Of course, summary justice was meted out to some of the most reviled 'puppets' if they fell in the hands of the people who had suffered under them. In one instance, the former head of the Secret Police in the City of Hangchow, Ch'en Ch'un-yu, was taken by a mob and after being paraded through the streets he was executed. In all it was estimated that 2,720 leaders of the Wang Ching-wei government were executed, with another 2,300 being sentenced to life imprisonment.

Weaponry of the Nanking Army

The equipment and weaponry used by the Nanking Army from 1940 to 1945 came from various sources. With only a few arms factories in Nanking-held territory, the regime had to rely on captured Nationalist arms or those donated or sold to them by the Japanese.

The quantity and quality of weaponry used by the various Nanking units varied greatly, with some units receiving the best available rifles, while others were lucky to receive any kind of firearm. Soldiers who came over from the Nationalists often did so as whole units with their commander and would obviously have brought their rifles and other arms with them. The Chinese Nationalist Army itself was armed with such a variety of rifles that obviously the same would follow for turncoats from that Army. Two of the main types of rifle in use were the Chinese-manufactured copy of the Mauser 98k rifle, known popularly as the 'Chiang Kai-shek', and the Hanyang 88, a copy of an earlier 1888 Mauser. In fact, numerous additional types had been bought by the Nationalist government to equip their army, and these would have found their way into Nanking Army service. Some rifles were manufactured in arsenals under the control of the Nanking Government, although usually in small quantities. The Ordinance Technical Report # 27 states that late in the war, small scale production of rifles in these arsenals took place. The Kwangtung Arsenal certainly manufactured Chinese Mauser 98k's during the period of Japanese Occupation. Small-scale production of the Japanese Nambu 19 automatic pistol also took place in a small arsenal in north China. Although they may have been produced for Japanese use, some probably were issued to Chinese 'puppet' officers. In 1941 the Japanese did sell the Nanking Government about 15,000 Mannlicher rifles from their 'war booty' stocks and these were supplied to the Nanking Army units most loyal to Wang Ching-wei. Up to 30,000 new Japanese Arisaka rifles were also supplied by the Japanese and were reserved for the best Nanking units. Reports state that the Capital Garrison divisions and the Salt Tax Police received all these weapons.

The well-organised arsenal in Taiyuan under the control of the 'semi-puppet' Yen Hsi-shan produced copies of the US Thompson sub-machine gun and some of these were sold to 'puppet' soldiers in the region. Machine guns in use were again of various types, with the Czech ZB–26 light machine gun in being in widespread use. When Japanese machine guns were issued to the 'puppet' soldiers they were not surprisingly the oldest models, with the Nambu Model 11 (1922) light machine gun and the Type 3 (1914) medium machine gun being the most common. French light machine guns were also reported in use with 'puppet' soldiers in the south of China, near the border with French Indo-China. These were presumably handed over by the Japanese from stocks taken from the Vichy French Garrison who were effectively under their control.

Mortars had historically always been widely used in China in place of other artillery pieces, which were always in short supply. The manufacture of Stokes-type mortars was relatively easy, and many local Chinese arsenals produced them. Many 'puppet' units had to rely totally on mortars for artillery support with the heavier calibre pieces being held at divisional or army level. Smaller calibre mortars of Chinese or Japanese manufacture were issued at regimental and battalion level, although there were only a few per unit. The better equipped 'puppet' units had up to 4 mortars per battalion while others were not so well off, with only about 1 per unit.

When small arms were not brought over by the defecting Nationalist soldiers they were supplied by the Japanese from 'war booty'. These arms were not usually supplied free, and the Nanking government had to buy them from the Japanese. Some very poor quality captured small arms were given to the Nanking Army without charge, but these must have been virtually useless. The Nanking Army units nearest to the capital were generally better armed than the units stationed in the outlying provinces.

Even when a 'puppet' soldier was issued with a rifle, the amount of ammunition he was allowed was strictly limited by the Japanese. The 'puppets' were usually limited to. at the most, 30 rounds of ammunition, and in fact some were only issued with 5 bullets each. Japanese thinking was that even if the 'puppet' soldiers went over to the Nationalists or Communists they could not take too much ammunition with them. Some Japanese rifles were issued, but their war industry had enough problems supplying their own troops without equipping the large number of 'puppet' troops as well. One 'puppet' unit in north China was given the task of garrison-ing a large strongpoint called 'Mafeng' from 1944, after the Japanese troops guarding it had been withdrawn. The 50 'puppet' troops holding the strongpoint were given 'old' and 'discarded' rifles and were issued with a bare minimum of ammunition by the Japanese.

The Japanese kept their 'puppet' troops short of heavy weapons, as they simply did not trust them not to go over to the Nationalists or Communists when the opportunity arose. When artillery was used by Nanking units during anti-bandit operations it was usually kept under the control of their Japanese advisors. Historically the Chinese Army had always been short of artillery and even during the civil fighting of the warlord era from 1912 to 1928, when millions of men were under arms in China, the number of field guns in service was small. The best equipped Nanking forces in the region of the capital under the direct control of Wang Ching-wei had the majority of artillery available and this still only totalled 31 field guns. In the spring of 1941 the Japanese did sell a small amount of equipment to Wang Ching-wei, and this included ten Model 1917 mountain guns.

The Nanking Army also had very few armoured vehicles, although 18 Japanese Type 94 tankettes were supplied in 1941 to give them at least a token armoured force. Reportedly the Japanese also supplied the Nanking Army with British heavy equipment they had captured at the fall of Singapore in early 1942. There were huge amounts of equipment captured at Singapore, including Bren gun carriers, Marmon-Herrington Mk III armoured cars and 4.5" howitzers. Much of this equipment had already been issued to the Japanese-backed Indian National Army, and it is not known what was left to issue to the Nanking Army. There is no photo-graphic or other evidence as to what equipment was issued, but the large number of Bren or Universal carriers available would suggest that some of this type of vehicle were amongst those supplied. The Japanese had enough problems trying to supply their own forces with new tanks and other armoured vehicles. They were not willing to sell or give new armoured vehicles to their Chinese 'puppet' allies in any quantity. Any armoured vehicles that they were willing to give them would be from captured stock or very obsolete Japanese types. Records show that the Japanese supplied the Nanking Army with 20 armoured cars in spring 1941, and about 24 motorcycles These could not obviously come from captured British stocks as Japan did not go to war with the Allies until 8 December that year.

Nanking Army Special Units 1940–45

Wang Ching-wei's Personal Forces

Like all other Chinese politicians before him, Wang Ching-wei wanted to raise a military force which he could rely on to keep him in power. With this in mind he raised the 'Capital Garrison' Brigade in May 1941, which was to be stationed in Nanking and perform garrison duties in and around the capital. This Brigade was to pro-vide a loyal and trustworthy unit which owed personal loyalty to Wang himself. The Brigade was a success and in due course Wang decided to expand it into a Division with an influx of former KMT officers and men in September 1942. It was then reinforced with the 14th Independent Brigade and renamed the 2nd Capital Garrison Division. This was because Wang had decided to raise another two divisions of Capital Garrison troops although why this first unit did not become the 1st Division is a mystery. The two new divisions were named the 1st and 3rd Capital Garrison divisions, giving Wang a sizeable personal army. These three divisions were given the best uniforms, equipment and training of all Nanking Army units. They were also given the lions share of what little heavy equipment – e.g. armour, artillery etc. – the Japanese were willing to sell or give to the Wang Ching-wei government. Wang set up a Gendarmerie Command for the capital with 300 men trans-ferred from the Gendarmerie Command in Peking. Another of the best Nanking Army units was reported to be the Nanking Police Protection Army, under the command of Liu yi. This force was one of the best-equipped of the Nanking units, and was made up of one Police Division, one independent brigade and one Training Battalion with a total strength of 10,000 men.

Salt Tax Police

This special 'elite' military force was set up in July 1940 under the command of Wang Ching–wei's Minister of Finance, Chou Fuo-hai. Although designated as a police unit, the Salt Tax Police was a military unit with a strictly military role. They were given the police title to get around the rule that no Chinese military force was allowed to serve in the city of Shanghai. Chou Fuo-hai wanted the Tax Police to be better trained and equipped than the average 'puppet' military unit. His aim was to prove to the Japanese that with their backing he could produce a well motivated and loyal force which was up to the standard of a regular Japanese Army unit. He laid the groundwork for the Tax Police from the start by opening a Central Revenue Police Academy in July 1940. This academy was supposed to provide a high quality officer cadre with loyalty not just to the Wang Ching-wei government but also to Chou personally. Recruits came from the 'Loyal and Righteous Army' and from KMT prisoners, especially those with previous service in the Nationalist Tax Police. Starting with a few hundred men the Tax Police were rapidly expanded to first 4,000 then 10,000 and eventually reaching a strength of about 30,000 men, although some sources say that the maximum strength reached was nearer 20,000. For most of their life the Tax Police were highly regarded by both the 'puppet' and Japanese leadership. Wang Ching–wei and his government counted them as one of their best units along with the Capital Garrison Divisions. The Japanese gave the Tax Police special treatment and issued them with precious brand new Arisaka rifles. They did, however, come to fear this unusually well trained and equipped 'puppet' unit and late in the war decided to move the bulk of the force out of the Shanghai region where they had been stationed. Most of the Tax Police ended the war fighting guerrillas in the Kiangsu and Chekiang provinces.

Canton -Kowloon Railway Force

The Japanese were constantly attempting to raise reliable Chinese units which could relieve the pressure on their own troops duties. Although they recognised the authority of the Nanking Government over most of occupied China they did sometimes raise forces which were independent of the Wang Ching- wei government. In October 1943 it was announced that they would be raising a force of five divisions in the Canton area to garrison the Canton-Kowloon Railway. This force was to be completely independent of the Nanking Government and was to operate directly under Japanese orders. The intention was that the whole Japanese garrison along the railway could then be sent to other areas of China or to the Pacific Theatre.

Nanking Military Academies

The first Military Academy to train officers for the Nanking regime was actually opened before the official launch of the government. In December 1939 the new Military Academy or 'Central Army Officer Training Group' was opened at Chenju near Shanghai in a disused Japanese Barracks under the command of General Yeh Peng, a forty-five year old former KMT officer. The Academy had an initial intake of 800 cadets made up

A mixed unit of Japanese and Nanking Chinese soldiers are pictured during an operation in February 1942. It would be unusual to see 'puppet' troops fighting at the side of their Japanese allies like this. Although Nanking Army units often went on anti-guerrilla sweeps with the Imperial Japanese Army they would normally be kept in separate units. In fact, they were often taken on operations with the Japanese to act as support troops and to take over any garrisoning duties.

The Mainichi Newspapers

of unemployed Northern soldiers, students and captured KMT troops. It was divided into 2 battalions or classes, with the experienced personnel in one and the younger students in the second. Senior students in the 1st Battalion were simply given refresher training and political indoctrination and in February 1940 a few were sent to take up posts in the 'puppet' army. The majority of the senior class however were kept back to form Wang's personal bodyguard. Students from the second class continued their training and after the official formation of the Nanking Government in March 1940 they were sent to a Central Army Officers' Academy in Wuhan. According to 'puppet' propaganda of the time the academy was unable to take all the young men who had applied to join from all parts of occupied China. From the photographic and other evidence available it seems that the academy was certainly given the best of everything. The intention was that the academy was to be expanded to allow for the rapid enlargement of the Nanking Army.

A Central Military Academy was established in Nanking in September 1941 with an initial enrolment of 1,000 cadets who were aged between eighteen and twenty-five. Any student who had graduated from a Senior Middle School was eligible for enrolment in the academy. The training course was to be two years after which they would join the Army as junior officers. Japanese officers on the reserve list were also recruited by the Wang Ching-wei government to act as military instructors. The classes opened in November with a particular emphasis on artillery training and mechanised warfare training. With the opening of the Central Military Academy the earlier Military Schools at Canton and Wuhan were closed down as training was centralised at the new institute. An Officers Training Corps was established in Nanking to train lower ranking officers from the newly organised armies of the Nanking Regime. There was also an Army Training Corps opened to give specialist training to Privates of the Nanking Army, and a Central Army First Grade Training Institute to continue this training for the brightest cadets. A US Intelligence report of April 1945 states that by the later stages of the war there was a branch of the Central Military Academy in Canton, and both a Military Academy and a Military Training Corps situated in Peking. The Peking academies were presumably to train officers and men for the Army of the Northern Political Council, which still had a large amount of autonomy from the Central 'puppet' government in Nanking.

Nanking Military Academies	
Central Military Academy	Nanking
Branch of Central Military Academy	Canton
Peking Military Academy	Peking
Military Training Corps	Nanking
Military Training Corps	Peking
Generals and Colonels Training Academy	Nanking

The Pacification Role of The Nanking Army 1940–45

Regular 'puppet' troops were usually given the more important roles of defending lines of communication such as railways. This was the case in the Canton region where regular 'puppet' troops made up a combined Chinese, Japanese force of 15,000 men to patrol the Canton-Sheklung railway line and to control area. The 45th and 30th 'puppet' Divisions, each of about 5,000 men, were also responsible for garrisoning the cities of the region. Along the railway were stone pillboxes or strongpoints every half a Li to protect the line from attacks by guerrillas. Efforts to control the rural population of Japanese-occupied China were mainly half-hearted, with not enough resources available. A programme of 'Rural Pacification' was decided on in early 1941 and a 'Rural Pacification Commission' was appointed on 26 May to formulate a policy. The aim was to control the population and to stop them aiding any guerrilla activity in their areas. A Rural Pacification Policy or Movement – 'Ch'ing-hsiang yun-tung' – was underway by July 1941 and called for the setting up of 'Model Peace Zones' – 'mo-fan ti ho-p'ing ti-ch'u'. These zones would be initially cleared of Communist or KMT guerrilla forces and there was to be efforts to develop their economies to make them attractive to the people living in them. Everyone moving within the zones was to carry ID cards and other documents, to be checked at regular checkpoints. Policing the Model Peace Zones was to be undertaken by regular 'puppet' soldiers, local militia or police. On 1 July 1941, work began on constructing a system of bamboo palisades in the area south of the Yangtze River. Once surrounded the blockaded area would be isolated by checking and searching all traffic in and out by means of gates guarded by Nanking soldiers and police.

In a posed propaganda photograph, a mixed patrol of Nanking Army and Japanese soldiers share a comradely smoke. It is doubtful whether the Japanese and their 'puppet' allies mixed to this degree in reality. Japanese soldiers were taught to regard all Chinese as racially inferior, so this close contact is most likely for the benefit of the camera.

Philip Jowett Collection

The Rural Pacification campaign had limited success and was only ever really viable in the areas under the direct control of the Wang Ching-wei government. These areas formed a rough triangle, with the three cities of Nanking, Shanghai and Hangzou at the angles. As part of the policy to control the rural population, small fortresses or strongpoints were built all over occupied China, but mainly in the north of the country, where the Communist guerrillas were most active. A typical strongpoint was described by Harrison Forman in his 1945 book *Report from Red China*. The strongpoints were made up of several blockhouses with a high wall surrounding a compound, with fixed broken glass and barbed wire on top of the wall. The fortress was surrounded by broad ditch, which was cut wider at the top and narrower at the bottom to make it difficult to climb out of. Each strongpoint in the area in which Forman was an eyewitness was garrisoned by about 60 Japanese and 60 'puppet' soldiers, who lived in separate quarters and didn't mix at all. These strongpoints were

also garrisoned at times by 'puppet' soldiers alone, and were found to be easy targets for guerrilla attack. Strongpoints or blockhouses were often easily isolated by the guerrillas, and the men garrisoning them could often be persuaded to surrender without a fight. Captured strongpoints often provided the Communist guerrillas with a welcome supply of arms with which to fight the Japanese and other 'puppets'.

The Pao-Chia System

By far the most effective method for controlling the Chinese population of occupied territory however was the tried and trusted 'Pao-Chia' system. This method was taken from the old Imperial system of collective responsibility, which placed the onus for good behaviour on the local population. Under this system each and every household had a designated 'head' who was responsible for the behaviour of his family. Above the household was the next tier of responsibility, which was the 'Chia' made up of 10 households. The head of the 'Chia' was called a 'Chia-Chang' and he was responsible for every person within his group. Next up from the Chia came the 'Pao' which was made up of ten 'Chias' or in other words 100 households. The leader of the 'Pao' was called a 'Pao-Chang' and he was appointed from amongst the 'Chia-Changs' by the government and he had a deputy. 'Pao-Chang's' were joined together with others groups to form a 'Ren-Pao' which was the largest group in the system. Only the 'Chia's ' or household heads were not chosen by the 'puppet' government so the other group heads would have been picked from the more reliable members of the community. The whole system was controlled at a local level by the 'puppet' police with the 'Ren-Pao' having to report to their nearest station for orders. Stations chiefs would then report to the district Police Commissioner who was under the control of the District Magistrate who then reported to his local Japanese Army Commander. The 'Pao-Chia' system meant that if any member of the community was found to have broken the law or aided the guerrillas in any way, the head of household would be held responsible and punished.

Although the 'Pao-Chia' system was a brutally effective way to control the population on a local basis it did not stop guerrilla activity from fighters coming from outside the area. These guerrillas often had little or no regard for punishments meted out to a population whose affiliation they often suspected anyway.

Anti-Guerrilla Units

Various militia and guard units were raised to enforce the Pao-Chia system and to protect the lines of communication in Japanese occupied-areas. It is often confusing when trying to decipher the different militias and guard units which were featured in 'puppet' sources. Some of these paramilitary forces were obviously of particularly poor quality and would be virtually useless. The Japanese and their Nanking government allies had enough difficulty raising regular forces and providing them with training, equipment and leadership. Any irregular forces recruited by the Nanking government would have received little in the way of training and weaponry and officers in command of these units would be totally unreliable.

Pao-Chia Militia

The militia raised to help police the 'Pao-Chia' system was a poorly-trained and very poorly-armed force with no combat value. No rifles were supplied by the Japanese and any they did manage to acquire would have had to have been captured from guerrillas. Every Chinese household under the scheme was ordered to provide at least one able-bodied man to serve in the militia. Japanese occupation forces organised the militia on a local basis so that the Pao-Chia did not become one coherent force which could have constituted a threat to them. Each village had to form its own Pao-Chia unit with, each household having to provide one adult male to serve in it. All males between the age of eighteen and forty were liable for militia service, with men under and over those age limits being liable to serve in the reserve force. There were two basic sizes of unit, the 'Chia' – Sub-district and 'Pao' – District, with a 'Chia-chang' in charge of the smaller unit and a 'Pao-chang' in charge of the larger. Local 'puppet' police were in overall charge of the 'Chia' units and the 'puppet' District Magistrate had jurisdiction over the 'Pao' units.

Pao-Chia militiamen were given rudimentary training in physical education, self-defence and rifle shooting. Rifle practice would have been limited by the shortage of firearms, which were only issued to the militiamen

This small unit of young men and women in Chiangsintien are being trained as Railway Guards to patrol the railways in Nanking Government territory. 'Puppet' forces such as this were used for guard and patrol duties on railways, factories and government buildings. Japanese soldiers formally employed in these roles w ere then released to serve in a more active role in China or were sent to bolster the beleaguered garrisons in the Pacific.

Imperial War Museum HU73378

on a very limited basis. The Pao-Chia were also given political education by the Japanese in an effort to persuade them to remain loyal to the occupying forces and their 'puppets'. This political education drummed into the militiamen that the Communists were the real enemy and that the Pao-Chia should unite with the Japanese Army to crush them. Militiamen were constantly told that they should see their service in the Pao-Chia as an honour and that there was no greater honour than to fight against the evils of Communism. Unfortunately for the Japanese, the Pao-Chia was badly motivated and organised and its lack of proper arms meant that it was of little use in a military capacity.

Peace Preservation Corps

A Peace Preservation Corps was also raised as a form of Rural Guard, who were not used to guard strategic guerrilla targets such as railways, but were instead village guards. This local militia force was nominally under the control of the 'puppet' Nanking Government, although it had in reality a great deal of independence. The Peace Preservation Corps operated largely in the 'no-regime' no mans land between Nationalist and Japanese-controlled areas. In reality the PPC was nothing better than bandits in the employ of the Japanese and often shifted its allegiance between them and the Nationalists. It was extremely unreliable and therefore not employed unless absolutely necessary as garrison troops. Its main occupation seems to have been the robbing and extortion of the local population. The Japanese actively recruited many of the local guerrilla groups and converted them into PPC's. This was done with little preparation, and any training of these former guerrillas seems to have been rudimentary at best. Any effort by the Japanese would have been largely wasted as whenever they withdrew from an area the men of the PPC's simply reverted back to their guerrilla role.

A new force of Volunteer Guard Units was also reportedly recruited to police the blockaded areas with its men receiving a basic military training. These Guard units were, as might be expected, extremely unreliable, and special care was supposed to be taken to recruit reliable officers for this force. Where the Nanking authorities were to find reliable and trustworthy officer material from was not explained in the propaganda bulletins.

Nanking Army Operations 1940–45

Hard information on operations undertaken by the Nanking Army during the 1940–45 period is almost impossible to find and usually regarded as unreliable. Nationalist sources usually gloss over the role of these 'puppet' troops for obvious reasons and generally underplay their significance. Nanking Government reports of the time would also, of course, be regarded as unreliable, as they tended to build up the role played by their troops. What is generally agreed is that the majority of Nanking Army operations were as support troops to the Japanese. One exception was an action that took place in the region of North Hunan and South Hupeh provinces by the 29th 'puppet' Division. The Division fought a pitched battle against Nationalist forces in the region and for once they did so without the support of any Japanese.

Nanking Army Operations 1943

Suhuai Drive – Febuary to March 1943
An operation against the 89th Nationalist Army and the Communist New Fourth Army in the Suhuai region of Kiangsu Province. The aim of the campaign was to attack the bases of both these armies and the Nanking Government claimed to have killed 1,800 and taken 7,000 prisoners.

Kiangpei Drive – February to March 1943
A Japanese led offensive to the North of Lake Tungting-Hu to attack the 118th Division of the Nationalist Army under the command of General Wang Ching-tsai. Japanese propaganda claimed that they killed 8,000 and took 23,200 prisoners of war and in their words 'Brought peace and order to that part of the country'.

Taihsing Spring Drive – April to May 1943
A drive against the 24th Nationalist Army based around the border between Shansi and Honan Provinces and the Communist forces in the Shansi, Chahar and Hopei Provinces. Japanese sources claim that the anti-Japanese forces suffered heavy casualties with 11,500 dead and 75,000 taken prisoner. The commanders of the 24th Nationalist Army, General Pang Ping-hsun and General Sun Tien-ying of the 5th Nationalist Army came over to the Nanking Government.

Drive into Kiangnan – May to June 1943

This campaign was launched against the 29th and 10th Nationalist Army Groups who were operating north of Tungting-Hu. The main aim of the operation was to capture the Kiangnan region which was the main grain producing centre in Central China. During the heavy fighting the Japanese used land, naval and air forces in concert with Nanking ground forces. Again, according to Japanese sources the Nationalists lost 43,700 dead and 6,400 prisoners of war. The final result was that the Nanking Government was able to extend its control over the whole of the grain-producing region of Hunan Province.

Drive Against North China Communists – September to November 1943

This drive was launched against the Communist supply bases in north China and was, according to the 'puppet' sources, highly successful.

The following reports appeared in a Nanking Government publication in 1943 and describe the operations of a number of 'puppet' armies during the 1940–43 period. Although they may exaggerate the success of these operations they do at least give some indication of how involved the 'puppets' were in actions against the Communist and Nationalist Guerrilla forces:

War Record of Peace Guard of Shansi 1943

The Peace Guard operated against Communist Guerrillas throughout the year and was also responsible for launching propaganda campaigns amongst the peasantry. They were heavily involved in collecting foodstuffs and helping bring in the harvest to supply both themselves and the Japanese.

Shansi Peace Guard Operational Record 1943	
Number of armed encounters	908
Enemy Casualties	4,010*
Prisoners Taken	859
Light Machine guns captured	14
Rifles captured	578
Revolvers captured	58
Rounds of ammunition captured	4,962*

* Presumably including civilian deaths claimed by the 'puppets' as armed guerrillas.

War Record of Wu Wen-hua's Army 1943

Nationalist General Wu Wen-hua came over to the Nanking Government in January 1943 with his 40,000-strong army. For the rest of 1943 his army was in action fighting alongside the Japanese against Nationalist forces. In May it was claimed that a joint Nanking-Japanese force including Wu Wen-hua's force defeated the 113th and 114th Nationalist divisions in the Lonan region in southern Shangtung Province. The 25,000-strong force of

Officers of the Nanking Army are seen at work with the mobile propaganda unit that was sent into the countryside to spread the word about the Wang Ching-wei regime. Three of the men are wearing standard officers' uniforms with the ski cap and would be almost indistinguishable from Nationalist officers. The man in the foreground could well be a 'Gunzoku' or civilian attached to the Nanking Army, and his uniform would be green in colour.

Imperial War Museum HU73373

Nationalists was reportedly expelled from the region with heavy losses. Wu Wen-hua's force also suffered heavy losses with 1,200 killed and over 3,000 wounded.

Wu Wen-hua Army Operational Record 1943	
Number of armed encounters	648
Number of Enemy encountered	518,400*
Enemy dead	6,684
Enemy wounded	11,543
Enemy prisoners	2,885
Heavy machine guns captured	12
Light machine guns captured	96
Artillery captured	1
Rifles captured	3,973
Revolvers captured	55
Hand grenades captured	8,397
Radio sets captured	3

*Almost certainly an exaggeration.

Selected Nanking Army Units 1940–45

Some units were formed to guard specific strategic targets such as railways, factories and other industrial installations. Two such units were the 'Kaifeng-Sinsiang Railway Protection Unit', with 200 men and the 'Tsiaoto Mine Garrison' which had 600 men. There were also reports of 'puppet' soldiers being used by the Japanese in the Burma Campaign as auxiliary troops. According to one intelligence report of December 1942, 30,000 troops from north and central China were sent to Burma via Hainan Island. There were also reports of Manchukuoan troops being used in the same campaign although it is impossible to confirm these facts. The fact that the Japanese did not trust their 'puppet' allies to serve in China suggests that it was unlikely that they would let them serve in foreign lands.

Detailed information on specific 'puppet' units usually came from intelligence reports from US, British or Nationalist agents. Most intelligence information featured lists of larger units, e.g. armies, divisions and regiments, without giving specific information regarding their organisation. One British report of 27 March 1943 does, however, go into a great deal of detail about the 'puppet' soldiers stationed in the Kongmun area near Canton in Kwangtung Province. The report stated that there were 1,000 'puppet' troops in the region distributed between the towns of Shekki, Tongka and Sunwui which included a small cavalry unit of 35 men. Regarding the organisation and equipment of the 'puppet' troops in the Kongmun area the source goes on to say that the regiment stationed there consisted of three battalions with each having four companies, each divided into four sub-units. According to the report, this regiment seems to have been extremely well armed, with the following equipment issued to each battalion: four small mortars, six 7.7mm calibre French 1937 machine guns and twelve machine guns of Czech manufacture (presumably ZB–26s). The agent also reported that some of the 'puppet' soldiers had as many as six grenades each and were armed with 'old' pattern rifles of non-Japanese manufacture.

In a rather futile attempt to raise the morale of the Nanking Regime and to bolster the people's support for it, this military band marched through the deserted streets of Nanking every morning playing martial tunes. Their uniforms are based on the full dress uniforms of the Nationalist Army which was normally only seen worn by the highest ranking officers on very formal occasions.

Imperial War Museum HU73376

Why this particular regiment should be so well armed is a mystery but the amount of equipment issued to different 'puppet' units varied greatly. Perhaps the local Japanese commander was a generous man or maybe this unit had proved itself in battle as a reliable one.

Intelligence reports also exist which detail the strength and equipment of the 'puppet' troops who garrisoned the Luichow Peninsula in the south of China in 1944. According to British Intelligence Report No. 4715, dated 3 November 1944 the strengths were as follows:

Table 6 – 'Puppet' Troops and Equipment, Luichow Peninsula, September 1944		
City	Men	Equipment
Hoi-hong	200	5 LMGs, 2 pieces of light artillery
Namphing	200	2 LMGs, 2 pieces of light artillery
Lung-Moon	80	1 LMG
Bac-Wo	100	1 LMG
Wushek	100	–
Ping-Wu	70	–

As the above table shows, the 750 men of the 'puppet' army in the peninsula had a total of 9 light machine guns. They were quite well off regarding artillery, with what the report describes as four small cannons. Although the report does not go into detail regarding the type of artillery, these cannons were most probably mountain guns that were in service with the Chinese army in quite large numbers.

A US Intelligence report of 9 May 1945 gave a detailed description of the 'puppet' units at Shanhsien in Honan Province:

Table 7 – Shanhsien Forces, May 1945		
Unit	Men	Equipment
1st Shanhsien Self-Protection Unit	800	600 rifles, 15 pistols, 4 LMGS
'Puppet' Advancing Army	2,000	500 rifles, 10 pistols
2nd Shanhsien Self-Protection Unit	300	150 rifles, 10 pistols
3rd Shanhsien Self-Protection Unit	200	100 rifles, 3 pistols

Reports by an OSS operative Captain Chiyoki Ikeda of the Hsien Field Command give some details of the strength and equipment of 'puppet' units in Honan Province in the summer of 1945, just before the end of the war. They show a great disparity in the level of weaponry that the different 'puppet' units have, with some units well equipped and others poorly armed. For instance two 'puppet' regiments in the vicinity of Hsinyang were relatively well equipped, with one having 2,000 men, 50 light machine guns, 4 heavy machine guns and 4 artillery pieces. The second unit had 3,000 men, 80 light machine guns, 6 heavy machine guns and 4 artillery pieces. Ikeda's report does not, however, explain what kind of artillery pieces these units had, although in all probability they were mortars. Four smaller units in the region around the city of Shanhsien were not so well equipped, with the 'puppet' 'Advancing Army' having 2,000 men on strength but only 500 rifles and 10 pistols between them. Two smaller units in the same area had respectively, 300 men with 150 rifles and 5 pistols and 200 men with 100 rifles and 3 pistols. The fourth unit was better equipped than the other three, with 800 men possessing 600 rifles and 15 pistols. This last unit had only gone over to the Japanese on 27 April, and this probably explains why it had four light machine guns in its armoury.

The ratio of equipment per unit of the Nanking Army varied greatly and was often directly related to the perceived reliability of the particular unit in the eyes of the Japanese military. 'Puppet' troops stationed in the Swatow area of Southern China were found to be unreliable and in 1943 they had their machine guns confiscated by the Japanese. They also had the majority of their ammunition for their rifles withdrawn and were only allowed five bullets each. One of the poorest equipped 'puppet' garrisons was the force that operated on the island of Hainan, off the coast of southern China. There were a total of 960 'puppet' soldiers and militia on the island possessing only two heavy and two light machine guns between them! The 'puppet' garrison of the

Luichow Peninsula, also in southern China, had a smaller number of troops than on Hainan but more equipment. There were only 750 men in the Luichow force and they were armed with 9 light machine guns

Autonomous Nanking Forces 1940–45

Some military forces raised by the Japanese or in outlying regions were almost totally Independent of the Nanking Government. Units in the south of China seem to have had a large degree of self government

Self–Governing Army of Kinhwa

Raised by the Japanese Military Police in the city of Kinhwa and commanded by two Chinese officers of rather dubious background. The 'Army' was split into two battalions, with the commander of the 1st Battalion being the proprietor of a local gambling den. He and the commander of the 2nd Battalion of the Army were both opium addicts and enjoyed an unsavoury reputation. Their army was reportedly only 150 men strong and was extremely 'top heavy', with over 20 officers on strength. The Army was raised specifically for an attack on the towns of Yungkang and Tsinyin, although their failure to capture either soon led to its disbandment by the Kempeitei.

Hainan Island 'Puppet' Forces

The island of Hainan, off the southern coast of mainland China, was occupied by the Japanese in February 1939. There were three types of 'puppet' units raised on the island – Pacification, Anti-Communist and Self Defence Troops. Pacification troops were organised along regular army lines in five battalions of 200 men each, making a total of 1,000 men. Although the best armed of the 'puppet' units on Hainan, the Pacification Troops were poorly armed. The equipment of the 1st Battalion of Pacification troops was recorded as two heavy and two light machine guns. The so-called Anti-Communist troops were lighter armed than the Pacification troops with only rifles and pistols, and had a total strength of 830 men in units of various sizes. Self Defence Troops were basically village militia, being given the job of protecting villages against guerrilla attack. These Self-Defence units were small, with only 15–20 men per village, the total being a tiny 130 men. There was also individual armed 'puppets' who acted as 'Village Guards' and were the worst armed of all. They would have been very lucky to have been given anything more lethal that a spear or sword.

The Western Suiyuan Army

Very little is known about the semi–independent army that existed in the western part of Suiyuan Province in Inner Mongolia. It is however nearly always included in the many orders of battle produced by Western intelligence. Its commander and titular head was Wang Ying, who had been an officer in the Inner Mongolian Army during the war, aiming to take Suiyuan Province in 1936–37. Presumably he had been able to carve himself out a fiefdom which he managed to rule independently of the main Inner Mongolian Government under the protection of the Japanese. All Western sources give his army a strength of 2,230 men in three divisions. According to reports from March 1943 these were made up of:

1st Division	1,000 men
2nd Division	630 men
3rd Division	600 men

Army of the North China Political Council 1940–45

Under the agreement reached between Wang Ching-wei, the Japanese and the Provisional and Reformed Governments, both 'puppet' regimes were officially unified. In reality however, although Wang Ching-wei was head of this new 'Reorganised' Government, north China still had its own identity. The Provisional government became the North China Political Council with Wang Ke-min at its head. Wang Ke-min and his new Council

took little notice of Wang Ching-wei's government and only paid lip service to it. In defiance of Wang Ching-wei they continued to fly the five barred flag of the Provisional Government until ordered not to by the Japanese. The former Provisional Government Army now also became officially part of the Army of the Reorganised Government in Nanking. However. effectively, most military forces in the north of China were still under the direction of the North China Council. The strength of the Army of the North China Political Council in October 1940 was reported to be 22 regiments, with 7 brigades of 2 regiments each and 8 independent and training regiments.

In November 1940 a new recruiting drive was launched to expand the regular armed forces available to the North China Political Council from 26,000 up to 41,000. In addition to this force there were 4,000 men of the former East Hopei Army still under arms who were kept as a separate army and given the task of patrolling the Peking-Sanhaikwan Railway. Another 4,000 men belonged to the Shantung Provincial Army, who were kept as a separate force also and stayed in their own province. The armed local 'puppet' police were estimated to number 63,000 and even though this was a sizeable force the large area covered by them meant that there were still only approximately 130 men to every district. The Internal Security Police were about 72,000 strong and although its role is not clearly defined this force seems to have been responsible for providing

In these two photographs we see a Nanking Army training class for the Japanese Type 3 medium machine gun taking place. Although an elderly piece of equipment in Japanese service, the Nanking Army would have been fortunate to receive many of these. They generally had to be content with captured war booty and any Japanese cast-offs they could get.

Philip Jowett Collection

officers to command the large militia force. Presumably the Internal Security Police were to form to 'backbone' of the poorly trained and even more poorly armed local militia. There was an average of 200 Internal Security Police per district and this meant that each village had between 1 or 2 to guard them. By November 1942 the North China Political Council's Army had undergone a further reorganisation, which had led to an establishment of 30 regiments. Although on paper the Army had expanded from 22 to 30 regiments, in actual, fact each unit was reported to be have fewer than 1,000 men. If this were really the case then the Army had actually shrunk from 41,000 to a force of under 30,000 men.

North China Armed Militia

A secret document issued by the North China Political Council on 28 September 1943 called for the formation of an 'Armed Militia' to help in maintaining the peace in north China. It also called for mutual co-operation between the Militia and the Japanese units stationed in the region. The Armed Militia was formed from amongst Japanese reservists and civilians resident in north China as well as amongst certain anti-Communist Societies such as the 'Red Spears'. Recruits also came from the members of the 'puppet' political organisation the 'Hsin Min' which had been set up to act as the one political party of northern China. The Youth Corps of the Hsin Min provided the vast majority of willing or unwilling recruits for the Militia. Recruits for the Armed Militia could also have come from the North Chinese 'puppet' organisation called the 'Tung Shan Sheh'. This group of traditional Taoists numbered 60,000 members in Hopeh, Shangtung and Kiangsu Provinces.

Sources report that the total number of Militiamen of all types reached 200,000, many of whom were armed only with spears. This new Militia was needed to take over garrisoning and other guard duties from Japanese units that had been withdrawn to other parts of China or had been transferred to the Pacific Theatre. According to the report, a certain Japanese division had been transferred from north China to Saigon in Indochina. When the Division was seen to still be operating in north China it was discovered that a cadre of Japanese had been left behind when they moved to Saigon. The ranks had then been filled with volunteers from the 'Armed Militia' who presumably were dressed in Japanese uniforms to complete the facade. This Armed Militia force was in fact a way for the North China Political Council to possess substantial forces independent of the Nanking Government. The North China Political Council were jealous of their independence from Nanking and needed more of their own military forces. Much of the information regarding the Armed Militia and its proposed independence from the central government was kept from both the Nanking Government and their Japanese advisors.

Table 8 – North China Political Council Army, Regiment Organisation, May 1941	
Regiment 'Tuan'	
	3 battalions of infantry
	1 machine gun company
	1 mortar company
	1 troop of cavalry
	1 signal company
Total	**1,650 men**
	27 automatic rifles
	9 machine guns
	9 mortars per regiment

One 1,500 strong unit of NCPC soldiers stationed fifteen miles from Peking shot their officers and ran away to join the guerrillas. In 1941 a Japanese officer admitted that there were an average of 50 engagements per day with guerrilla forces in north China. The main role of the NCPC Army was to guard the railways and roads from guerrilla attacks. At first the Provisional Government were allowed few military forces of their own, but this changed after the Communist 'Hundred Regiments' offensive. The Japanese realised that they needed a stronger 'puppet' force in north China to help them control the region. The loyalty of the 'puppet' troops in northern China was always in question and the Japanese were always trying to purge any disloyal elements. In August and September 1942 they did arrest a number of 'puppet' officers who were particularly suspect and some of these were executed as an example. At the same time the Japanese disbanded a few 'puppet' units that had proved particularly unreliable. Unfortunately for them if they had disbanded all the disloyal units in north China there would have been very few 'puppet' troops left. In 1943 the Japanese decided to break down the NCPC forces into smaller units by reducing the size of their divisions to 5,000 each. At the same time they decided to limit the amount of bullets per soldier to 30 rounds each.

The Inner Mongolian Army 1940–45

When the various 'puppet' governments of China were unified under the Wang Ching–wei government in March 1940, Inner Mongolia retained its separate identity. Although under the firm control of the Japanese Imperial Army which occupied its territory the Inner Mongolian Army of the 1940–45 period was, in theory, an independent force.

'Puppet' propaganda claimed in 1941 that the Inner Mongolian Army had a strength of 50,000 men, but this was a totally false figure. The Army's strength was probably more in the region of the 18,000 that was reported by Allied intelligence. By 1943 the Inner Mongolian Army had been reduced in size, and there were probably only between 4,000 and 10,000 men in the Inner Mongolian Army organised in between four and eight cavalry divisions. The Army was almost entirely composed of cavalry, with little in the way of heavy equipment, what there was being under the control of Japanese troops stationed there. Its troops were usually given the usual 'puppet' soldiers' role of guard duties and limited anti-guerrilla operations under the supervision of the Japanese.

Recruitment into the Inner Mongolian Army was by conscription, with all ordinary Mongolians liable for service, the only exception being Buddhist monks. As late as 1944 the Japanese attempted to recruit the Inner Mongolian youth by ordering the formation of a Youth Corps for boys and young men aged between fifteen and twenty. The intention was for a four month training course after which the cadets would join the 'puppet' Police Corps or Army.

Inner Mongolian Army Reorganisations 1939–44

A reorganisation of the Inner Mongolian Army in 1939 led to the transfer of all ethnic 'Han' or Chinese to the 1st, 2nd and 3rd divisions. In 1940 the designations of these three divisions were changed to the 1st, 2nd and

Two Nanking Army troops in a trench are preparing to fire what looks like a locally-produced light mortar. The Nanking Army suffered from a lack of all equipment and was kept purposely short of anything heavier than small arms. All artillery, including mortars, was usually kept for the more reliable personal troops of Wang Ching-wei in the Nanking region.

Philip Jowett Collection

3rd brigades of the 'Mongolian Regional Pacification Force' or 'Ch'ing An Tui'. This new force was to be responsible for the war against the various guerrilla groups and was under the control of the Public Security Bureau. In 1943 the Japanese combined the 4th and 5th divisions of the Inner Mongolian Army with the 7th and 8th divisions. These new strengthened and upgraded divisions were given the new designations of the 8th and 9th. The Japanese intention was that rather than having a larger number of weak divisions it was preferable to have a few more substantial ones. The Inner Mongolian Army had proved unreliable to the Japanese and the large number of desertions and heavy casualty list meant that by 1943 it only had a strength of two divisions and five so-called 'Defence' Divisions. The Defence Divisions were made up of local militia and other 'security' forces, and although each unit had three regiments, only one of these was capable of carrying out operations. A final reorganisation in 1944 led to the 1st, 2nd and 3rd 'Ch'ing An Tui' brigades being combined with the various garrisons of Chahar province to form four upgraded divisions. These 'divisions' were hardly worthy of the name and in fact only had about 2,000 men each. All this tinkering with the Inner Mongolian Army organisation could not alter the fact that it was a weak force. From the early 1940s until the end of the war it performed the same duties as the other 'puppet' armies, namely guard and local garrison duties which released the Japanese Army for more combative roles. The final organisation of the Inner Mongolian Army at the end of the war gave it six divisions, three independent brigades, five defence divisions and one 'Pao An Tui' 'Security Force' Regiment.

The Soviet Invasion of Inner Mongolia, August 1945

As with all other 'puppet' governments the Inner Mongolian regime's end came with the defeat of the Imperial Japanese Armed Forces. Soviet forces invaded Inner Mongolia at the same time as Manchukuo and soon crushed any organised resistance from the 'puppet' army. The Leavenworth Papers report on the Soviet invasion of Manchukuo in August 1945 includes the Inner Mongolian Army as part of the forces defending Inner Mongolia along with units of the Japanese Kwangtung Army. This paper gives the Inner Mongolian Army a strength of 44,000 men in five/six cavalry divisions/brigades. When estimating the size of the Inner Mongolian Army perhaps the US intelligence sources were unaware of just how small a Inner Mongolian division was? Certainly the figure of 44,000 sounds far too high, and to raise an Army of this size would have meant the forcible recruitment of just about every male in the country.

As the huge Soviet forces advanced into Inner Mongolia they met limited resistance from small detachments of Mongolian Cavalry. The 17th Army and the 6th Guards Tank Army easily pushed aside the 1st Inner Mongolian Cavalry Division, which was stationed north of Kalgan on the border between Mongolia and Inner Mongolia. Throughout the Soviets relentless advance the only opposition to them came from the Kalgan-based Inner Mongolian forces and small Japanese units. Heavy fighting did take place on 15 August at Kanbao, when the Soviet-Mongolian Cavalry Mechanised Group was faced by a substantial Inner Mongolian force. This force was made up of the 3rd, 5th and 7th Inner Mongolian cavalry 'divisions' who were the only defenders of the city. After two days heavy fighting with the Soviet attack spearheaded by the 27th Motorised Rifle Brigade the Inner Mongolians were defeated. Soviet units took 1,635 Inner Mongolians prisoner and captured the city while any surviving Mongolians fled. Any surviving Inner Mongolians would have in most cases been incorporated into the Chinese Communist forces in the region. These men would have faced the KMT forces which contested Inner Mongolia with the Communists during the Civil War of 1946–49.

CHAPTER FIVE

'Puppet' Air Forces and Navies 1931–45

Manchukuoan & Chinese 'Puppet' Air Forces 1932–1945

Manchurian Paramilitary Airline (MKKK)

A Manchurian Aviation Company was formed in 1932 to provide an airline for the new state which could also act in times as war as a military air arm. The 'Manchu Kokuyuso Kabushiki Kaisha' or 'MKKK' operated a number of transport planes including Fokker Super Universals supplied by Japan, home-produced Mansyu Hayabusas and a single American-made Clark GA 43 transferred form Japan Airlines. The MKKK's repair shops at Fengtien produced the Fokker Super Universal as the Manko Type 1 and also the British De Havilland Puss Moth trainer as the Manko Type 3. In 1938 a number of German aircraft were bought to reinforce the MKKK. These were a few Messerschmitt Bf 108 light transport and communications 'planes and 10–12 Junkers Ju 86Z–2 transports which had the dual role of civilian transports and, in time of war, improvised bombers. Some reports state that the Bf 108s were employed as ambulance planes, and were in fact 'loaned' to the Japanese to be used in this role.

Aircraft of the MKKK were to see action on the side of the Inner Mongolian Army during the campaign in Suiyuan province in 1936. An 'Independent Volunteer Battalion' of the MKKK comprising 13 planes flew in support of the invasion of Nationalist-held Suiyuan.

Table 11- Aircraft of the MKKK in Service 1932–45	
Clark GA43 Transport	1
De Havilland DH80A 'Pussmoth' trainer/communication plane	12
De Havilland DH80A 'Manko' Type 3 trainer/communication plane	15
De Havilland DH85 'Leopard Moth' communications plane	1
Fokker FV11/3M transport	2
Heinkel He 116 communications plane	2
Junkers Ju 86Z–1 transport/improvised bomber	10
Junkers Ju 86Z–2 transport/improvised bomber	10
Mansyu Hayabusa transport	30
Messerschmit Bf 108D 'Taifun' liaison plane	15
Mitsubishi Ki–57 'Topsy' transport	10
Nakajima Ki–34 'Thora' transport	12
Tachikawa Ki–54 'Hickory' transport	1+

Manchukuo Aircraft Manufacture

A Manchurian aircraft industry was set up under the auspices of the Japanese and even managed to design its own transport plane . The 'Mansyu Hayabusa' was a six-seater light transport which was used by the Manchukuo Airline and Air Force as well as by some Japanese Airlines. The Nakajima Ki–27 fighter was also produced by Manchukoan factories for service with its own Air Force and the Japanese. The Mansyu Aircraft factory in Harbin produced 1,379 Ki–27s, of which only a handful were used by the Manchukuoan Air Force.

A Junkers 86Z-2 transport and improvised bomber of the Manchukuoan paramilitary airline, the 'Manchu Kokuyuso Kokuyuso Kaisha' or MKKK. The MKKK was designed to act as a civilian airline with the capacity to be used in time of war in support of the Manchukoan Army. The Junkers 86 was bought from Germany because of its capability to perform both roles, as it started life in its home country as an airliner and was converted into a medium bomber by the Luftwaffe.

Aerospace Publishing

The Manchukuo Air Force 1932–45

The Manchukuo Air Force was formed in February 1937 when 30 volunteers from the Manchukuo Army were sent to Harbin for training. The volunteers were then sent to Xinjing Airfield where they were formed into the first air unit under the command of 1st Lieutenant Uta. At first the Air Force had only one old Nieuport-Delage Ni–D29 fighter which had formed part of the equipment of the Japanese Air Force during the invasion of Manchuria in 1931. The 'fledgling' Manchukuo Air Force was expanded with the addition of a number of Nakajima Type 91 fighters and Kawasaki Type 88 light bombers. The aircraft were operated as part of the Japanese Air Force and sported Japanese insignia, were flown by Japanese pilots and serviced by Japanese ground crew. At this stage the Japanese were not prepared to have an independent Manchukuo air arm, and kept the force under their complete control. A second air unit was formed in Fengtien followed by a third in Harbin during 1938–1939 and in July 1940 the new headquarters of the Manchukuo Air Defence was established in Xinjing. At the same time the Japanese finally decided to form a modern Manchukuoan Air Force with modern equipment and Manchukoan pilots. As part of this process a flying school was opened in Mukden on 1 April 1940 to give Manchukuoan pilots training, the school training both military and civil pilots. The expansion programme suffered a severe blow however, when in January 1941, 100 trained pilots of the Manchukuoan Air Force who were stationed near Harbin rebelled. After murdering some of their Japanese instructors they fled in three trucks and tried to join the guerrillas before being captured and court-martialled. This setback obviously did not stop the development of the new Air Force, which underwent reorganisation later that year.

Manchukuo Air Force Organisation 1941:
1st Air Unit (Xinjing)
2nd Air Unit (Fengtien)
3rd Air Unit (Harbin)
Tongliao Independent Air Unit
Flying School

Three fighter squadrons were formed from cadets from the flying school in 1942 and the typical strength of a squadron was as follows:

1st Squadron- 11 Officers (5 Japanese and 5 Chinese), 12–14 NCO's, 90 Privates.

The Air Force was supplied with a number of training and transport aircraft including Tachikawa Ki–9 and Ki–55 trainers and Tachikawa Ki–54 and Mitsubishi Ki–57 transports. Kawasaki Ki–32 light bombers were to provide the only bombing capacity of the Manchukuoan Air Force but there were unconfirmed reports of 6 Mitsubishi Ki–21 medium bombers being supplied in 1943. In 1942 the Manchukuo Air Force received its first fighter aircraft with the supply of Nakajima Ki–27s. These fighters were presented to the Air Force on 'Aviation Day' on 20 September 1942. Money to pay for the fighters came largely from Manchukuoan companies who were 'encouraged' by the Japanese to donate funds. In 1943 some of the Ki–27s were taken over by the Japanese who also recruited some of the Manchukuoan pilots to fly them. A small number of Nakajima Ki–43s were given to the Manchukuoan Air Force in 1945 to try and intercept American B–29 Superfortresses raiding

Mukden. The aging Ki–43s along with the older Ki–27s were given the estimated time of arrival of the bombers by Japanese intelligence. They would then take off 20 minutes before they were due to arrive and climb to 7,000 metres and then make one head on pass before the B–29s flew out of range. Because of the inferiority of the Nakajima Ki–27 Manchukuoan pilots were also given 'Kamikaze' training with the intention of their making suicide attacks on the B–29s. At least one pilot must have been willing to undertake a kamikaze attack as in December 1944 it was reported that a B–29 was destroyed by a Ki–27 which crashed into it. As the war drew to a close it became obvious that the main threat to Manchukuo would now come from the Soviet army poised to attack on the northern border and not from the B–29s . To meet this new threat the Manchukuoan pilots training was then changed to ground attacks on Soviet tanks and these would include 'Kamikaze' tactics. All the fighter and trainer aircraft left in the Manchukuoan Air Force would be employed in these attacks. When the Soviets did invade Manchukuo in August 1945 they overwhelmed the Japanese Army and Air Force completely. The Manchukuoan Air Force had almost ceased to exist by this time but there were reports of clashes between their aircraft and the Soviets, although these were isolated incidents.

Table 12 – Manchukuoan Air Force: Aircraft in Service 1932–45	
Kawasaki Ki–32 light bomber	1+
Kawasaki Type 88 light bomber	1+
Mitsubishi Ki–30 'Ann' light bomber	1+
Mitsubishi Ki–21 bomber	6
Nakajima Type 91 II fighter	1+
Nakajima Ki–27 'Nate' fighter	12
Nakajima Ki–43 'Oscar' fighter	3
Nakajima LB–2 medium bomber	1
Northrop 2F BXN2 Gamma 2E attack bomber	1
Tachikawa Ki–9 'Spruce' trainer	6+
Tachikawa Ki–54 ' Hickory' transport	1+
Tachikawa Ki–55 'Ida' advanced trainer	1+

China Aviation Company – A 'Puppet' Airline

In an attempt to provide air communication throughout the territories controlled by the various 'puppet' Chinese governments an airline was set up by the Japanese and their client states in 1938. The China Aviation

This Manchukoan Nakajima Ki-27 fighter was one of the first modern aircraft provided to the air force in 1941. The black inscription down the fuselage identifies the Manchukoan company which sponsored its purchase. Most of these aircraft were bought for the air force by oil, steel and other industrial companies.

Aerospace Publishing

A line of Manchukuoan Nakajima Ki-43 'Oscar' fighters are warmed up on a Manchurian airfield in the last days of the war. Only a handful of these fighters were in service with the Manchukuoan Air force to try and counter B-29 raids. Although obsolete by Japanese standards, they were the most up to date fighters that the Manchukuoans operated.

Aerospace Publishing

Company – 'Ching Hua' Ltd – was jointly financed to the tune of six million yen by the Provisional Government, Reformed Government, Inner Mongolian Government, Kwangtung Army, Japanese Air Transport Company and the old Chinese airline, the Huitung Aviation Company. The airline had airmail and passenger routes from Peking-Shanghai, Shanghai-Hankow, Shanghai-Canton, Peking–Darien and Peking-Taitung. Although the China Aviation Company was never used in a paramilitary role like the MKKK in Manchuria, it did provide a valuable transport link between different parts of 'puppet' China. Nearly all its passengers were Japanese as it was almost impossible for ordinary Chinese to obtain a ticket. It was used to ferry both civil and military Japanese personnel from one 'puppet' government centre to another.

Reformed Government Air Force 1938–40

Although hardly deserving the title of 'Air Force' the short-lived Reformed Government in Nanking did start to try and train pilots for a future force. A number of training gliders, possibly as many as 40, were bought from the Japanese, these being either the Fikuda Ki–23 or Hikari 6.2 models. The gliders carried the Japanese roundel on the wing and fuselage and on the rudder the five bars taken from the Chinese Republican flag in use with the Reformed Government. From the top to bottom of the rudder the colours were red, yellow, blue, white and black.

Nanking Air Force 1940–45

Plans to develop an air arm of the Nanking Government began in May 1941 with the founding of an Aviation School with an intake of 100 pupils. At the same time the Japanese presented the Nanking Air Force with its first aircraft, described at the time as being specially developed for them. They were in fact 3 Tachikawa Ki–9

Four Japanese officers of the Manchukoan Air Force are dressed in a mixture of Japanese and Manchukoan uniforms. The field caps all have the five-coloured enamel star of Manchukuo, and the officer on the far right, Colonel Matsumoto, has a Manchukuoan decoration on his left breast pocket. The cross is the '3rd Class Bravery Badge of Manchukuo' and is described as an army rather than an imperial award. Colonel Matsumoto was pothumously awarded the rank after his suicidal attack on a US B-29 bomber over Manchukuo in spring 1945.

Ransei Kai

These Tachikawa Ki-9 'Spruce' trainers were presented to the Nanking Air Force in 1941 as the first step in establishing an air arm for the Wang - Ching wei regime.The Ki-9's sport the new roundels of the Nanking Air Force, which were almost identical to the Nationalist ones but with an added red outer circle.

Philip Jowett Collection

In another view of the same ceremony, a line of mixed Japanese and Nanking Chinese officers are presented to Wang Ching-wei in front of a couple of Tachikawa Ki-9's. The Nanking Air Force pilots are wearing their distinctive uniform with the peaked cap while next to them is a Nanking Army officer. To the right of the picture are two Japanese officers, who are probably part of the instruction team.

Philip Jowett Collection

basic trainers which were handed over with great ceremony and then flown over Nanking by their Chinese pilots. Other aircraft were to follow, including further Ki–9s and Tachikawa Ki–55 advanced trainers supplied in 1942 and the 'ancient' Avro 504 trainer in former use with the Japanese. Transport aircraft included a Fokker Super Universal used as a personal transport by Wang- Ching wei. Others types were the Mitsubishi Ki–57 medium and Tachikawa Ki–54c light transports along with Nakajima Ki–34 eight-passenger planes, which were all supplied in 1942. At least one L2D3 transport was supplied, being a Japanese license-produced copy of the US DC–3. There were also reports that 20 ex-Nationalist Savoia Marchetti–72 transports captured by the Japanese were handed over to the Nanking Air Force, but this seems doubtful. Plans were published in early 1942 to expand the Air Force substantially with orders for a few score of Japanese aircraft placed but never fulfilled. There was only one true combat aircraft in service with the Nanking Air Force, a Soviet Tupolev SB bomber from the Nationalist Chinese Air Force. This aircraft (registration 0202) had been flown to Nanking by its crew, who were given a substantial reward by the Japanese. Another SB bomber had defected to Nanking in September 1940 but it is not known if this plane was also put into service with the 'puppet' air force. This bomber with the registration 'C9' had been flown to Ichang where the crew of Captain Chang Ti-chin and Lieutenants Tang Hou-lien and Liang Wen-hua surrendered their plane before being allowed to fly on to Nanking. They were also given a sub-

Lieutenant General Noguchi of the Manchukoan Air Force is wearing Japanese officers' service dress with the addition of the five-coloured star cap badge and Manchukuoan ranks on his shoulder boards.

Ransei Kai

stantial reward each by the Wang Ching-wei Government, quoted as $30,000 for the Captain and $20,000 each for the two lieutenants. On 10 July 1940 a report in the South China Morning Post stated that on 10 June "A Chinese airman attached to the Chungking Air Force recently came flying from the sky to surrender himself ...". The pilot "... Tan Shih-chang, aged thirty, airman of the Air Transport Battalion of the Chungking regime, hopped off from the Chengtu Aerodrome in Szechwan in an American-made Beechcraft 17 transport plane and landed at a place in the Japanese-occupied areas." There were reports that this Beechcraft 17 was in fact employed by the Nanking Air Force on transport duties. These defections to the Nanking Regime by Nationalist pilots were isolated incidents and the vast majority of their men stayed loyal to Chiang Kai-shek.

The Nanking Government did have some grand plans for the expansion of the air force with the building of an aircraft factory and the opening of a Central Aeronautical Research Institute. It was intended that the Nanking Air Force would be supplied with a number of Nakajima Ki–27s to form a fighter squadron but these came to nothing. The Japanese simply did not have enough confidence in the Nanking Air Force to make it a real combat force and were worried that its pilots might desert with their aircraft to Nationalist territory. Japanese fears were well founded as the morale of the Nanking Air Force was never very high and as the war progressed it got worse. Approaches were made by certain officers in the Nanking Air Force towards the end of the war to the Nationalist Chinese Secret Service about defecting *en-masse*. They were told by the Secret Service not to do this, as this would only incite the Japanese to attack Nationalist airfields. News reports of 1945 do state however that some pilots did defect to the Nationalist side with their planes, although there are no exact figures as to the number.

Table 13 – Nanking Government Aircraft in Service 1940–45

Avro–504 trainer	1+
Beechcraft–17 transport	1
Fokker Super Universal transport	1
L2D3 Transport	1
Mitsubishi Ki–57 transport	1+
Nakajima Ki–34 'Thora' transport	1+
Tachikawa Ki–9-kai 'Spruce' trainer	3
Tachikawa Ki–54 'Hickory' transport	3
Tachikawa Ki–55 'Ida' advanced trainer	1+
Tupolev SB bomber	2

There were reports in the *South China Morning Post*, 26 June 1941, that the 'puppet' authorities in Canton in South China were planning their own air arm. Although under the supposed control of the Wang Ching-wei Government in Nanking the Canton regime enjoyed some local autonomy mainly due to their isolation from the rest of Japanese-occupied China. According to the report, the Cantonese planned to form an Air Squadron with a number of planes supplied by the Japanese. These plans seem to have been quite well developed as the report also says that the aircraft of this squadron would carry ensigns very similar to the Nationalist aircraft. We do not know for definite if these plans came to anything, but if they did, then presumably the force would only consist of a handful of trainers and transports at most. Reference is often made in what little documentary evidence we have on Chinese 'puppet' air arms to a 'Cochin Chinese' Air Force and the Nanking government's air force is sometimes referred to by this title. Cochin China is not, in fact, part of China and was instead the name for the southern province of French Indochina, in what is now the People's Republic of Vietnam. The markings of the air arm are described and illustrated as similar to the Nationalist Chinese governments. These are the white sun on a blue circle, as with the Nationalists, but with a slightly different design as the white rays of the sun are connected around the edge instead of remaining separate until they touch the outside of the sun (see colour plate C). The sun emblem appeared on the fuselage and on the wings, and a tricolour of red, white and blue was carried on the rudder. Although it is purely conjecture, perhaps the Cochin Chinese Air Force was the air arm that was mentioned in the South China Post in 1941?

Mention should also be made of the Inner Mongolian Air Force, which was formed during the fighting in Suiyuan province in 1936. Suiyuan was one of the three provinces that made up Inner Mongolia and was partly controlled by the Central Chinese Government and partly by the 'puppet' Government. The Japanese had been flying in support of their Inner Mongolian allies during the campaign to try and wrest Suiyuan from the control of the Nationalist Chinese government. Although the number of aircraft employed by the Japanese was

At the presentation ceremony for the Tachikawa Ki-9's a line of senior Nanking Air Force officers stand in front of the aircraft. Most of the Chinese officers are wearing the new 'western' type of uniform with peaked cap while the officer fourth from right wears the standard Nanking khaki uniform with field cap

Philip Jowett Collection

A young 'puppet' soldier guards the Nationalist Tupolev SB-2 bomber '2002' which has been flown to Wang Ching-wei government territory by its deserting crew. This bomber was the only offensive aircraft definitely in service with the Nanking Air Force, although there are reports that another SB-2 was also flown to Nanking territory during the war.

D.Y. Louie

small they played a significant role in what was a small but vicious war. The Japanese decided during the fighting to present the Inner Mongolians and their leader Prince Teh Wang with six aircraft that had been flying in their support as a gift from the Japanese Emperor. All the planes were painted bright yellow and had a motif showing a 'demon-quelling club' painted on the wings and on the fuselage. The demon-quelling club is a Buddhist symbol usually described as a three-pronged dagger. There is no record of what types of aircraft were given to the Inner Mongolians but the Japanese aircraft which flew in this campaign were a mixture of fighters and light bombers. Types of these Japanese aircraft in service at the time included the Nakajima Type 91 and Kawasaki Type 92 fighters and the Kawasaki Type 88 light bomber. Prince Teh Wang was also given his own personal aircraft in 1937 along with a Japanese pilot to fly him around on official duties.

The Manchkuoan and Nanking Navies 1931–45

The Chinese Navy

Historically the Chinese Navy had always had a limited role, mostly restricted to river and coastal patrols. The Imperial Chinese Navy had been destroyed by the Japanese Imperial Navy during the Sino-Japanese War of 1894–5. This destruction of the Chinese sea-going fleet led to a period of decline and after the fall of the Imperial Government in 1911 any remaining naval forces were divided up amongst the various warlords. Although attempts had been made by the Nationalist Navy in the 1930s to both expand and modernise the fleet any improvements were largely cosmetic. Even though the Nationalist Navy had seen improvements its role was still the limited one of river patrol and coastal defence. It was therefore surprising that when naval forces were raised by any of the 'puppet' governments they were to perform the same limited role.

The Manchukuoan Navy 1931–45

Immediately after the start of the Manchurian Incident in September 1931, the North Eastern KMT Navy Minister Shen Hung-lieh and the Fleet Commander Hsieh Kung-che deserted their posts. This desertion of the Nationalist Naval forces in Manchuria by their leaders left a power vacuum that the invading Japanese were quick to fill. They were contacted by a Captain Yin Tsu-ch'ien, who offered to bring over the Naval forces in the region over to the Japanese authorities. After a meeting with Lt-Commander Sasaki of the Japanese Manchurian Special Organisation the Captain agreed to hand over the five gunboats of the fleet in Harbin on 15 February 1932. This acquisition of former Nationalist Chinese ships allowed the establishment of the 'Kobou Kantai' River Defence Fleet, which was established under the Manchukuo Military Government on 1 March. On

This landing party of the Manchukoan Navy are wearing the winter version of their uniform with navy blue caps, jersey and trousers. The uniform was basically the same as that worn by various navies at the time. All the men are armed with Japanese Arisaka rifles and have Japanese cartridge belts.

Philip Jowett Collection

16 April the first actions of the River Defence Fleet were along the Sungari River when it thawed in support of the Japanese Imperial Army. These military actions to suppress Chinese resistance in the cities of Fuchin, Suiping and Tungkiang continued until the 18th. Throughout 1932 the fleet continued to support the Japanese and their Manchukuoan satellite troops in actions along the Sungari. In 1933 the fleet was taken further a field down the Sungari River and into the Amur and Ussuri Rivers. Also in the same year an expansion of the River Defence Fleet took place with the gunboats, *En-Min*, *Hui-Min* and *P'u-min* being delivered from Japan. On 25 August two gunboats made in Japan, *Daido* and *Rimin* were added to the fleet. Two other gunboats, the *Ta-Tung* and *Li-min*, were sent from Japan in sections and after being reassembled in Harbin were conveyed up the Amur River to join the Fleet on 7 September.

Japanese Naval Forces In Manchukuo

When the Japanese Imperial Army invaded Manchuria in 1931 a naval contingent known as the Special Naval Organisation under Rear Admiral Kobayashi Shozaburo was sent in support of the Kwangtung Army. This temporary body was soon made permanent under the title 'Resident Manchurian Navy' and was given responsibility for the naval defence of Manchukuo until local forces could be trained for the role. During operations against the large anti-Japanese guerrilla armies of Ma Chan-shan in the early 1930s the RMN found that it was unable to cope alone. The Manchukoan River Defence Fleet was found to be totally inefficient and could not be relied upon to assist them. So the RMN had to request for Japanese reinforcements and a portion of the Japanese Naval force stationed on the North Chinese coast was despatched to help.

This force was given the name 'Sungari Naval Despatch Unit' and besides assisting the RMN it was also charged with training the River Defence Fleet to eventually take over its role. As with the Manchukuoan Army, the Japanese initiated training programmes with the hope of improving the poor performance of the Fleet. Three Manchukuoan naval commanders were sent on a tour of Japanese naval installations in January 1934 at Yokosuka, Kure and Sasebo. This visit was followed by the sending of a class of ten Manchukuoan naval students to the Yokosuka Naval Academy in March, where they underwent training in navigation and gunnery. After also taking in visits to military and air force academies, the students returned to Manchukuo in August 1934. In another attempt to increase the efficiency of the RDF a number of Japanese Naval reservists and retired personnel were attached to the Manchukuoan Navy from 1932. The Japanese held ranks from 2nd Lieutenant up to the rank of Captain and were approximately 300 in number. The Japanese were divided up into the following roles:

20	Naval instructors (from 1932)
20	Crew of old-pattern gunboats
35	Crew of newly-built gunboats
70	Crew of *Shun-tien* and the *Yang-min*
60	Crew of *Ting-pien* and *Chin-jen*
40	Crew for ships built up to 1939

The River Defence Fleet was effectively out of action from November to April every year, as all the rivers in Manchukuo freeze over during the winter. During this six months of inactivity the vessels of the fleet were laid up in either Harbin or Heiho. Servicing and re-arming of the ships took place during the winter as well as re-equipping them. Meanwhile the ships' crews were given naval training as well as further training in land operations in case they were needed to fulfil a military role. From 1935 into 1936 this winter training took place in special compounds and enabled an increase in the fleet's strength of 180 crew when the men boarded their vessels on 26 April.

In November 1938 the Japanese RMN in Manchukuo was officially disbanded and the defence of Manchukuoan waterways was left to the River Defence Fleet. Officially this was done because of the increased efficiency of the River Defence Fleet which meant that a Japanese Naval presence was no longer required. Unofficially the constant disputes between the Japanese Navy and Army in Manchukuo over which service should be responsible for the defence of the border region were to blame. Because the River Defence Fleet was now solely responsible for the defence of Manchukuo's river system it was thought prudent to increase its military capacity. For this reason a land combat element was formed consisting of two units of 500 men each, with six companies per unit. Other additional land units with a total of 2,000 men were formed for specific guard duties, including a unit to guard the Fengman Dam. This total included 300 Japanese personnel and 800 taken from the crews of the River Defence Fleet. 50 naval guardsmen were assigned to the naval base at Darien for steamboat protection duties.

Many of the Japanese instructors had been recalled to Japan when the RMN had been disbanded and their job had been left to a smaller number of reservists and retired personnel. The River Defence Fleet was dealt a further blow when in 1941–42 two-thirds of the remaining Japanese personnel were called back to Japan. This left many of the RDF ships under the command of Manchukuoan officers who were not really up to the job, as up to 50% of the Manchukuoan vessels had formally been under Japanese command and were now under the command of insufficiently trained Manchukuoan officers. Not surprisingly the standard of the RDF went down drastically for the last few years of its existence. By 1945, when the Manchukuoan Navy was called upon to perform its role it had deteriorated to the point where, when faced with the might of the Soviet Navy, it simply disintegrated.

Shipbuilding

Japanese companies began to open shipbuilding facilities in Manchukuo with Kawasaki buying the Sukoda Dockyard in Harbin capable of producing ships up to 500 tons. At the same time the shipbuilder Harima

The *Hai-feng*, photographed in 1934, was a 184-ton river gunboat that was launched in 1933 and served in the Manchukuoan River Defence Fleet during the 1930's. Its main armament was a pair of 7cm guns as well as a number of anti-aircraft machine guns.

National Maritime Museum Greenwich, N6098

expanded into Manchukuo and were given most of the work by the Manchukuoan Navy. At first the gunboats were built in Japan and then disassembled and rebuilt in Harbin in Manchukuo. Later the whole of the ship-building process was undertaken by Harima in its Manchukuoan shipyards and factories. On 1 June 1943 the Harima facilities were converted into an arsenal under Manchukoan Government control but these were largely destroyed by fire in 1944.

'Kanchazu Island Incident', June–July 1937

Problems on the 3,000km border between Manchukuo and the Soviet Union had been an almost constant problem since the mid-1930s. Clashes on land between the Japanese and their Manchukuoan satellites and the Soviet Union and their Mongolian allies occurred in 1938 and 1939. These were preceded however by a naval clash in the vicinity of Kanchuazu Island between a Soviet river force and gunboats of the Manchukuoan River Defence Fleet. The incident was caused by the Soviet revoking a 1934 agreement for the navigation of the rivers in the Manchukuoan-Soviet border region. Soviet naval and land forces provoked the incident by blockading the Amur River in the Kanchazu River area in June 1937. A Manchukoan gunboat went to investigate this transgression on 20 June and came under fire from two Soviet gunboats which had crossed into Manchukuo territory and returned fire. Three other Soviet gunboats also crossed into Manchukuoan waters and attacked ships guarding Heiho.

Soviet forces began to gather on their side of the border and continued to occupy small islands around Kanchazu. After a protest by the Japanese Ambassador in Moscow on 29 June the Soviets again encroached into the waters to the south of the island and clashes occurred with Manchukuoan naval and land forces. A twenty-minute engagement resulted in the sinking of a Soviet gunboat and the damaging of another, which withdrew. The Soviets had already agreed to withdraw and the incident was settled at the Shigemitsu-Litovinov Conference on 2 July.

Border disputes between the armies of Manchukuo and the Soviet Union occurred on a regular basis during the 1930s. In fact, between 1933 and 1943 there were reportedly 1,600 boundary disputes between the Soviet Union and Manchukuo. The vast majority of these were provoked by the Soviets as they tried to 'test the mettle' of the Manchukuoans. Although in many of these disputes the respective navies were not directly involved some incidents did take place on the Sungari and Amur Rivers. Two disputes involving the Manchukuoan Navy were the 'Toanchin Incident' of May 1939 and the 'Xingkai Incident' of May 1941.

The *Tatung* was a 65-ton river gunboat of the Manchukoan Navy, built in 1933, and possessed a 15cm howitzer as its main armament, as well as being armed with three heavy machine guns.

Philip Jowett Collection

The Manchukuoan Navy vessel *Shun-tien*, photographed in 1936, was a 270-ton river gunship built in 1934 by Harima, with a main armament of a 15cm gun and two 12cm anti-aircraft guns, plus six mounted 13mm machine guns.

National Maritime Museum Greenwich, N6094

The Soviet Invasion, August 1945

On 9 August, the Soviet Army, Navy and Air Force began a massive invasion of Manchukuo which swept away both Japanese and Manchukoan defence forces. At the time of the Soviet invasion the Japanese-Manchukuoan fleet had a much reduced strength of 5 gunboats, 12 armoured motorboats, 10 reconnaissance craft, 3 large and 110 small landing craft as well as a few auxiliary vessels. The Fleet was stationed in the estuary of the Sungari River at the outbreak of the fighting and they retreated into Harbin. On 9 August Manchukuoan naval defences were made up of the 1st and 2nd squadrons, which were detailed to guard the Sungari River bridge in the upper stream above Harbin. The 3rd and 5th squadrons were to guard the bridge over the lower Sungari. On 15 August the 2nd Squadron, made up of the *His-Chun* and the *Yang-Ch'un* was ordered to move to block the advance of the Soviet Amur Fleet along the Sungari. For the rest of the campaign the Manchukuoan Fleet was to put up very little resistance to the Soviet Amur River Fleet, which, like the Soviet land forces, had overwhelming numbers on their side.

On 9 August the Amur fleet, with 127 ships, moved against the defences of Heiho. The fleet included 1 monitor, 5 gunships, 24 armoured boats, 10 minesweepers and 11 escort boats. With such overwhelming force the town fell, the defending Manchukuoan fleet losing 6 motorboats. At the same time, on the Sungari River, the Soviet fleet of 25 ships supported their ground forces against Manchukuoan attack. Before the fleet could see action however the Manchukuoan crews mutinied and murdered 5 Japanese officers including Squadron Commander Matsuo. Other mutinies had taken place on the 14th and the 15th, the first taking place when two 32-ton ships and two 10-ton gunboats tried to flee the fighting, although these were pursued by the *Li-Min*, which captured them. On 15 August, the Manchukuoan Captain of the *Hsing-Ya* took his ship towards the lower Sungari after taking on board the crew of the *Ta-Tung*. The ship was soon captured by the Soviets, who shot all the crew apart from the Captain, who acted as a pilot for them. With the announcement of the defeat of the

Japanese Empire on the same day the crew of *Hsing-Jen* mutinied and shot its commander 1st Lieutenant Ishikawa. Insurrections also took place at the various training and support establishments, with a few Japanese officers being killed in the process.

Table 9 – Organisation of Manchukuoan River Defence Fleet

1st Squadron	*Ting-pien, Chin-jen*
2nd Squadron	*Shun-tien, Yang-min*
3rd Squadron	*Ta-Tung, Li-Min*
4th Squadron	*His-chun, Yang-Chun*
5th Squadron	*Hsing-Ya, Hsing-Jen*
1st Gunboat Group	*Hui-Min, Pu-Min*
2nd Gunboat Group	*Hsiang-Yun, Ching-Yun*
3rd Gunboat Group	*Hai-Tien, Hai-Yang*
4th Gunboat Group	*Hsiao-Chiang, Chin-Chiang*
5th Gunboat Group	*Wai-Mung, Chen-Ming*

Table 10 – Manchukuoan Navy Vessels 1932–45

Name	Launched	Type	Displacement (tons)	Crew	Armament
Hai-wei	1916	Destroyer	755	110	3 x 12cm, 3 x MG
Ting Pien	1935	River Gunship	290	90	3 x 12cm, 6 x 13mm MG
Chin Jen	1935	River Gunship	290	80	3 x 12cm AA, 6 x 13mm MG
Shun Tien	1934	River Gunship	270	80	3 x 12cm AA, 6 x 13mm MG, 15cm Howitzer
Yang Min	1934	River Gunship	270	70	2 x 12cm, 3 x MG
Hai Feng	1933	River Gunship	184	?	2 x 7cm, 2 x MG
Hai Lung	1933	River Gunship	184	?	2 x 7cm, 2 x MG
Li Sui	1903	River Gunship	350	74	2 x 5cm, 2 x MG
Li Chi	1895	River Gunship	362	62	2 x 8cm LT, 2 x 8cm Mrt, 2 x MG
Chiang Ching	1900	Gunboat	360	63	2 x 8cm LT, 2 x 8cm Mrt, 2 x MG
Chiang Pien	1900	Gunboat	360	65	2 x 8cm LT, 2 x 8cm Mrt, 2 x MG
Chiang Tung	1903	Gunboat	250	53	2 x 8cm LT, 2 x 8cm Mrt, 2 x MG
Tatung	1933	Gunboat	65	31	15cm Howitzer, 3 x MG
Limin	1933	Gunboat	65	31	15cm Howitzer, 3 x MG
Chimin	1934	Gunboat	20	13	3 x Heavy MG
Wenmin	1934	Gunboat	20	13	3 x Heavy MG
Emin	1933	Gunboat	15	14	3 x MG
Huimin	1933	Gunboat	15	14	3 x MG
Pumin	1933	Gunboat	15	14	3 x MG
Hai Kuang	1933	Gunboat	45	?	1 x 5cm, 2 x MG
Hai Jui	1933	Gunboat	45	?	1 x 5cm, 2 x MG
Hai Jung	1933	Gunboat	45	?	1 x 5cm, 2 x MG
Hai Hua	1933	Gunboat	45	?	1 x 5cm, 2 x MG
Shuan An	1935	Gunboat	42	?	1 x 5cm, 2 x MG
Shuan Kai	1935	Gunboat	42	?	1 x 5cm, 2 x MG

Key:	AA – Anti-aircraft	LT – Low-trajectory
	MG – Machine-gun	Mrt – Mortar

Nanking Navy 1940–45

Northern China

The Navy of the Reorganised Government of Wang Ching-wei was created by the Japanese on 13 December 1940. This new naval force was based in the north of China with an inauguration ceremony taking place at Liukung-tao, Weihaiwei. In attendance at the inauguration were high-ranking officials of the 'puppet' Nanking Government including the Vice-Chief of the Nanking Naval General Staff, Chang Hsi-yuan as well as Vice-Admiral Mitsuyashi Shimizu, the commander-in-chief Japanese Naval Force in North China. Ships handed over to the new Navy by their Japanese benefactors included the *Yung Siang* of 730 tons and the *Tung Chun* of 322 tons. Other ships included the *Min Teh*, *Tung Hai* and the *Hai Ho* as well as 4 unnamed vessels. The naval bases at Tsingtao, Lienyunchiang, Chefoo and Liukung-tao were also handed over to the Navy. At Liukung-tao the Nanking Government established a naval station and training barracks under Vice-Admiral Chao Pei-chun as the commanding officer. In a typically creeping telegram of gratitude Wang Ching-wei thanked Rear-Admiral Shimada the Commander-in-Chief of the Japanese Imperial Navy in China with the words "The Naval forces of your country have rendered valuable assistance in the naval reconstruction of our country and in response to your goodwill, our country will certainly struggle harder for the mutual prosperity of both countries and the peace of East Asia".

The former Nationalist cruisers, *Ning Hai* and *Ping Hai*, two of the most modern and powerful ships of the KMT Navy, were refloated by the Japanese. Both cruisers had a displacement of 2,500 tons with the former launched in 1931 and the latter in 1932. They were given a thorough refurbishment before being handed over to the Nanking Navy with much pomp and circumstance. They formed a useful propaganda tool for the Japanese, who allowed the Nanking Navy to operate the ships until 1943, when they took them into their service. In March 1941 a Kiangyin Defence Company was formed to defend the strategic approaches to the capital at Nanking. A Naval Defence Corps was established at the same time at Weihaiwei for the purpose of centralising control over the Nanking naval units in north China.

A British intelligence report of January 1944 stated that the Nanking Navy was under the direct command of the Navy Minister, Jen Yuan-tao. The Navy was involved purely in coastal patrol work and was well equipped for this limited role. According to the report, based on information taken from 'puppet' publications, the total strength of the Navy was 19 warships, 12 gunboats of the Chiangping and *Chiangan* class,

A crew of a Nanking vessel load a light howitzer during a training exercise wearing working fatigues and Japanese field caps. The Nanking Navy had a large number of smaller vessels such as gunboats in their inventory but was purely a coastal and river patrol force.

Philip Jowett Collection

These crewmen of the Nanking Navy are wearing the summer version of the uniform, of square rig with blue collar and black silk. The black cap tally has the name of the ship in white characters on the front.

Philip Jowett Collection

President Wang Ching-wei reviews the Nanking Navy along with high-ranking Japanese officers and is dressed in the uniform of a Chinese Admiral. The Nanking Navy was a purely coastal and river patrol force and acted in support of the Japanese Imperial Army and Nanking Army.

Philip Jowett Collection

24 small-sized 'special' gunboats and 6 survey craft. In addition the report stated that a further 37 naval craft and gunboats had been under construction since 1942. These craft included 13 gunboats of the 'D' type and 18 gunboats of the 'E' type which were ordered from the Mitsui dockyard in Japan. It is not known how many of these Japanese gunboats were delivered but photographic evidence indicates that at least 6 were in service.

Naval academies and training facilities run by the Nanking authorities in 1944 included a Central Naval Academy, a Sailors' Training Camp and a 'Surveyors' Training Camp. There were also two naval regiments of marines, one based at Canton and the other at Weihaiwei.

Kwangtung Naval Command

The Kwangtung Naval Command, which was under the overall command of the Nanking Government of Wang Ching-wei, had a force of 7 shallow-draught gunboats and 1,000 troops. This so-called 'South China Navy' had Kan Chee Yuen as commander-in-chief and Chan Bun as commander of the Naval Defence. On 30 November 1941 the Canton River Garrison was abolished and reorganised into the Canton Harbour Garrison. The purpose of this reorganisation was to unify the naval forces in Kwangtung Province and bring them under central government control. According to a Nanking Government Publication several cruisers, gunboats and speedboats were put under the control of the Canton Harbour Garrison. These vessels were given the task by the Nanking Government of assisting the Japanese Imperial Navy in patrolling the south Chinese coastline.

Uniforms of Manchukuo 1931–40

1. Manchukuoan Infantry Private 1934
2. Manchukoan Artilleryman 1934
3. Manchukuoan Infantry Officer 1940
4. Manchukuoan Infantry Private 1940

Uniforms of Manchukuo and Inner Mongolia 1936–45

5. Manchukuoan Cavalry Trooper 1942
6. White Russian Volunteer Bugler, Manchukuoan Army 1942
7. Inner Mongolian Irregular Soldier 1936
8. Inner Mongolian Standard Bearer 1940

PLATE A

Aircraft of MKKK and Manchukuoan Air Force 1931–45

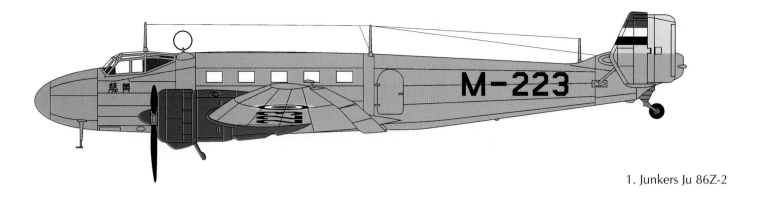

1. Junkers Ju 86Z-2

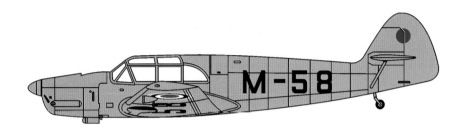

2. Messersschmitt Bf 108D Taifun

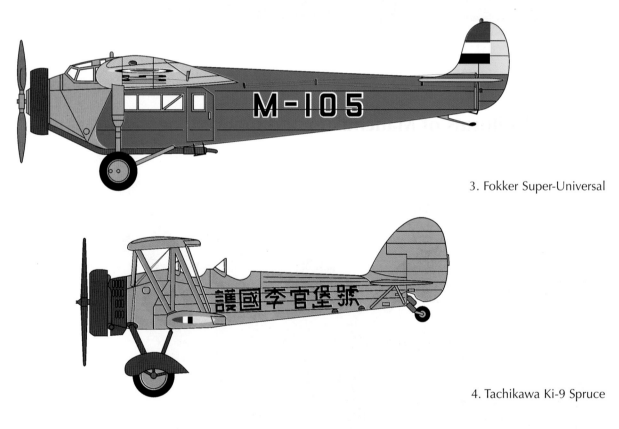

3. Fokker Super-Universal

4. Tachikawa Ki-9 Spruce

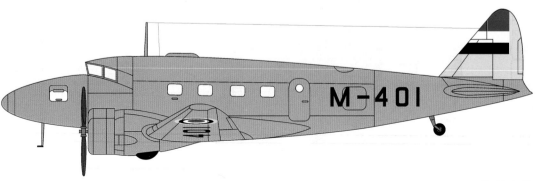

PLATE B

5. Nakajima AT-2 (Ki-34)

Aircraft of Manchukuo and Nanking Air Forces 1931–45

6. Nakajima Ki-27b

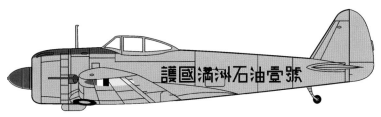

7. Nakajima Ki-43 - II-ko Oscar

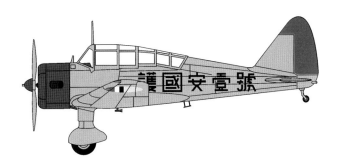

8. Tachikawa Ki-55

9. Tachikawa Ki-9 Spruce

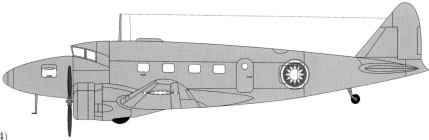

10. Nakajima AT-2 (Ki-34)

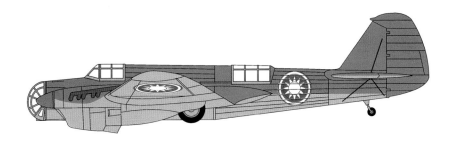

11. Tupolev SB-2bis

PLATE C

Chinese 'Puppet' Armies 1936–40

1. East Hopei Infantryman, East Hopei 1936

2. Provisional Government Officer, Peking 1939

3. Reformed Government Soldier, Nanking 1939

4. Captain Instructor, Central Military Academy, Shanghai 1939

Uniforms of Nanking Army 1940–45

5. Nanking Army Private 1941

6. Nanking Army Sergeant, Standard Bearer 1941

7. Nanking Army Private 2nd Class 1943

8. Nanking Army 'Shang-wei' Captain, 4th Division 1945

PLATE D

Notes to Colour Plates

PLATE A
FIGURES 1–4: UNIFORMS OF MANCHUKUO 1931–40
1. Manchukuoan Infantry Private 1934: This Manchukuoan soldier is wearing the uniform worn by the 'new' Army of the Empire of Manchukuo in the early 1930s. With his grey cotton tunic and trousers along with his peaked cap he is dressed in a similar uniform to his enemies, the anti-Japanese guerrillas operating in the countryside. For this reason Manchukuoan soldiers of this period were often seen wearing yellow armbands to distinguish them from the guerrillas who wore red ones. His collar tabs are in the red of the Infantry branch and his shoulder tabs are in the red with gold stars, in the same system as the Japanese Army. The Manchukuoan Army was mainly armed with rifles and other weaponry captured, like this Mannlicher, from the Nationalist Young Marshal's Army, who the Japanese chased out of the region when they invaded in 1931.

2. Manchukoan Artilleryman 1934: This crewman of one of the mountain guns which made up the main weaponry of the artillery branch of the Manchukoan Army is wearing a similar uniform to figure 1. The main difference is that he is wearing a typical Chinese straw sun hat of the type worn by all Chinese armies including the Manchukuoan Army on campaign. His collar tabs are in yellow, the Manchukoan branch colour of the Artillery and have silver insignia and numerals on them, which indicate which unit this man belongs to. He is armed, as were most of the early Manchukoan Army, with a captured rifle taken from the armouries of the defeated Nationalist Armies in Manchuria.

3. Manchukuoan Infantry Officer 1940: This officer is wearing the new type uniform which had developed during the 1930s with a series of dress regulations beginning in 1932. By 1940 the Manchukoan officer was wearing a quite distinctive uniform although made out of the same Japanese khaki cloth as the Japanese Army officer. Manchukuoan Army officers usually wore the peaked cap, which had largely been replaced in the Japanese Army by the field cap. Again, the Manchukoan Army continued to carry their ranks on the shoulder boards, a practice which had been phased out of the Japanese Army in the late 1930s.

4. Manchukuoan Infantry Private 1940: This Private wears the Manchukuoan uniform made of Japanese khaki material which had gradually been introduced during the 1930s. The field cap is a type which was unique to the Manchukuoan Army and differed from the Japanese pattern in the shape of the crown. Shoulder boards continued to be worn by the Manchukuoan Army long after they had been discarded by the Japanese Army and were maroon coloured for all branches. The collar tabs are in the red of the Infantry arm and have silver Arabic numerals on to indicate which unit he belongs to (see text). Equipment carried by this soldier is standard Japanese issue, as is his Arisaka rifle, which was also the main type in use with the Japanese Armed Forces. Because he belongs to one of the model units based around the capital he is probably better dressed and equipped than the majority of Manchukuoan troops.

FIGURES 5–8: UNIFORMS OF MANCHUKUO AND INNER MONGOLIA 1936–45
5. Manchukuoan Cavalry Trooper 1942: This Cavalry trooper illustrates the winter fur hat worn by the Manchukoan Army with fur-lined earflaps tied on top. The soldier's collar patch is in the green of the Cavalry branch and has a square insignia on the right side, which also indicates his branch. His rank is worn on the shoulder bars. Fur hats came in several slightly different versions, as with the Japanese Army, and had the usual five-coloured enamel star on the front. He is armed with the most up to date Japanese Cavalry carbine, the Type 44, and carries his ammunition in the larger single pouch worn by the Japanese Imperial Army.

6. White Russian Volunteer Bugler, Manchukuoan Army 1942: This White Russian Volunteer of the Manchukuoan Army 'Asano' Brigade wears a Japanese-style field cap instead of the type worn by the rest of the army. On his cap he wears the five-coloured enamel star of the Manchukoan Army while above his right breast pocket he wears the special insignia of the White Russians in service with this force. The same Russian cross insignia is carried on the brassard of his trumpet and obviously signifies the Tsarist origins of the White Russian volunteers.

7. Inner Mongolian Irregular Soldier 1936: A uniform of sorts is worn by this irregular cavalryman of Prince The Wang's Army during the campaign in Suiyuan Province in 1936–37. The blue 'deel' tunic was a common item of clothing in this army and the colour of the sash and turban would have varied from tribe or Banner to Banner. Although many of the Prince's armies were poorly armed others managed to acquire modern weaponry. This man is well armed with a brand new Czech ZB26 light machine gun, probably captured from the Nationalist Chinese Army or donated by the Japanese.

8. Inner Mongolian Standard Bearer 1940: This man is an Inner Mongolian infantryman from the regular army which fought along with the Japanese Army until the end of the war in 1945. He is carrying the Inner Mongolian Army flag which was manufactured in Japan and has the yellow Mongol composite bow as its centrepiece. The soldier's uniform is basically a Japanese model with steel helmet and mid-blue coloured shoulder tabs with the same rank system as the Manchukuoan Army. It is doubtful that many of the Inner Mongolian Army were this well dressed, although photographic evidence proves that at least some 'model' or elite units were.

PLATE B
PROFILES 1–5: AIRCRAFT OF MKKK AND MANCHUKUOAN AIR FORCE 1931–45
1. Junkers Ju 86Z-2: Registration M-223, Manchu Kohku Kabushiki Kaisha (Manchurian Air Transport Co) 1938/40. Several of these transport/bombers were used by both the MKKK and the MAF. Aircraft is Light Grey overall with Dark Blue engine nacelles/ housings and spinners, with MKKK roundels in four positions. These were (from the outside) yellow, black, white, blue and red. Registration numbers are black and appeared on both wing surfaces and the fuselage sides. Manchukuo colours in (from the top) red, blue, white, black and yellow are present on all vertical tail surface sides. Japanese characters under the cockpit are black.

2. Messersschmitt Bf 108D Taifun: Registration M-58, Manchu Kohku Kabushiki Kaisha (Manchurian Air Transport Co) 1938/40. Taifuns were used by the paramilitary MKKK for light transport, ambulance and reconnaissance duties. Aircraft is light grey overall with MKKK roundels in four positions. These were (from the outside) yellow, black, white, blue and red. Registration numbers are black and appeared on both wing surfaces and the fuselage sides. In addition, there is a dark red disc on the tail.

3. Fokker Super-Universal: Registration M-105, Manchu Kohku Kabushiki Kaisha (Manchurian Air Transport Co) 1933. Aircraft fuselage is dark blue with natural metal nose and black cowl ring. Wings and tail are yellow with MKKK roundels as described above. Manchukuo colours are also present on the vertical tail surfaces. Registration numbers are in black on the fuselage and wings, with the fuselage registration being outlined in white. Undercarriage legs, wheel covers and tail-skid are natural metal.

4. Tachikawa Ki-9 Spruce: Serial unknown, Manchukuo National Military Force Air Corps, 1938–39. This trainer is orange overall, with black cowling, forward fuselage, undercarriage, legs and spats. MNMFAC roundels are applied in four wing positions, in (from top) red, blue, white, black and yellow. The fuselage script indicating the donor of the aircraft (usually an industrial Manchukuoan company, e.g. Mukden Steel Works) is in black.

5. Nakajima AT-2 (Ki-34): Registration M-401, Manchu Kohku Kabushiki Kaisha (Manchurian Air Transport Co) 1936. Twelve AT-2's were used by the MKKK, all of which bore registrations in the 400 series. Aircraft is natural metal overall. MKKK roundels as described above are applied in four wing positions. Manchukuo colours are also present on the vertical tail surfaces. Registration numbers are in black on the fuselage and wings.

PLATE C
PROFILES 6–11: AIRCRAFT OF MANCHUKUOAN AND NANKING AIR FORCES 1931–45
6. Nakajima Ki-27b: Serial unknown, Manchukuo National Military Force Air Corps 1944. This aircraft is finished in an overall light gull grey-green scheme. MNMFAC roundels are applied in four wing positions, in (from top) red, blue, white, black and yellow. The fuselage script indicating the donor of the aircraft is in black. A red, white device is also used on the vertical tail surfaces. Note the absence of wheel spats.

7. Nakajima Ki-43 – II-ko Oscar: Serial unknown, Manchukuo National Military Force Air Corps, 1944/45. This aircraft is finished in an overall light gull grey-green scheme. MNMFAC roundels are applied as described above. The fuselage script and anti-glare panel are black, Spinner is red.

8. Tachikawa Ki-55: Serial unknown, Manchukuo National Military Force Air Corps, 1943. This Ki-55 is natural metal overall, with black cowling and red rudder. MNMFAC roundels are applied in four wing positions, as described above. The fuselage script, indicating the donor of the aircraft, is in black.

9. Tachikawa Ki-9 Spruce: Serial unknown, Reorganised Government of China Air Force, 1941. This trainer is orange overall, with black cowling, forward fuselage and undercarriage legs. RGCAF roundels are applied in four wing positions and on the fuselage sides, consisting of a white sun on a blue disc, surrounded by red, white and red concentric rings.

10. Nakajima AT-2 (Ki-34): Serial unknown, Reorganised Government of China Air Force, 1940. Aircraft is pale grey overall. RGCAF roundels as described above are applied in four wing positions and on fuselage sides. No other markings are carried.

11. Tupolev SB-2bis: Serial unknown, Reorganised Government of China Air Force, 1940. Aircraft is finished in mid-green on the upper surfaces with pale grey undersides. RGCAF roundels as described above are applied in four wing positions and on the fuselage sides. No other markings are carried. This aircraft was the only documented combat aircraft of the RGCAF having defected from the Chinese Nationalist Air force although there were reports of another defecting Tupolev.

PLATE D: CHINESE 'PUPPET' ARMIES 1936–40
1. East Hopei Infantryman, East Hopei 1936: The Army of the 'puppet' state of East Hopei wore a variety of uniforms and this soldier is wearing his old uniform from service in the former Peace Preservation Corps. This uniform was made up of a simple grey cotton peaked cap, tunic and trousers worn with white puttees. Insignia on the cap is the enamel five-coloured star, which had been in use with the pre-1928 Republican Chinese Army.

2. Provisional Government Officer, Peking 1939: Provisional Government Army uniforms were a real mixture of types and this officer seems to have adapted his former Nationalist uniform with puppet insignia. The field cap is the 'ski' pattern in common use with the Nationalist officers to which he has attached a five-coloured enamel star. This same insignia was worn by the Chinese Republican Army from 1912 to 1928 and the colours were taken from the five barred Republican flag. Republican five barred flags were adopted by both the Provisional Government in Peking from 1937 to 1940 and the Reformed Government in Nanking from 1938 to 1940.

3. Reformed Government Soldier, Nanking 1939: This soldier belongs to the Pacification Department of the fledgling army of the Reformed Government of China. He is dressed in nondescript light khaki cotton uniform with a Japanese field cap. On the front of the field cap is the insignia which was used only by the Reformed Government Army (see D). Ranks do not appear to have been worn by the other ranks although higher ranking officers had a system of sorts. He is armed with a captured Chinese 'Chiang Kai-shek' Mauser which was manufactured under licence in China in large numbers.

4. Captain Instructor, Central Military Academy, Shanghai 1939: The Central Military Academy was opened near Shanghai to train recruits for the Army of the proposed Reorganised Government of China. At the time that the Academy was opened Wang Ching-wei was still negotiating with the Japanese over the government's structure. This instructor wears a green-khaki uniform which must have been produced especially for the academy as it does not appear to have been worn by other units of the Army. The cap badge on the peaked cap is a gold eight-pointed star on a laurel wreath and the ranks worn on the collar are the same as worn by the Nationalist Army.

FIGURES 5-8: UNIFORMS OF THE NANKING ARMY 1940–45
5. Nanking Army Private 1941: He is wearing the Winter version of the Nanking Army uniform which was again almost the same as the Nationalist grey wadded cotton type. One important difference between the Nanking Army uniform and the Nationalist one is the design of the enamel cap badge (see D). Whether his uniform would have been a captured one or one manufactured by a factory under the Nanking Government is not known. What we do know is that his Mauser 98k rifle would have been captured by the Japanese during their earlier fighting against the Nationalists and sold by them to the Nanking Army.

6. Nanking Army Sergeant, Standard Bearer 1941: This standard bearer of the Nanking Army wears a uniform which is basically identical in every detail to the Nationalist Army model. The M35 German steel helmet was worn in large numbers by the Nationalist Army and captured ones were turned over to the Nanking Army. His flag is the national Chinese flag as used by the Nationalist party since 1928 with the addition of the yellow pennant. The pennant was added at the insistence of the Japanese and it proclaims the 'anti-communist' nature of the Nanking Government.

7. Nanking Army Private 2nd Class 1943: This Private 2nd Class is from a Nanking Army unit in the Kongmun region of Southern China and wears the units cloth patch above the left breast pocket. His cap is modelled on the Japanese field cap but is manufactured in a local Chinese factory. The cap badge is the Nanking Army type (see D) and although this soldier does not carry a rank many of his comrades wore theirs on their left sleeves. This form of rank appears to have been in use with soldiers who were uniformed on a local basis rather than from a central government depot. He is armed with a Japanese Taisho-11 1922 light machine gun which although elderly was still in widespread use with the Japanese Army. The Nanking Government would have had to pay for the machine gun, as the Japanese rarely gave arms away for nothing unless they were of no use to them at all.

8. Nanking Army 'Shang-wei' Captain, 4th Division 1945: As a Captain or Shang-wei in the Nanking Army this officer had managed to get himself a smart uniform made out of Japanese khaki wool material. The 'ski' type field cap has the Nanking Army enamel badge on the front and his collar carries the new rank system introduced in about 1945. The left collar patch continues to carry the same rank system as in the Nationalist Army while the right hand collar now carries the unit number instead of the 3 stars. He is armed with a Japanese Nambu-14 automatic pistol which is carried in the holster on the right side of his Japanese issue officer's belt.

CHAPTER SIX

Uniforms of Manchukuoan and Other 'Puppet' Chinese Armed Forces 1931–45

Manchukuo Army Uniforms 1931–45

The Manchukuo Army of the early 1930s mostly wore the uniforms they had worn previously during their service with the Young Marshal's Army. These uniforms consisted of grey cotton tunic, trousers which were worn with woollen puttees and a grey cotton peaked cap.

The peaked cap worn in the early years of Manchukuo was usually of unkempt and scruffy appearance with a leather chin strap. On the peaked cap was worn a five-pointed enamel star which replaced the previously worn sun badge of the KMT. The star was divided into five coloured sections which were, clockwise from the top section, yellow, black, white, blue and red. These colours were the same as used on the five-pointed star of Republican China 1911–28 but in a different order.

In the early days of the 'new' state's army the Manchukuoan soldiers and their anti-Japanese adversaries wore basically the same uniform. To try and make it easier to recognise 'friend from foe' at a distance the Manchukuoan soldiers wore yellow armbands in contrast to the guerrillas red coloured ones.

A new model peaked cap was introduced in the dress regulations of December 1932 but was almost identical to those worn by the Young Marshal's forces.

As new uniform items were introduced in the early to mid 1930s they would have been worn concurrently with old uniform items. Manchukoan units serving in outlying and isolated garrisons would have continued wearing their pre-1931 uniforms for a lot longer than troops in the capital and other big cities. With the first dress regulations of 28 December 1932, new collar branch of service colours were introduced to replace the previously worn Nationalist ones:

Chart 1 – Collar Branch of Service Colours (from 1932)

Infantry	Red	**Cavalry**	Green
Artillery	Yellow	**Engineers**	Brown
Transport	Blue	**Military Police**	Black
Pioneers	Purple	**Supply Corps**	Silver
Medical Corps	Dark Green	**Veterinary Corps**	Purple
Legal Corps	White	**Musicians**	Pale Blue

Ranks worn on the early Manchukuoan Army from 1932 to 1937 were identical to the Japanese Imperial Army system and were worn on red cloth transverse shoulder bars. In 1937 the rank bar colour was changed to maroon with the same rank system.

One insight into the uniform situation in Manchukuo is given by witnesses to the visit of the International Lytton Commission, which visited the new state in May 1932. The visit was carefully staged by the Japanese to try and impress on the Lytton Commissioners that Manchukuo was a truly independent and sovereign state. Military displays had to be hastily arranged and Japanese soldiers in Manchukuoan uniforms provided the Guard of Honour. Presumably the Europeans who made up the Commission were not expected to recognise the difference between the Japanese and Manchurians. Other guards around the capital, Hsinking, were made up of recently recruited former Manchurian bandits. They had been quickly kitted out in 500 new Manchukuoan uniforms to replace the unkempt ones they had worn when joining the Japanese.

A bugler of the Manchukuoan Army is wearing the early pattern uniform worn by them until the late 1930s. The peaked cap could vary slightly in design and in the shade of grey cotton it was made of. His equipment is all Japanese issue and includes the 'old' model water bottle and leather haversack. We can just see his unit flag in the background, which had a yellow field with, at top, four stripes of, from top to bottom: red, blue, white and black.

Masuo Fujita

Later Manchukuoan Uniforms

During the 1930s a series of dress regulations- beginning with the first on 28 December 1932 – gradually introduced a unique Manchukuoan uni- form. Although based on the Japanese Imperial uniform it did have several unique features, by the late 1930s this model had completely replaced the improvised uniform of the early part of the decade. The uniform consisted of a Japanese M90 (1930) khaki or 'mustard-khaki' coloured five-but- ton tunic with breast and waist pockets, breeches which were generally tucked into woollen puttees and Japanese-pattern brown leather boots. Winter tunics and trousers were made from woollen material while summer versions would be made from light cotton cloth in a lighter shade of mate- rial than the winter version. Summer headgear came in two types, the first model, known as the '1st Army Hat' in the regulations, was a peaked cap. The peaked cap had a leather peak and chin strap with the five-coloured enamel star on the front. A '2nd Army Hat' was introduced in May 1938 and was based on the Japanese Army field cap but had a slightly different appearance. It differed from the Japanese pattern in that the crown at the front was raised slightly, in the same manner as the Austro-Hungarian cap of the First World War period. The cap badge on the second model cap was usually stitched onto a cloth back- ground although the older metal types were also still used. Khaki painted Japanese M32 steel helmets were also worn by some Manchukuoan troops but these retained the Imperial Army badge. Winter headgear was a fur-lined hat with ear flaps which could be worn down or tied over the crown. This winter hat was the same as the Japanese pattern and probably came from their stores with the addition of the same cloth badge as on the 2nd Army Hat.

Acting Corporal's ranks were also shown by a cloth chevron worn on the upper right sleeve of the tunic. This chevron was inverted with the top two-thirds red and the bottom third gold cloth.

Manchukuoan Collar Insignia

On the collar tabs which were in the branch colour (see above) were a system of metal numbers and badges which indicated which unit and sub-unit a soldier belonged to. This system was fairly simple when first introduced but with amendments being made throughout the 1930s it became far more complicated.

The first system was introduced with the first dress regulations on 28 December 1932, having a metal Arabic number on the right tab which showed the main unit. On the left tab were Roman numerals which indicated the secondary or sub-unit. For instance, a number 8 on the right tab would be for the 8th Regiment with the Roman numeral 'II' on the left tab indicating the 2nd Sub-unit, e.g. company.

Chart 2 – Manchukuoan Army Ranks, May 1937-August 1945

Tsung-ssu-ling	'Field Marshal' – National orchid symbol nearest collar and three stars on gold background piped in gold on shoulder boards.
Shang-chiang	'General'- three stars on gold background piped in gold on shoulder boards.
Chung-chiang	'Lieutenant General' – two stars on gold background, piped in gold on shoulder boards.
Shao-chiang	'Major General' – one star on gold background, piped in gold on shoulder boards.
Shang-hsaio	'Colonel' – three stars on maroon coloured shoulder board, edged in gold with two gold stripes.
Chung-hsaio	'Lieutenant Colonel' two stars on maroon coloured shoulder board, edged in gold with two gold stripes.
Shao-hsaio	'Major' – one star on maroon coloured shoulder board, edged in gold with two gold stripes.
Shang -wei	'Captain' – three stars on maroon coloured shoulder board, edged in gold with one gold stripe.
Chung-wei	'Lieutenant' – two stars on maroon coloured shoulder board, edged in gold with one gold stripe.
Shao-wei '2nd	Lieutenant' – one star on maroon coloured shoulder board, edged in gold with one gold stripe.
Chun-wei	'Warrant Officer' – one gold stripe on maroon shoulder board, edged in gold.
Shang-shih	'Colour Sergeant' – three stars on maroon coloured shoulder board on one gold stripe.
Chung-shih	'Sergeant' – two stars on maroon coloured shoulder board on one gold stripe.
Shao-shih	'Corporal' – one star on maroon coloured shoulder board on one gold stripe.
Shao-shih Ch'in-	*wu-che* 'Acting Corporal' – three stars on maroon shoulder board.
Shang-teng-ping	'Lance Corporal' – three stars on maroon shoulder board.
I-teng -ping	'1st Class Private' – two stars on maroon shoulder board.
Ehr-teng-ping	'2nd Class Private – one star on maroon shoulder board.

In the dress regulations of 19 September 1934 a series of metal circular badges was introduced for Training Schools and Guard Units. The Guard Unit badge was a gold disc with an intricate pattern of interlocked Chinese characters highlighted over a yellow enamel background. Training School badges were the same shape and size but had a different intricate design on them.

Things got a lot more complicated with the introduction of the dress regulations of May 1937 when the use of circular disc badges was extended to other branches of the Army. A square badge was to be used for Cavalry and Horse Artillery and this has basic design as the circular type with gold highlighted Chinese characters on a yellow enamel background. A series of badges were also introduced for certain types of troops which were attached to larger units. These badges were for Transport, Artillery, Machine guns and Anti-Aircraft Artillery troops and were worn on the left collar tab. The use of Roman numerals also seems to have been changed with Arabic numerals taking their place. A few examples of this confusing system are:

Right Collar Tab–17 in Arabic Numerals, Left Collar Tab–1 in Arabic Numerals.
(17th Infantry Regiment–1st Sub-unit)

Right Collar Tab–6 in Arabic Numerals, Left Collar Tab–6 in Arabic Numerals.
(6th Infantry Regiment Command Section)

Right Collar Tab-Square badge, Left Collar Tab-Crossed Cannon.
(Horse Artillery)

Right Collar Tab–21 in Arabic Numerals, Left Collar Tab-Stylised Machine gun.
(21st Infantry Regiment-Heavy Machine gun section)

Other insignia shown on the collar included a disc with a Roman numeral in the centre for the Military Police which was worn on the right collar. A star on the left collar tab was for Officer trainees and a metal harp for Musicians.

Other Insignia

As with their Japanese masters the Manchukuoan Army wore very little in the way of special insignia on their uniforms. A light brown cloth arm badge was worn for distinguished service in the Army on the upper arm. At

This Manchukuoan soldier takes aim with his Arisaka rifle during rifle training under the supervision of a Japanese instructor. The soldier has a canvas haversack on with a rolled blanket fastened by straps. We can just see a metal '3' on the left collar tab and, although not visible in the photograph, a metal disc is on the right tab. The disc indicates that he belongs to a training school, and the '3' indicates that he is from the 3rd Sub-unit of the School. An interesting note is the Japanese caption attached to the photograph, which claims that Manchukuoan soldiers have two meals a day, at 9 a.m. and at 5 p.m. It goes on to say that they were offered another meal at midday but refused it as it was not their normal practice to eat so much! Food served to the Manchukuoan soldier was, according to the caption, kaoliang, rice and vegetables, with meat being served once or twice a week.

Robert Hunt Library

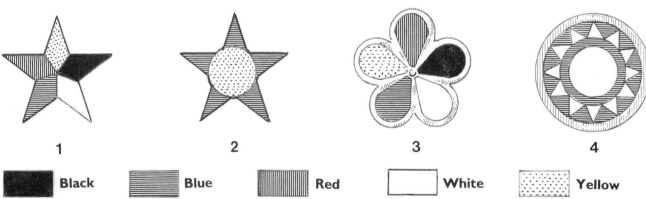

Figure 1: *Manchukuoan Army Cap Badge.* The badge was worn in this basic form on the caps of other ranks in the Manchukuoan Army and in the early days was often the only distinctive insignia worn by the newly-raised Army.

Figure 2: *Inner Mongolian Army Cap Badge.* As the Inner Mongolian Army was issued with Japanese Army uniforms from the late 1930s onwards this new cap badge was issued.

Figure 3: *Reformed Government Cap Badge.* The short-lived Reformed Government issued some of its troops with Japanese uniforms and these men wore this unique cap badge. Other 'puppet' governments used the pre 1928 Republican five coloured star and this insignia was an adaptation of those.

Figure 4: *Nanking Army Cap Badge.* Although the Nanking Army in general wore the same uniform as the Nationalists they did have a distinctive cap badge with a red outer rim.

the bottom of the badge were yellow chevrons, with one for Enlisted men and two for NCO's. There were a few types of metal badge worn by certain special types of troops, including an oval shaped copper badge with 2 crossed Manchukuo flags coloured in enamel for Headquarter Guards.

Cap Badges

Although the ordinary Manchukuoan soldier wore a simple five-coloured enamel star cap badge other specialist troops did wear other designs. Bodyguard troops had a silver cap badge in the form of a wreath formed from rice stalks with the five-coloured star at the top. Headquarters guards wore an oval shaped metal badge with crossed enamel Manchukuoan flags on.

Manchukuoan Army Equipment

The soldier of the new Manchukuoan Army was equipped in the same way as he had been when in the service of the Young Marshal before 1931. As with nearly all Chinese soldiers of that period he would have a canvas bandolier with pockets for ammunition and, if he was lucky, a water bottle and canvas bread bag. During the early 1930s the Japanese began to supply some new equipment to the Manchukuoan Army and the best units would have been quite well equipped. However until the late 1930s when the reforms and regulations introduced throughout the decade began to take effect the vast majority of ordinary soldiers in the Manchukuoan Army would be badly equipped. Photographic evidence shows that the soldiers seen in propaganda pictures of the time had the same standard of equipment as their Japanese counterparts. Obviously these were the 'model' units and the Manchukoan soldiery in the outlying areas of the 'puppet' state were not so fortunate. By 1938 things had improved and the following were the standard issue to the 'modernised' Manchukuoan Army.

Chart 3 – Manchukuoan Army Equipment 1938–45

1 Haversack (either new type canvas or old brown leather type)

1 Canvas Food Bag.

1 Brown leather belt with three ammunition pouches (two worn at front and one reserve worn at back) and scabbard for
Arisaka bayonet.

1 Water bottle (various Japanese issue models)

1 Mess Tin

Personal Equipment:

1 Blanket

1 Padded Quilt

1 Padded Mattress

1 Personal Hygiene kit

Equipment used by the modernised Manchukuoan Army included two types of backpack, one of which was a haversack type and the other a stiff leather type. Other equipment included a food bag and a metal water bottle, usually the Japanese model. Ammunition belt and pouches were also the Japanese brown leather type with twin pouches.

Manchukuoan Auxiliaries

The first Manchukoan volunteers who attached themselves to the Japanese invaders often wore their own civilian dress, presumably with yellow cloth armbands to distinguish them from the anti-Japanese guerrillas. Manchukuoan irregulars were also photographed as part of the Jehol Invasion force in 1933 wearing a mixture of civilian clothes and a few items of uniform. As the majority of Manchukuoan soldiers in the early days wore their old uniforms from service in the Young Marshal's Army the men in civilian dress were probably new recruits who had not served in the Nationalist Forces. These Manchukoan irregulars were also seen with white

Manchukoan Imperial Guardsmen wearing their very distinctive full dress uniform, consisting of leather helmet, blue jacket and red trousers. The lances carried by the Guardsmen have pennants based on the design of the Manchukoan flag and have in the fly the vertical stripes, from the lance outwards, of red, blue, white and black, with the remainder of the pennant yellow.

Philip Jowett Collection

flags with a star in the centre, which appears to have been red in colour. Local Defence Guard units were dressed in cast off Japanese uniforms with peaked caps, which appear to have been M1930 model types.

Japanese Adviser Uniforms

The uniforms worn by the large number of Japanese advisers in the Manchukoan Army were at first Japanese. Their uniforms were usually of the M1930 pattern uniform with the ranks carried on the shoulder straps of the tunic and the peaked cap with red hat band. A distinction is drawn between the uniforms of the Reserve list and Active list officers with the former having old, shabby and faded uniforms and the latter wearing brand new ones. The comparison between the old and new uniforms was particularly apparent in the condition of the red band which was badly faded on the Reserve officers hats. Eventually as the advisers were fully incorporated into the Manchukuoan Army they were issued with 'puppet' army officers uniforms with the distinction of a grey band around the cap.

White Russian Uniforms

The White Russian units of the Manchukoan Army wore the same basic uniform as the rest of the Army, but with their own insignia added. A five-pointed enamel star in the usual five colours of the Manchukuoan Army was worn on the field cap. Field caps worn by the White Russian appear to have been the Japanese khaki type instead of the Manchukuoan model. The rest of the uniform was made up of Japanese khaki shirts and trousers worn with brown cavalry boots or shoes with woollen puttees. On the right chest of their uniforms the White Russians wore a cloth badge which was white St Andrew's cross edged in red with a blue centre. (see plate A)

Manchukuoan Dress Uniforms 1932–45

A new dress uniform of the Manchukuoan Army was introduced in January 1934, just in time for the coronation of Pu-Yi as Emperor of Manchukuo. The uniforms were to be worn by the Palace Guard at the coronation and the Japanese ministers in charge in Manchukuo would certainly have wanted to make an impression on the world's press, who were in attendance. Unfortunately for the Japanese, the 'comic opera' appearance of the uniforms only served to reinforce the west's perception of the Manchukuo Empire and its new Emperor as a Japanese invention.

The dress uniform was made up of a blue wool tunic with fancy gold epaulettes and very intricate cuff insignia. Stiff high collars had gold decoration on with the design becoming more intricate the higher the rank. Enlisted men's tunics were single- breasted with seven gold buttons down the front, while officers were double breasted with two rows of seven gold buttons down either side of the chest. Around the waist was worn a gold sash with three red bands around it. Plain red breeches were worn with the tunic and these were tucked into high black leather boots. The helmet was black polished leather, conical in shape, with a brim around, and was similar in shape to the type worn by the US Police in the early 1900s. This rather strange design was based on the helmets worn by the famous Manchu cavalry, which came south from Manchuria during the 17th Century and conquered all of China. These foreign barbarians set up the Manchu Dynasty in 1644, whose emperors ruled China until the Revolution of 1911; Pu -Yi had been the last of the Manchu dynasty. These helmets had been worn by the Manchu warriors closest to the Emperor, who were known as 'Princes of the Iron Helmet'. Around the edge of the brim was silver metalled decoration and around the base of the helmet was a decorated silver metal band. On the front of the helmet was a gold badge with an enamel five-pointed star in the centre in the normal Manchukuoan colours. The exact design of the badge varied depending on the rank of the wearer and the unit to which he belonged, with special designs for bodyguard units, for instance. Officers' helmets had a metal pommel into which dyed horse hairs were fixed, these hung down in a fringe which reached to the bottom of the hat around the back and side.

Most of the Palace Guard carried 9ft lances with long triangular pennants based on the Manchukuo flag with from the pole outwards, red, blue, white and black vertical stripes and the rest of the field in yellow. Just below the spear point and above the pennant was a red horsehair tassel. They would also be armed with a dress sword based on the Japanese army model and manufactured there.

Manchukuoan Army musicians had their own dress uniform which was similar to the Japanese Imperial Army version. It consisted of a long blue tunic, red trousers and a peaked kepi which was red and blue instead of the Japanese red model. The kepi was divided by 10mm braid around the band half way up the cap with the top half of the hat blue and the bottom half red. Going up from the gold braid band were vertical braids going up the top half of the hat at the front and back and at each side. These braids went over the crown of the kepi forming a cross on the top in the same way as the French Foreign Legion cap. The kepi varied in shape from the Japanese model, which was higher at the back, whereas the Manchukuoan version had a flat top. Attached to the front of the kepi was a white feather plume over the cap badge, which was a five-coloured star over a rose bush forming a garland. Officers wore the same pattern kepi but this was all blue instead of the blue and red type worn by other ranks. The tunic had seven gold buttons down the front, and a high collar and cuffs which were decorated in gold with the higher ranking having more decoration. At the back of the tunic the tailcoat had red facings with gold buttons at the top.

Provisional Government Army

and North China Political Council Uniforms 1938–45

The Army of the Provisional Government formed in Peking in December 1937 wore a variety of uniforms with no standardisation. Most soldiers wore simple uniforms of light khaki cotton jackets and trousers worn with woollen puttees. Headgear for other ranks was either a Japanese field cap or a light khaki cotton peaked cap. Both types of hat had a 'Republican' enamel cap badge, which was a five-pointed enamel star divided into five coloured sections. The colours of the star were taken from the old Chinese five barred flag used as the national flag from 1911 to 1928. Its colours were from the top and clockwise red, black, white, blue and yellow and these were mounted on a silver frame. Another form of insignia which was used concurrently with the five-coloured star was a metal eight-pointed star mounted on a laurel wreath. This form of badge was seen in use with a number of units in north China although its origin is not clear. It continued in use after the supposed unification of all pro-Japanese governments in China in March 1940 under the leadership of Wang-Ching wei. In actual fact, the Provisional Government was virtually left in charge of the north of China although under the name of the

Left: An officer cadet of the Provisional Government Army poses for the camera holding a Japanese 'kendo' martial art sword. The cadet wears a khaki cotton uniform with a peaked cap bearing an eight-pointed star design. On the shoulder boards of the jacket and the cuffs are two eight pointed stars, which, if we follow the Republican rank system, would make him a lieutenant.

Ronald Ill

A high-ranking officer of the Provisional Government Army is wearing an improvised uniform made up of a KMT ski-type officer's cap and tunic with 'puppet' insignia. The insignia is a simple five-coloured enamel five-pointed star, which was also used by the pre-1928 government of China. He also has a Japanese 'Shin-Gunto' sword, which were issued by the Japanese to higher-ranking Chinese 'puppet' officers.

The Commercial Press (Hong Kong) Ltd

Northern Political Council. The Council's armed forces remained intact and kept its old insignia until the end of the war in 1945. Officers of the Provisional Government Army wore the same uniform as the other ranks or wore their old Nationalist Army officers uniforms with new insignia added. This insignia was the five-coloured enamel star which the same design as used on the other ranks field caps.

Reformed Government Army Uniforms 1938–40

The Reformed Government was a short-lived regime with little resources and little time to organise and equip its army. Early units of the Reformed Government Army wore a mix of uniforms, and photographs of these troops on parade show a real 'rag-tag' line up of soldiers. The basic uniform was a light khaki cotton jacket, trousers and woollen puttees worn with a variety of headgear including Japanese field caps and both German M35 and Japanese steel helmets. Although these simple uniforms were quite easy to have manufactured but they were most likely captured Nationalist ones with the insignia removed. As for the helmets, the German M35s were obviously captured Nationalist ones, while the Japanese models were donated to the 'puppet' troops by their Japanese masters. In the last year of the life of the Reformed Government a Pacification Department was set up to try and combat guerrilla activity. The Pacification Department managed to supply their recruits with a better standard of uniform. Although these uniforms were basically the same khaki cotton ones as the rest of the Reformed Government Army they did at least manage to 'kit' a whole unit out in the same dress. Pacification troops wore the Japanese khaki field cap with the cap badge of the Reformed Government on the front. This badge was a five-petalled enamel flower with each petal being a colour taken from the Chinese Republican flag of 1911 to 1928. This flag had been adopted by the Reformed Government as well as by a few other of the 'puppet' Governments. The colours were, clockwise from the top, red, black, white, blue and yellow and these were mounted on a silver frame. Officers of the Pacification Department wore Japanese officers uniforms with the officers version of the field cap and the same cap badge as the other ranks. A system of ranks does appear to have been in use with the higher-ranking officers of the Reformed Government Army. These ranks appeared on gold coloured collar patches and seem to have followed the same system as the Nationalist ones. In place of the three-pointed gold star in the Nationalist Army the Reformed Army had small eight-pointed stars. Higher-ranking officers in the Provisional and Reformed Government armies were issued with Japanese officers' swords of the 'Shin-Gunto' pattern. These traditional-style swords had been issued to the Japanese Army from the mid-1930s as part of the revival of the Samurai warrior 'ethos'. Those swords issued to 'puppet' army officers were almost certainly of inferior manufacture as the Japanese would have regarded it as too great a honour for the Chinese to carry superior types. Presumably the Japanese military presented the swords to 'friendly' Chinese officers who would carry them as a mark of their authority. Shin-Gunto's are not seen in service with Nanking

Jen Yuan-tao was the Minister of Pacification in the Reformed Government and went on to hold many offices under the Wang Ching-wei Regime from 1940. He is wearing a Japanese officer's uniform with the officer's version of the field cap bearing the unique enamel badge of the Reformed Government. The badge was in the shape of a flower with each petal one of five different colours. On his collar he has a gold rank patch with two eight-pointed stars, which indicate he is a Lieutenant General.

Philip Jowett Collection

Army officers and they appear to have been withdrawn from use after 1940. This would have made sense as the Nanking Government did not want to appear to be a quasi-Japanese organisation.

Nanking Army Uniforms 1940–45

The army raised by Wang Ching-wei's Nanking Government reflected the belief by its leaders that it was the true National Government of China. Wang Ching-wei proclaimed that his version of the Nationalist Party were the true disciples of Sun Yat-sen, the founder of the Kuomintang. Regulation uniforms worn by the Nanking Army therefore followed almost the identical pattern as Nationalist models with a few modifications. Only the Capital Guard divisions and other élite units and bodyguard units seem to have been issued with regulation uniforms and the majority of Nanking soldiers wore non-regulation dress.

Enlisted Men's Summer Uniform

There were two main versions of the Nanking Army's uniform for enlisted men, a lightweight summer one and a heavier padded winter version. The summer uniform was made up of a light khaki cotton jacket, trousers or shorts and woollen puttees. Various shades of khaki material were used for the summer uniform but a light sandy khaki was the most common. The jacket was single-breasted and had two breast and two waist pockets and there were usually five buttons down the front. A fold-down collar carried the soldiers rank on the left-hand side (see below) and his unit number on the right side. This was a departure from the Nationalist collar ranks, which had the rank on both sides. Soldiers who came over to the Nanking Government with their commanders continued to wear their KMT uniforms. In many cases they would have continued to wear the uniform with the old Nationalist insignia until new 'puppet' ones could be issued. Some units took their Nationalist insignia off their uniforms and were issued with simple armbands to distinguish them. The Japanese were worried, of course, that both their Nanking Allies and Nationalist foes wore identical uniforms. They worried that 'friendly fire' situations could happen and tried to persuade the Nanking Army to use clearly different insignia, flags etc. Wang Ching-wei's insistence that his men wear KMT uniforms as the 'true' Nationalist Army of China could have caused great problems. The fact that the Japanese Imperial Army and regular Nationalist forces rarely came into conflict after 1940 meant that this was not a great problem. These regulation uniforms were worn mainly by the so-called 'Capital Guard Divisions' which made up the personal Army of Wang Ching-wei in the vicinity of Nanking.

A sentry of the Inner Mongolian Army on guard outside an official building of the 'puppet' government of Prince Teh Wang. He wears a Japanese-type field cap and a cotton uniform, probably grey in colour. His personal equipment includes a canvas bandolier, which was a strictly Chinese item and not used by his Japanese allies.

Masuo Fujita

Non-Regulation

and Regional Nanking Uniforms

The vast majority of troops officially under the control of the Nanking Government served in the outlying provinces. Here they were effectively beyond the control of the central government and had to rely mainly on their own devices for both uniforms and equipment. Many of the 'puppet' soldiers of the Nanking Army came over in large numbers from the Nationalist side with their commanding officers. These men continued to wear their former army uniforms and more often than not they removed the Nationalist insignia. As a temporary measure units in the field would often be issued with coloured armbands in an attempt to distinguish them from loyal Nationalist troops.

Newly recruited 'puppet' soldiers who had not served in the Nationalist Army had to rely on local sources of uniforms or on their local Japanese Army commander. The simple cotton uniforms worn by regional troops were easily manufactured in local factories or workshops. They were manufactured out of low-grade cotton material in various shades of khaki According to intelligence sources at the time, the general rule that was applied to the uniforms of the 'puppet' troops were that the officers wore Japanese uniforms and the other ranks wore Nationalist uniforms with Nanking insignia. This is not usually borne out by the photographic evidence, which shows the highest ranking officers of the Nanking Army wearing Nationalist officers uniforms. Perhaps this is explained by the fact that the majority of contemporary photographs show the best uniformed units of the troops directly under the command of

Wang Ching-wei in the vicinity of Nanking. The rule therefore might be that the officers of the Army in and around Nanking wore Nationalist type uniforms and those in the outlying provinces were issued with uniforms by the Japanese. Other ranks wore basically old Nationalist uniforms in winter and summer versions with the troops from the better divisions having better uniforms.

In many cases the 'puppet', Nationalist and Communist troops wore similar uniforms with little in the way of insignia to distinguish them. From what little evidence we have on the 'puppet' soldiers in the countryside it seems that they wore the light khaki or grey cotton uniforms in summer and the padded blue cotton uniforms which faded to blue grey with wear in winter. A large number of regional 'puppet' soldiers were lucky to receive a uniform of any type and many local militia wore their civilian clothes. Armbands were worn with the civilian dress and appear to have been made of white cloth with a suitable inscription in Chinese or Japanese text. These inscriptions would usually proclaim the anti-communist role of the unit that the wearer belonged to.

For obvious reasons the Nanking government propaganda machine did not want these second-rate units to be photographed and most surviving images are of the better dressed units of the Central Nanking Army. Footwear with both uniforms would be either black canvas gym type shoes, army boots or civilian leather shoes. Some boots may have come from Japanese Army stocks although the Nanking Army was usually expected to clothe its troops from its own resources. Many of the Nanking Army's recruits were former Nationalist soldiers and many units came over to the Wang Ching-wei Government *en-masse*. These men would have worn their former uniforms as they were identical to those worn by their new employers.

Japanese Model Uniforms

Nanking Government soldiers who served in some of the outlying provinces were not under the firm control of the Wang Ching-wei Government. These troops relied on their local Japanese garrison to supply them with both arms and uniforms. Many of these soldiers were given cast-off Japanese uniforms onto which they added 'puppet' insignia. Any Japanese uniforms issued to the 'puppet's would have been the M90 '1930' pattern which was officially obsolete from 1938. Japanese pattern uniforms were also manufactured in local factories and the material type and colour of these would vary from region to region. Some 'puppet' units were reported to be wearing a mixture of uniforms with one 200-man unit having 40 of its members dressed in Japanese uniforms while the rest wore civilian or KMT uniforms. A 'puppet' unit stationed in southern Shensi in 1944 were all issued with Japanese uniforms. This particular unit had been moved into the area to take the place of Japanese troops who had been transferred to Honan Province. Whether the unit was issued with Japanese uniforms in an attempt to fool the local population that the Japanese were still present is not known.

Nanking Army Headgear

Field Caps

The most common for of headgear worn with the summer uniform was a field cap or 'ski' cap, so called because it resembled the caps worn by German and Austrian mountain troops in the Great War. The 'ski' cap was made of the same cotton material as the rest of the uniform and had fold-down side panels which fastened with a button on the crown and had two small brass or wooden buttons at the front. Above the buttons at the front was the cap badge, which was a small enamel blue circle with a white sun with twelve rays. This badge was identical in every detail to the one used by the Nationalists, and of course most would have come from captured sources. A newly designed badge was introduced for the Nanking Army, which was basically the same as the Nationalist one but with one small but very important difference, the Nanking Army cap badge had a red border around the outside of the circle. These new design badges were definitely issued to the officers of the Nanking Army although whether, in the circumstances, they ever were issued to the rank and file is doubtful. They almost certainly would have been worn by the bodyguard units and by those Nanking troops who would have appeared on parade in the capital. These troops were always smartly turned out and were given the best uniforms and equipment. to give a good impression to any outsiders. Other hats were locally manufactured in the Japanese field cap style and these again seem to have been of inferior materials. Surviving examples of these show that they were usually of very poor manufacture and because of war shortages seldom had leather chin-straps and were replaced by cloth ones.

Steel Helmets

Steel helmets were not worn by the majority of Nanking Army soldiers, only the Capital Garrison divisions being issued them in any numbers. Most of the CGD soldiers wore the grey painted M35 German steel helmet which had been the main helmet worn by the Nationalists in the 1930s. These came from the vast numbers of captured helmets that the Japanese had stockpiled after their victories against the Nationalists from 1937 to 1940. The other model of helmet in widescale use was the British/American Mk I, which again had been in service with the Nationalists. Insignia on the helmets conformed with the Nationalists' types with, on the M35, a white KMT sun on a blue circle on the left-hand side, while a larger version of the stencilled insignia was worn on the front of the Mk I helmet.

Winter Uniforms

The winter uniform was made up of a 'wadded' cotton loose-fitting jacket made of blue wadded cotton which quickly faded to a blue-grey colour with wear. Trousers were made of the same padded blue-grey material and were worn with woollen puttees. These same 'peasant'-type winter clothes were also worn by Communist and KMT troops, leading to difficulties in differentiating between 'friend or foe'. Headgear would be either a blue-grey version of the summer 'ski' cap or a fur-lined hat with fold-down earflaps. Both forms of hat would have the usual blue sky and white sun cap badge on the front. Although the winter uniform was very unmilitary looking and made the wearer look rather ungainly, it did keep the wearer warm.

Nanking Army Insignia

The Nationalist Army wore various types of insignia on their uniforms and the Nanking Army followed suit to some extent. Unit insignia could be worn on the left sleeve or left breast of the jacket and was usually a simple white cloth square with black Chinese characters which denoted the wearer's unit and commanding officer. Some Nanking soldiers wore armbands in place of the unit patch and these may well have been plain white, again with black Chinese characters. In the Nationalist Army the unit patch was often edged in the branch colour e.g. red – infantry, yellow – artillery, and this practice seems to have been continued in the Nanking Army. Certainly the better dressed and equipped units of central China that were under the direct control of Wang Ching-wei adhered to the correct use of insignia. More remote regular 'puppet' units seem however to have adopted their own insignia and although few examples were noted at the time a record of the badge of a unit in the Kongmun region of south China does exist. This badge, recorded in a British intelligence report of 1943, shows a light blue cloth patch with a dark blue border and a complicated yellow and green design in the centre.

Chart 4 – Nanking Army Branch Colours (From 1940)			
Infantry	Red	**Cavalry**	Yellow
Artillery	Blue	**Engineers**	White
Mediacal	Green	**Supply Corps**	Purple
Divisional Train	Black	**Military Police**	Pink
Topographical Engineers	Brown	**Legal Corps**	Grey
Musicians	Orange		

Nanking Army Ranks

The rank system of the Nanking Army was similar to the Nationalist Army's apart from a few very important details. There were only 3 General Officers ranks in the Nanking Army instead of the 5 in the Nationalist Army, with the highest ranks of 'T'e-chi Shiang-chiang' (Field Marshal) and 'I-chi Shang-chiang' (Senior General) not existing. Ranks were shown by a system of three-pointed gold metal stars on various backgrounds but in the Nationalist Army these were on both the left and right-hand collar. In the Nanking Army the system was the same for the three grades of General Officer as in the Nationalist Army, but from Colonel down, the right-hand collar had the soldier's unit number in Arabic numerals in gold metal. As Commander-in-Chief of the Nanking Armed Forces as well as president of the regime, Wang Ching-wei wore a unique rank on his officers uniform. His rank was shown by three gold three-pointed stars on a gold background-the same as 'Shang-Chiang' (General) but at the front of the patch was a small Kuomintang white sun on blue sky badge.

Chart 5 – Nanking Army Ranks 1940–45	
Shang-Chiang	'General' – three stars on gold background on left and right collar patches
Chung-Chiang	'Lieutenant General' – two stars on gold background on left and right collar patches.
Shao-Chiang	'Major General' – one star on gold background on left and right collar patches.
Shang-Hsao	'Colonel' – three stars on left collar patch, Unit number on right-hand collar patch both edged in gold with two gold bars on branch colour background.
Chung-Hsao	'Lieutenant Colonel' – two stars on left collar patch, Unit number on right-hand collar patch, both edged in gold with two gold bars on branch colour background.
Shao-Hsao	'Major' – one star on left collar patch, Unit number on right-hand collar patch, both edged in gold with two gold bars on branch colour background.
Shang-Wei	'Captain' – three stars on left collar patch, Unit number on right-hand collar patch, both edged in gold with one gold bar on branch colour background.
Chung-Wei	'Lieutenant'- two stars on left collar patch, Unit number on right-hand collar patch, both edged in gold with one gold bar on branch colour background.
Shao-Wei	'2nd Lieutenant' – one star on left collar patch, Unit number on right-hand collar patch, both edged in gold with one gold bar on branch colour background.
Chun-Wei	'Warrant Officer' – no star on left collar patch, Unit number on right-hand collar patch, both edged in gold with one gold bar in the centre.
Shang-Shih	'Colour Sergeant' – three stars on left collar patch, Unit number on right-hand collar patch, both with blue bar behind on branch colour background.
Chung-Shih	'Sergeant' – two stars on left collar patch, Unit number on right-hand collar patch, both with blue bar behind on branch colour background.
Hsia-Shih	'Corporal' – one star on left collar patch, Unit number on right-hand collar patch, both with blue bar behind on branch colour background.
Shang-teng Ping	'Lance Corporal' – three stars on left collar patch, Unit number on right collar patch-both on branch colour background.
I-teng Ping	'Private Trained' – two stars on left collar patch, Unit number on right collar patch, both on branch colour background.
Ehr-teng Ping	'Private Untrained'- one star on left collar patch, Unit number on right collar patch, both on branch colour background.

Some local 'puppet' soldiers were known to wear their ranks on the arm instead of the collar and these were the usual three-pointed stars system. A First Class Private had three stars, a Second Class Private two stars and a Third Class Private one gold circle.

Nanking Officers' Uniforms

Officers in the Nanking Army divisions in the vicinity of the capital wore a single-breasted khaki wool jacket with two breast pockets and two waist pockets with a stand-and-fall collar having the usual collar rank patches. The colour of the uniform varied, but a brown shade of khaki seems to have been the most common. Trousers worn with the jacket were either breeches worn with high leather boots or straight trousers or 'slacks' worn with shoes. In the field, officers wore the same basic uniform as the enlisted man but the cloth would be a higher quality and it would be tailored to a higher standard. Other 'puppet' army officers in units in the outlying provinces of Japanese-occupied China wore Japanese officers' uniforms. These uniforms were probably issued by the Japanese because the 'puppet' officers in the more remote provinces who had come over from the Nationalists would have needed new clothes to replace their 'tatty' old ones. Unlike the officers of earlier

Chinese 'puppet' armies, the Nanking Army officer rarely wore the 'Samurai' style Japanese officers sword. They instead wore the 'sabre' style officers' sword, and these may have been Japanese or Chinese, as the latter was usually manufactured in Japan.

Nanking Air Force Uniforms

The uniforms of the 'tiny' Nanking Air force were usually restricted to the handful of officers in command positions. Surprisingly, an entirely new design of uniform was introduced for the Nanking Air Force officer based on Western uniforms. It consisted of a khaki peaked cap, wool jacket with open collar worn with white shirt and black tie and khaki wool 'slacks' worn with leather shoes. On the upper lapel of the jacket were coloured tabs whose colour is a mystery, as neither the Chinese Nationalist nor the Japanese had a branch colour for their air forces. These may have been sky blue as used by the Manchukuo Air Force, but this is conjectural. Above the left breast pocket were worn a pair of stylised wings similar in design to those in use with the Japanese Air Force. The peaked cap had a lighter coloured band around it and a gold woven cap badge with a winged propeller mounted on a wreath on the front with a gold button above this.

Nanking Navy Uniforms

The Navy wore Japanese naval uniforms, which, for the ordinary sailors, were very similar to those worn by the Chinese. Ratings wore white jumper, trousers and cap with the jumper having a large blue 'jean' collar with a white border, cap tallies were black, with the name of the sailor's ship in Chinese. Officers wore white jacket and trousers with a white peaked cap. High-ranking Nanking naval officers wore the Chinese black high collared tunic with black lace trim around the collar and down the front edge and bottom of the jacket. This was worn with black trousers and black peaked cap with gold trimming and a gold woven cap badge. The cap badge was in the design of a wreath with a gold anchor in the centre and a blue sky and white sun badge above it. The Nanking naval ensign was introduced in 1942, and was the same flag as used by the Army but without the yellow pennant and with a white cross over the field.

Other Uniforms

'Rikugun Gunzoku' Uniforms

The Japanese Army had a corps of civilians who performed military support tasks and administration duties such as clerical staff and translators. This organisation, known as 'Rikugun Gunzoku' or 'Army Civilian in Military Employ', was supposed to take over many of the everyday and routine jobs that would otherwise have had to be undertaken by regular Japanese Army officers. A similar organisation was set up under the Nanking regime and wore the same kind as uniforms as their Japanese counterparts. These uniforms were usually made up of a Japanese field cap, Western style jacket with shirt and tie and straight trousers. The field cap, jacket and

A mobile propaganda unit of the Nanking government is led by Lieutenant Colonel Po Shi-chou of the Nanking Army, who was a graduate of the Shanghai Political Academy. Propaganda units like this would go out into Japanese controlled areas and try and convince the villagers of the legitimacy of the Wang Ching -wei regime. The Lieutenant Colonel is wearing the same uniform as an officer in the Nationalist Army but for some reason he has no rank patches on his collar.

Imperial War Museum HU 73374

Nanking Army soldiers on a winter march, dressed in what appear to be Japanese-issue winter coats. Presumably units like this, which is operating alongside a Japanese anti-guerrilla unit, would have received a little of their ally's surplus uniforms and weapons. The men in the foreground have canvas covers over their ZB-26 light machine guns to protect them from the cold.

Philip Jowett Collection

trousers were made from green wool cloth and the shirt from the same colour cotton with a grey tie. The Nanking Government 'Gunzoku' are described as wearing brown leather leggings with brown leather boots. A ranks system for the Japanese 'Gunzoku' was made up of 5 basic ranks, 'Chokunin' (equivalent to a regular Army General Officer) with 2 grades, and 'Sonin' (equivalent to a Field or Company Officer with five grades), 'Hannin' (equivalent to the Regular Army ranks Warrant Officer down to Corporal with four grades). Two lower ranks of 'Yatonin' and 'Sonota' are described as other ranks and were presumably equivalent to the various classes of Private in the Japanese Army. These ranks were indicated on the jacket by a five-pointed interlinked star in various colours which was worn on a circular badge on the left sleeve.

'Chokunin' – gold star on a green background edged in gold
'Sonin' and 'Hannin'- yellow star on a green background
'Yatonin' – white star on a green background
'Sonota' – red star on a green background

The 'Gunzoku' organisation in China would presumably have been under the overall control of higher ranking Japanese officials and most Chinese personnel would have been in the two lowest ranks of 'Yatonin' and 'Sonota'.

Military Cadets

Cadets of the Central Military Academy set up near Shanghai in 1939 wore Nationalist-type uniforms made out of green cotton cloth. The uniform consisted of a peaked cap, cotton tunic and breeches worn with woollen puttees. The Academy was set up just before the inauguration of the Wang Ching-wei government in Nanking. Because the academy was opened while the situation of the various 'puppet' governments was in transition the insignia worn on the cadets uniforms were a mixture of the old and new. The cadets had a white cotton patch above the left breast pocket and on the left upper sleeve. Ranks were worn on the collar and were the same as those used by the Nationalist Army and adopted by the Nanking Army from 1940. The peaked cap had a gold cap badge with an eight-pointed star, which was a symbol seen in use by the Provisional Government pre-1940. The cadets were very smartly turned out, as befits a group of officer trainees who were hoped to be the nucleus of a new and well organised army for the Nanking Government.

Inner Mongolian Army Uniforms 1936–45

The Inner Mongolian soldiers who fought in the early fighting in Suiyuan were mainly dressed in their traditional civilian clothes. A long blue padded cotton tunic or 'deel' was worn which reached down to the ankle and was worn with an orange sash around the waist. Headgear was either a lambs' wool hat or a coloured turban wrapped around the head. The colour of the turban varied with each 'Banner' having a distinctive one. Equipment worn by the early Inner Mongolian soldiers was pretty basic, usually only a leather bandolier for cartridges was slung over the left shoulder. Some Inner Mongolian soldiers were dressed in a loose fitting cotton jacket and trousers worn with a peaked cap. When soldiers were pictured wearing this type of uniform they usually belonged to one of the Mongol Princes Bodyguards.

In 1936 a new uniform was seen in use, said to be modelled on the Nationalist Chinese uniform. This uniform had a loose-fitting grey cotton jacket worn with grey cotton trousers tucked into woollen puttees. A scruffy peaked grey cotton cap was worn with this uniform and looked rather like those worn by the Russian Army in the Great War. Insignia is reported as being worn on the cap but it is not sure what exactly the design of this badge was. It probably included the 'yin-yan' symbol which appeared on Mongolian flags of the time, or another favourite symbol of a horse archer. Photographs of the time show a small metal circular cap badge on the peaked cap and this may well have been a simple 'yin-yan' symbol. Equipment worn with this new uniform included a new canvas bandolier, which was worn over the left shoulder and then wrapped around the waist.

Li Shou-hsin's contingent in the 1936 Suiyuan Campaign wore Manchukuoan uniforms and insignia as they were seconded from that Army. Manchukoan uniforms worn at this time would have been the early pattern grey type with peaked cap.

By 1937 the Inner Mongolian Army was seen by Western eyewitnesses wearing what they described as Japanese uniforms with 'puppet' insignia and ranks. One US visitor to Inner Mongolia in June 1940 said that there were a large number of 'puppet' officers and soldiers in the capital. He also commented that they wore Japanese uniforms with 'puppet' insignia and ranks. Although some Inner Mongolians were undoubtedly dressed in full Japanese issue uniforms this was not usually the case. Inner Mongolian soldiers wore padded cotton uniforms with tunics and trousers, worn with woollen puttees by the infantry. The Inner Mongolian cavalry wore either Japanese brown leather boots or the soft suede boots traditionally worn by Mongolians.

Headgear worn by the Inner Mongolian Army after 1937 included Japanese fur hats, peaked caps and field caps similar to the Japanese model. All types of headgear had the Inner Mongolian insignia on the front, this being a blue enamel five-pointed star with a yellow disc in the centre (see Figure 2, above).

Ranks in use with the Inner Mongolian Army from 1937 to 1945 were based on the same system as used by the Manchukuo Army at the time. Stars were worn on the shoulder boards of the uniform as with the Manchukuoan Army but were backed with mid-blue cloth instead of the maroon. The rank of 'Shang-Chiang' or General was only held by Prince Teh Wang, the first Commander-in-Chief, and by Li Shou-hsin the second C-in-C. Although Prince Teh Wang held the rank of General in the Inner Mongolian Army he seems to have never worn military uniform. Li Shou-hsin, the Inner Mongolian Army Commander-in-Chief for most of the war, wore a Japanese officers' uniform from an early date and was pictured wearing the 1930 model uniform with officers' field cap. He also carried a traditional Japanese 'Shin-Gunto' officers' sword, which were often presented as gifts to 'puppet' officers.

Uniforms Of Minor 'Puppet' Governments 1935–45

East Hopei 1935–37

The Army of the 'puppet' State of East Hopei was made up of former soldiers of the 'Peace Preservation Corps' or 'Pao-An-Tui'. This Corps had been formed to act as a Military and Police force for the Demilitarised Zone, north and east of Peking in 1933.

At first the East Hopei Army wore its old uniforms of pale grey cotton jacket and pale grey cotton trousers tucked into white woollen puttees or leggings. Headgear was a pale grey cotton peaked cap with a white band around and insignia was, until 1936, the old Nationalist type.

Amazingly, the East Hopei Regime continued to fly the Nationalist flag for the first year of its existence even though they were in open rebellion against the National Government. In November 1936, on the first anniversary of the founding of East Hopei, the old five barred flag of the Republic 1911–28 was unveiled as its new symbol. At this time the insignia worn on the uniforms also changed to the five-coloured enamel star as used by the Republican Government up to 1928. At least some elements of the East Hopei Army received winter uniforms at this time, including padded overcoats with fur collars and fur-lined hats. High-ranking officers of the East Hopei Army were issued with Japanese officers' uniforms worn with the Japanese peaked cap with the five-coloured star badge on the front.

Ranks in use with the East Hopei Army were based on those used by the Chinese Republican Army 1911–28. In the Republican Army they were worn on the shoulder boards but in the East Hopei Army they were worn on the collar. The patches were straight at the front of the collar and came to a point at the back and had a system of gold five-pointed stars, with a General having three gold stars on a gold background and a Captain three gold stars on a gold bar with a red background.

The 'Great Way' Government 1937–40

The 'puppet' Government of the Greater Municipality of Shanghai was known as the 'Ta -Tao' or 'Great Way' Government. Its armed force was made up of a Paramilitary Police Force, which acted as the state's army. The 'Ta-Tao' Police had simple uniforms of light khaki cotton jacket with a white collar and trousers with light khaki woollen puttees. When on traffic duty the Ta-Tao Police wore white over sleeves on their jackets to make them more visible. As most people tended to ignore any signals given by the Ta-Tao these sleeves were really a waste of time! A peaked cap in light khaki cotton with a black peak and a white band was worn with a round cap badge on the front. The exact design of the cap badge is not known but following the example of other 'puppet' armies it may have been taken from the regime's new flag. This flag had a yellow field with a disc in the centre with the old Chinese 'T'ai Chi' or 'yin-yan' symbol in green and red, the badge was almost certainly based on this symbol. A winter version of the uniform was the same design but made out of heavier duty black cotton cloth, with the peaked cap having a white band around the sides. 'Ta-Tao' Police cadets reportedly wore Japanese military uniforms and the fifty or so female recruits would have worn the same uniform with a khaki skirt instead of trousers. 'Ta-Tao' Police wore little equipment and had only a Sam Browne leather belt with two ammunition pouches to carry rounds for their Mauser rifles.

Peace Preservation Corps 1933–37

The Peace Preservation Corps or 'Pao An-Tui' recruited to police the Demilitarised Zone in the north of China from 1933 were supposed to be a totally neutral force out of the control of both the Chinese and the Japanese. In reality though, they were often coerced into acting on a local basis as 'puppet' troops by the Japanese. They wore a variety of coloured uniforms, which were usually based on the same basic cotton uniform of peaked cap, cotton jacket and trousers worn with puttees and black shoes. The uniforms came in three basic colours, light khaki, grey and black with all the uniforms having a white band around the peaked cap. Little is known about specific uniforms worn by particular 'Pao An-Tui' units, but one eyewitness stated that there was a regional variation in the summer uniforms This source stated that the 'Pao An-Tui' in the eastern part of the Demilitarised Zone wore pale grey cotton uniforms and that those in the western part wore light khaki uniforms. He then rather oversimplifies the complex loyalties of the various units by saying that the eastern units were far more likely to become 'puppet' troops than the western units. White woollen puttees appear to have been worn with all the various coloured uniforms and must of been a distinguishing feature of the 'Pao An-Tui' dress. When units of 'Pao An-Tui' were operating as Japanese 'puppets' they often wore insignia to distinguish them from the still 'neutral' units. One such unit for the town of Hsiang Ho, 35 miles from Peking, wore a black cotton uniform and added a red stripe around the red band of the peaked cap. On the left sleeve of the jacket they wore a white cloth armband with the words 'Farmers Militia' written in Chinese characters in black ink. Equipment used by the 'Pao An-Tui' was cast-off Chinese military gear, and because of the non-combat role of the force only the poorest quality would have been issued to them. From photographic evidence it appears that their equipment would have consisted of a simple leather belt with a couple of ammunition pouches.

Other 'Puppet' Uniforms 1933–37

The Japanese slowly encroached into Chinese territory in the Demilitarised Zone to the south of the Great Wall during the mid 1930s. They often sponsored the setting up of locally-based and short-lived regimes which would take over part of a province and usually had a capital based in a small town. Military forces to support these regimes were usually recruited from the 'Pao An –Tui' (see above) and from local bandit elements. Uniforms would be the usual mix of scruffy cotton military items and civilian dress while the former 'Pao An-Tui' wore their old uniforms. Little is known about the insignia worn by the military forces of these governments but they did invariably fly the old Chinese Republic five-barred flag. At least some of the 'puppet' soldiers of these armies were described as having distinctive 'puppet' insignia based on the colours of the five-barred flag. In all probability, if insignia was worn, it would be the five-coloured enamel cap badge as worn by the 1912–28 Republican Army.

'Puppet' soldiers in Shansi Province in the 1940s wore light khaki cotton uniforms with the now archaic looking Northern Chinese peaked cap. These uniforms were never issued under any kind of regulations and we often only have photographic evidence to identify the various types. The 'puppet' quasi-military organisation the 'National Peace and Salvation Party' formed by General Hwang Ta-wei in Canton in February 1940 had its own uniform. Officers and men of this organisation wore Nationalist type uniforms with the addition of Japanese field caps. Although photographs of this group clearly show the basic uniform worn by Hwang and his men, their insignia is not visible. At the meetings of the 'National Peace and Salvation Party' and its sister organisation the 'South China Association for the Promotion of Peace' the five-barred flag was flown, which would indicate that the five-coloured star cap badge was worn. The formation of the Wang Ching-wei Government in March 1940 meant that the Canton 'puppet' organisation was absorbed into the new central regime along with its military forces.

Anti-Communist militia or self-defence corps in the north of China were formed from members of various political and paramilitary groups. These included the 'Red Spears' and the youth corps of the Hsin Min party, which was the political organ of the Provisional Government and its successor, the North China Political Council. The militia were nearly always dressed in civilian clothes and firearms were in short supply, so most were armed with crude spears. White cloth armbands with a suitably anti-communist slogan were worn by the militiamen, these having to be bought by the volunteers from the Japanese.

'Puppet' Army Equipment

As with all Chinese armies of the period the average 'puppet' soldier would have had very little in the way of equipment. Ammunition would usually be either carried in a canvas bandolier with small pockets sewn into it and slung over one shoulder or in a simple satchel or bread bag. Canvas bread bags could be easily manufactured locally by the 'puppet' governments or provided by the Japanese. Blankets were also often used to carry the soldier's gear and rice ration by the simple method of folding them into a U-shaped bedroll and tying them at the bottom with string. Although primitive, this makeshift carryall did at least provide a means of carrying kit when nothing else was available. The Nanking Army also adopted a sort of back pack fashioned by rolling a blanket into two rolls and securing them together by means of canvas straps. The back pack was then carried on the back and secured by two canvas shoulder straps.

'Puppet' soldiers issued with Japanese rifles would have been supplied with the brown leather belt and ammunition pouches which went with them. Because of the small amount of ammunition issued to individual soldiers and also due to war shortages a single pouch would usually be worn. When captured Chinese Nationalist rifles were issued it also follows that available belts and pouches will also have been issued with them.

Basic utensils carried by the 'puppet' soldier would include a rice bowl and hopefully a water bottle. Water bottles would be either captured Nationalist models which came in two models based on the German Army type, or donated Japanese models. If Japanese water bottles were issued, they would presumably be the older model. The Japanese did issue their Chinese 'puppet' allies with equipment captured from the British army stores in Singapore and these may well have included water bottles, packs, etc.

'Puppet' Unit Flags

Manchukuo Unit Flags

Command flags used by the the Manchukoan Army came in two sizes. For larger units, the flag measured 100cm long x 80cm deep. The flag for smaller units was 78cm x 68cm and had the same design, which was a yellow field in the bottom half with the top half made up of five bars divided equally from top to bottom, red, blue, white and black. In the bottom left corner of the larger flag was a 24cm high x 21cm wide white patch which carried the name and number of the unit, the smaller flag had the same patch but proportionally smaller. The pole was topped with a tip having a yellow tassel under it, and the flag itself had a yellow fringe around it.

Inner Mongolian Army Flags

Early Inner Mongolian forces flew a flag of archaic appearance with a yellow field and a Chinese ragged or 'invected' fringe in blue. Down the hoist of the flag were two parallel columns of black characters, one in Chinese and the other in Mongolian script. Presumably the script referred to the independence struggle of the Inner Mongolians against the central Chinese government. During the 1930s the Inner Mongolian Army was presented with a new flag, designed and manufactured in Japan. Measuring 80cm x 70cm, the flag had a sea blue field with a 10cm yellow border around the edge. On the centre of the mid-blue field was a yellow design in the form of a Mongol composite bow and nine arrows, and the whole flag was trimmed with a red fringe. The flagpole was made of lacquered oak with silver leaves decorating it and had a tip with a black hair tassel ornament under this. Attached to the flagpole under the black tassel were two smaller red tassels and fastened to the pole under the flag were two yellow tassels. (see Plate A, Figure 8)

Provisional Government Army Flag

Photographic evidence shows that the soldiers of the short-lived Provisional Government carried small unit flags based on the five-barred flag of the Chinese Republic. This flag was seen carried before a parade of Provisional Government troops in Peking in 1939. Although the colours of the flag are not conclusively known a little educated guesswork points to the following. The field was white with a red border and had the five-barred flag in the canton and three red five-pointed stars in the upper fly. The three red stars probably indicated the number of the unit.

Nanking Army Unit Flags

The Nanking Army flag followed almost exactly the pattern used by the Nationalist Army and was red with in the centre a blue rectangle with a white sun and rays symbol in the middle. Dimensions of the red flag and blue rectangular varied slightly from flag to flag. Down the hoist of the flag was a white cloth panel which bore the unit name and number in black Chinese characters.

Orders of Battle

Creating an authoritative order of battle for the 'puppet' armies in China and Manchukuo is almost impossible due not only to the lack of textual evidence but also to the biased nature of what little information does survive. All sources for information on the order of battle for 'puppet' troops had their own agendas when reporting them. The differences of opinion between Japanese, Chinese Communist and Chinese Nationalist sources are of course largely due to their own particular political bias. There is also however often a difference of opinion between United States and British Intelligence reports which makes the task of producing an accurate orbat even harder. The US and British intelligence departments were not too concerned with the Chinese 'puppet'armies, who they regarded as of little combat value. They produced numerous lists of units, which nearly always contradicted each other, so this example should be viewed in that context. The order of battle below is taken from a British intelligence report of 17 March 1943, and is one of the more measured and fair of those available. It should not however be taken as an authoritative list.

**ORDER OF BATTLE CHINESE
'PUPPET' TROOPS (MARCH 1943)**
North China (Under North China Political Council)
Peace Preservation Army 'Peking'
Commander in Chief: General Chi Hsieh

1st Group Army	3,000
2nd Group Army	3,000
3rd Group Army	3,000
4th Group Army	3,000
5th Group Army	3,000
6th Group Army	3,000
7th Group Army	3,000
8th Group Army	3,000
9th Group Army	3,000
Total	28,000 men

Gendarmerie Corps
Commander: Shao Wen-kai
Total   18,000 men

1st Provisional Army 'Suihsien'
Commander: Chang Lang-feng

14th Temporary Division	3,780
15th Temporary Division	3,000
16th Temporary Division	2,000
17th Temporary Division	2,000
18th Temporary Division	2,000
Total	12,780 men

4th Central Provisional Army 'Fengshou'
Commander: Liu Kai-tai
Total   2,000 men

7th Temporary Division 'Pengpu'
Commander: Wang Chan-lin
Total   2,000 men

21st Temporary Division 'Tsinghua'
Commander: Chen Yu-shan
Total   2,000 men

24th Route Army 'Sinsiang'
Commander: Chang Wei-ming
Total   2,000 men

101st Group Army
Commander: Tien Wen-ping
Total   3,000 men

102nd Group Army 'Shunteh'
Commander: Kao Te-lin
Total   3,000 men

105th Group Army
Commander: Liu Hua-nan
Total   3,000 men

'Peace Herald Army' 'Anyang'
Commander: Liu Hung-tsu
Total   5,000 men

'Army for the Development of Asia' 'Taiyuan'
Commander: Wu Chin-ying
Total   4,000 men

Pacification Commissioners Forces 'Kaifeng'
Total   2,000 men

Peace Preservation Force 'Singsiang'
Commander: Yang Pei-chi
Total   1,000 men

Hopei Pacification Army 'Anyang'
Commander: Chu Lieh-wu
Total   3,000 men

Guerilla Forces on Hopei Border 'Puyang'
Commander: Li Cheng-hua
Total   1,400 men

Anti-Communist Route Armies
Commander: Liu Pei-chen

1st Route Army	4,000
2nd Route Army	4,000
3rd Route Army	4,000
Total	12,000 men

Communist Suppression Troops in Southern Hopei 'Hantan'
Commander: Wu Shou-sung

Total	1,500 men

1st People's Communist Suppression Army of Shangtung 'Linchu'
Commander: Yang Pin

Total	3,000 men

2nd People's Communist Suppression Army of Shangtung 'Changchiu'
Commander: Kao Sung-po

Total	1,800 men
Total for North China	93,280 men

EAST CHINA (UNDER NANKING GOVERNMENT)
1st Area Army 'Lower Yangtze, North Anhwei and South Kaingsu'
Commander: Jen Yuan-tao

1st Division	3,432
2nd Division	4,144
3rd Division	3,195
4th Division	2,227
5th Division	2,837
6th Division	1,625
7th Division	2,575
7th Independent Brigade	550
8th Independent Brigade	550
9th Independent Brigade	820
Training Brigade	868
Total	25,343 men

2nd Area Army 'Eastern Honan'

Total	20,898 men

1st Group Army 'Taihsien'
Commander: Li Chang-chiang

24th Division	3,000
25th Division	800
26th Division	800
27th Division	800
28th Division	800
Independent Brigade	1,000
1st–8th Independent Divisions	3,000 each
12th Independent Brigade	800
13th Independent Brigade	800
14th Independent Brigade	800
Total	34,400 men

2nd Group Army
Commander: Tsang Cho

32nd Division	600
33rd Division	600
34th Division	600
35th Division	600

1st Independent Brigade	400
2nd Independent Brigade	400
Total	3,200 men

Kiangsu Honan Border Defence Headquarters 'Eastern Honan and Northern Anhwei'

4 Divisions	2,575 each
Total	10,300 men

'Army for National Salvation by Peace' 'Lunghua & Shanghai'
Commander: Yuan Ying-chieh

1st Route Brigade	1,000
4th Route Brigade	1,000
5th Route Brigade	1,000
10th Route Brigade	1,000
11th Route Brigade	1,000
Total	5,000 men

Army for the Development of Asia and National Reconstruction 'Shanghai'
Commander: Huang Chia-pen

1st Route Brigade	1,000
2nd Route Brigade	1,000
3rd Route Brigade	1,000
Total	3,000 men

Temporary 2nd Army 'Soochow'
Commander: Liu Pei-hsu

10th Division	9,180
13th Division	9,590
Total	18,770 men

Allied Army for Peace 'Nanking'
Commander: Hu Chang-yung

1st Division	4,000
2nd Division	4,000
Total	8,000 men

Temporary 19th Division 'Taihing'
Commander: Tsai Hsin-yuan

Total	7,059 men

Temporary 22nd Division 'Nanghwa'
Commander: Liu Hsiang-tu

Total	2,100 men

Temporary 28th Division 'Paohing'
Commander: Pan Nan-cheng

Total	5,000 men

Kiangsu Peace Preservation Troops
Commander: Li Shih-chua

Total	1,500 men

North Kiangsu Field Headquarters
Director Tsang Cho

Total	1,000 men

North Kiangsu Garrison
Commander: Ma Yang-hsien

Total	1,500 men

**Pacification Troops for
Honan Kiangsu Border Area 'Shangchiu'**
Commander: Hu Yu-kun
Total   800 men

Nanking Garrison
Commander: Li Chu-yi
Total   3,500 men

Nanking Gendarmes
Commander: Shen Chen-kang
Total   1,000 men

**1st Detachment of Bandit
Suppression Army for Central Anhwei 'Hofei & Tsaohsien'**
Commander: Tu Hai-lan
Total   1,200 men

Wuhu Garrison
Commander: Tnag Yu-sen
Total   1,500 men

Chekiang Peace Preservation Troops 'Hangchow'
Commander: Ting Ta-pang
Total   1,500 men

East Chekiang Pacification Command 'Hsiaoshan'
Commander: Wang Tsung-lin
Total   2,000 men

Total for East China   159,570 men

CENTRAL CHINA (UNDER NANKING GOVERNMENT)
Pacification & Field Headquarters for Wuhan Area
Director Yeh Peng
Total   2,000 men

Pacification Army
Commander: Wang Pu-ching
Total   8,000 men

Temporary 11th Division 'Kwangshui & Yingshan'
Commander: Li Pao-lien
Total   4,000 men

Temporary 12th Division 'Sinyang'
Commander: Chang Chi-huang
Total   2,500 men

Temporary 13th Division 'Ichang'
Commander: Liu Chen-hua
Total   5,000 men

Temporary 14th Division 'Lungchuanpu'
Commander: Liu Kwei-tang
Total   4,000 men

Temporary 23rd Division 'Tangyin'
Commander: Lu Chao-yuan
Total   3,500 men

Army for National Construction by Peace
Commander: Liu Tien-hsuing
1st Division   3,000
2nd Division   2,000
3rd Division   2,000
5th Division   1,000
Total   8,000 men

**Army for Co-ordination with Imperial Japanese Force and
for Reformation**
Commander: Liu Hsiao-yueh
Total   2,000 men

Peace Preservation Command for Western Hupeh
Commander: Hsiung Kuang
Total   2,000 men

People's Troops of the Republic of China 'Nanchang'
Commander: Chu Ta-ching
Total   1,500 men

**Troops for Co-ordination with Imperial Japanese Forces in
Kiangsi 'Nanchang'**
Commander: Teng Ju-cho
Total   1,500 men

Pacification Troops for North Kiangsi 'Kiukiang'
Commander: Ma Yueh-kuei
Total   4,000 men

Peace Preservation Troops at Nanchang
Commander: Wan Hsi
Total   1,000 men

Total for Central China   49,000 men

SOUTH CHINA (UNDER NANKING GOVERNMENT)
Pacification Commissioner of Kwangtung 'Canton'
Commissioner Chen Yueh-tsu
Total   1,500 men

Canton Pacification Headquarters -'Canton'
1st–9th Divisions
Total   12,060 men

20th Division 'Canton'
Commander: Fang Yi
Total   3,000 men

30th Division 'Swatow'
Commander: Cheng Hsi-hsun
Total   5,000 men

**Pacification Troops for
Fukien Kwangtung Border Area 'Swatow'**
Commander: Huang Ta-wei
Total   4,000 men

Fukien 'Army for National Salvation by Peace'
1st Group Army   4,000
1st Route Brigade of 1st Group Army   2,000

2nd Route Brigade of 1st Group Army	2,000
3rd Route Brigade of 1st Group Army	2,000
2nd Group Army	3,000
1st Route Brigade of 2nd Group Army	3,000
2nd Route Brigade of 2nd Group Army	1,000
Total	17,000 men

South China Commission 'Chungshan & Paichao'
Acting Director Cho Chiu

Total	1,000 men

Kwangtung Naval Station 'Nanti'
Commander: Chao Kuei-chang

Total	1,500 men

South China National Garrison Army
Commander: Wang Hui

Total	1,600 men

East River Garrison 'Shumchun'
Commander: Chang Kuei-fu

Total	1,000 men

Bandit Suppression Troops
for Tungkun, Tsengshing, Paoan Area
Commander: Liu Tang

Total	1,500 men
Total for South China	47, 660 men

INNER MONGOLIA & SUIYUAN
Inner Mongolian Army
Commander: Li Shou-hsin

4th Cavalry Division	900
5th Cavalry Division	900
6th Cavalry Division	800
7th Cavalry Divsion	800
8th Cavalry Divsion	1,000
Total	4,400 men

Pacification and Garrison Army 'Kweisui'
Commander: Ting Chi-chang

1st Group Army	700
2nd Group Army	500
3rd Group Army	500
Total	1,700 men

Self Government Army of Western Suiyuan 'Paotou'
Commander: Wang Ying

1st Division	1,000
2nd Division	630
3rd Division	600
Total	2,230 men

Peace Herald Army of the Northwest 'Mochiaotang'
Commander: Tang Ching-sheng

1st Division	500	
2nd Division	500	
Total		1,000 men

Charhar and Suiyuan Self Government Army 'Hsuanhua'
Commander: Li Hsing-tso

Total		1,000 men

Peace Preservation Troops for Chunker Banner 'Saratsi Tangshanyaotsu'
Commander: Chi Tzu-hsiang

Total	800 men

Mongolian Self Government Army of Pin Banner 'Pinkwangfu'
Commander: Pao Shan

Total	3,000 men

Mongolian Self Government Army of Po Banner 'Powangfu'
Commander: Han Se-wang

Total	3,000 men

Total for Inner Mongolia and Suiyuan	*17,130 men*

MANCHUKUOAN ARMY
Manchukuoan District Armies

1st Army District	23,400
2nd Army District	23,400
3rd Army District	23,400
4th Army District	23,400
5th Army District	23,400
6th Army District	23,400
7th Army District	23,400
8th Army District	23,400
9th Army District	23,400
10th Army District	23,400
Total	234,000 men

Manchukuoan Mixed Brigades

1st–13th Brigades	4,000 each
Total	52,000 men

Gendarmarie Corps 'Changchun'
Commander: Wang Yu-chin

Total	24,800 men

Guards Detachment -'Changchun'
Commander: Wang Ke-chen

Total	4,000 men

Chengteh Garrison Troops
Commander: Shao Pen-liang

Total	8,000 men

Harbin Garrison Troops
Commander: Li Wei-yi

Total	6,000 men

Total Manchukuoan Army	*328,000 men*

TOTALS

North China	93,280
East China	159,570
Central China	49,000
South China	47,000
Inner Mongolia & Suiyuan	17,130
Manchukuo	349,510
Total	694,640

APPENDIX B

'Puppet' Military and Civil Leaders 1931–45

General Chang Ching-hui

Born in 1871 he became a bandit leader before serving in the army of the Manchurian warlord Chang Tso-lin. He chose to join the Japanese in Manchuria 1931 and eventually became the Manchukuoan Minister of War and then Prime Minister. Described at the time as being largely illiterate, he personified the Japanese problem with recruiting puppet leaders of the right calibre.

General Chi Hsieh-yuan

A former Warlord Army commander during the Civil Wars of the 1912–28 period, he was born in Hopei in 1879. He joined the Japanese after the fall of Peking in August 1937. Although he had been in retirement he became the Peace Maintenance Minister under the Provisional Government. After serving the Japanese for several years he was reportedly dismissed by them in early 1945 for 'squeezing a little too much'. In other words, he was making a little too much profit and abusing his position just a little too much for even the Japanese. He suffered the fate of most high ranking 'puppet' officials at the end of the war and was executed in 1946.

Fu Siao-en

Second Mayor of 'Ta-Tao' 'Puppet' Government in Shanghai in succession to Soo Hsi-wen, he was born in Chekiang in 1871. He was a magistrate under the Chinese Imperial Government pre-1912 and went on to serve in various industrial posts. Forced into exile by the Nationalists in 1927 he returned to lead the new puppet government in Shanghai in 1938.

Huang Ta-wei

Leader of the pro-Japanese National Peace & Salvation Party formed in the South of China in early 1940 he was one of the prominent puppet leaders in the south. He later commanded the 4,000 Nanking Pacification Troops in the Fukien-Kwangtung area.

Jen Yuan-tao

Began his military career at the Paoting Military Academy and went on to serve as a Brigade Commander in the Nationalist Army. In March 1938 he became a Vice-Minister and Acting Minister of Public Security in the Reformed Government in Nanking. He went on to hold numerous posts under the Wang Ching-wei Government from 1940 including the command of the 1st Front Army and Minister of the Navy.

Liang Hung-chih

Born in 1883 he was a government official in Warlord China from 1911 until the victory of the Nationalists in 1928. When the Japanese were searching around for anyone who would be willing to serve in their Reformed Government in Nanking in 1938 and no other higher profile candidate could be found they called on Liang. He was head of the Reformed Government until its takeover by the new Reorganised Government of Wang Ching-wei in March 1940. He then went into virtual retirement but did not escape justice at the end of the war, when he was executed by the Nationalists on 9 November 1946.

Li Shou-hsin

Commander in Chief of Inner Mongolian Army and Vice Chairman of the Federated Autonomous Mongolian Government at Kalgan. He was a native of Jehol province and originally served in the Manchukuoan Army as a Brigade Commander.

Soo Hsi-wen

First Mayor of the 'Ta-Tao' 'Puppet' Government in Shanghai he was born in 1892 and was a graduate of Waseda

University. When the Japanese set up the 'puppet' 'Great Way' or 'Ta Tao' government in Shanghai in November 1937 he was installed as the leader of the regime with the title of Mayor. He was a failure in this role and was forced to stand down by the Japanese and was made Chief Secretary under the new Mayor, Fu Siao-en.

Prince Teh Wang (Mongol name – Demchukdongrob)

Mongol Prince of the West Sunid Banner, born in 1902, he was one of the main leaders of the fight for Inner Mongolian independence from China. After attempting to gain autonomy for the region from the Nationalist Government for a number of years he threw in his lot with the Japanese in early 1936. He then led a military campaign to extend the territory under his control into Suiyuan province. Although defeated in this campaign the outbreak of full-scale war between Japan and China in July 1937 allowed him to be established at the head of a new Inner Mongolian 'puppet' state known as 'Meng-Chiang' or Mongol Borderlands. This new state was under the total control of the Japanese and Prince Teh Wang soon became disillusioned. He escaped death at the end of the war in 1945 and was allowed to go into retirement but was eventually handed over to the Communists after their victory over the Nationalists in 1949. After 14 years of imprisonment he was released in 1963 and was allowed to teach at the Inner Mongolian University until his retirement.

Wang Ching-wei

Born at Canton in 1885 he was a young revolutionary and made his reputation by attempting to assassinate the Imperial Prince Regent. He was condemned to life imprisonment but released after the overthrow of the Emperor in 1911. Later he went on to serve as Sun Yat-sen's secretary in the last few years of the founder of the Nationalist Party's life. He became a prominent member of the Nationalist Party serving in various roles throughout the 1920s and 1930s. During this period he was to be frequently in opposition to Chiang Kai-shek, the leader of the Nationalists. He was expelled from the party in early 1939 when it was discovered that he had been holding discussions with the Japanese. For the whole of 1939 he negotiated with the Japanese about becoming the head of a new 'Nationalist' government in Nanking and was inaugurated as its leader in March 1940. For the rest of his life he was the head of the Reorganised Government in Nanking and played out this purely 'puppet' role until his death in a Tokyo clinic in 1943. Wang Ching-wei's motives have been long debated and he was certainly not alone in his belief that resistance to the Japanese was futile and only by co-operation with them could China prosper.

Wang Ke-min

Head of the Provisional Government in Peking from December 1937 to March 1940 when the regime was incorporated into the Nanking Government. He had served in government posts in Peking during the 1920s when the government was under the control of various Warlords. After a short period in exile in Hong Kong he was asked by the Japanese to head the new 'puppet' government in Peking. After March 1940 he continued to serve the Japanese on the largely autonomous 'North China Political Council'. At the end of the war he was imprisoned by the Nationalist Government and died in prison in December 1945.

General Wang Ying

He was one of the commanders of one of the contingents of the Inner Mongolian force which invaded Suiyuan in 1936. He had previously been known as a notorious bandit leader in Suiyuan and brought his band over to Prince Teh Wang. He later went on to become the commander of North West Autonomous Army and the 'Self Government Army of West Suiyuan' from 1940.

Yin Ju-keng

Born in 1888 he graduated from the Waseda University before serving in various roles in Warlord government before 1926 and then going on to serve the Nationalists and becoming Commissioner of the Luantung Area of the demilitarised zone in 1933. He then proclaimed the area as the Autonomous Government of East Hopei in opposition to the Nationalist Government. After the Tungchow Mutiny in 1937 he was removed from his office by the Japanese but went on to serve in various puppet offices until 1945, he was arrested by the Nationalists at the end of the war and shot in 1946.

Nanking Army Commanders 1940–45

Lieutenant-General Fu Shang-ying

Formerly a Fengtien Army Commander under the Manchurian Warlord, Chang Tso-lin he was made Director General of the Military Training in Nanking from April 1940.

General Chang Lan-feng

Commander-in-chief of 2nd Puppet Army Group made up of 5 divisions totalling 20,000 men. Chang was reportedly trusted by the Japanese although even he was called to Peking in 1944 to answer rumours of his possible defection.

General Hu Yu-k'un

One of the Christian generals' former subordinates, he was captured by the Japanese in fighting on the Suiyuan Provincial border in 1938. After agreeing to join the Japanese he went on to command the Kiangsu-Honan Pacification Army from September 1941. He also became the commander of the Paoting Military Academy from approximately the same date.

General Li Chang-kiang

General Li was a former Nationalist Deputy Commander of guerrillas in the Shangtung-Kiangsu-Anhwei Special War Zone. He went over to the Nanking Government with 30,000 of his men and was appointed Commander in Chief of the 1st Group Army.

General Pang Ping-hsun

Commander of Nationalist 24th Army he went over to the Nanking Government in May 1943. He was formerly a high ranking officer under the Christian Warlord Feng Yu-hsiang. He became Commander-in-Chief of the Nanking 5th Group Army District which was stationed in Western region of the Lunghai Railway. According to reports at the time, he lived in virtual retirement and had as little to do with the Japanese as possible.

General Sun Liang-cheng

Commander of 18,000 well-armed 'puppet' troops in the Kaifeng and South Shansi region. In July 1943 he was appointed C-in-C of the North China Peace Maintenance and in November as a member of the Nanking Military Inspection Corps.

General Sun Tien-ying

Commander of Nationalist 5th Army, went over to the Nanking Government in May 1943, then became Commander-in-Chief of the Nanking 6th Group Army District in the Southern Sector of the Peking-Hankow Railway. He had been a former subordinate of General Pang Ping-hsun (see above) in the forces of the Christian Warlord.

Lieutenant -General Sun Liang-cheng

A former subordinate of the 'Christian Marshal' Feng Yu-hsiang, he was in command of an army of several divisions when he defected to the Nanking Government in 1942. He took part in a military mission to Japan in May 1943 and then became Commander-in-Chief of the 2nd Group Army District of the Nanking Army in the region of Yangchow and Hwaian.

General Wen Ta-ko

Commander of the Nationalist Training Division and the 19th Nationalist Army Corps he went over to the Nanking Government in November 1942. He was given command of the temporary 31st Division of the Nanking Army.

General Wu Hua-wen

He brought his 40,000 men over to the Nanking Government in January 1943 and was given command of the Nanking 4th Army Group District which garrisoned the Southern Sector of the Tientsin-Pukow Railway.

General Yang K'wei-yi

Former Secretary General of the Hupeh Provincial Government Committee, he was denounced as a traitor by the Chiang Kai-shek Government. He joined the Nanking Regime and became Deputy Chief Of Staff of the General Staff, Military Affairs Commission.

Marshal Yeh P'eng

Formerly commander of Wuhan Garrison under the Nationalists, he joined Wang Ching-wei's government and was Commander of the 'puppet' military academy opened near Shanghai in 1939. His later career in the Nanking Army included his appointment as a member of the Nanking Military Affairs Commission in September 1941. In April 1943 he was appointed War Minister and in May of that year he led the Nanking Military Mission to Japan.

Japanese Officers Involved
in China and Manchukuo 1931–45

Captain Takayoshi Tanaka

He was involved in China from the late 1920s and was behind various intrigues, helping to engineer a military clash between the Japanese and Chinese in Shanghai in 1932. His main involvement in puppet China was as the Head of the Special Service Agency for Inner Mongolia. Tanaka was the main Japanese organiser of the Inner Mongolian invasion of Suiyuan in 1936 and regarded the campaign as his own personal project. Forced to retire by Prime Minister Tojo because of his opposition to the attack on the US in 1942.

Colonel Doihara Kenji

Known in the Western Press as the 'Lawrence of Manchuria' he was the chief architect of Japanese intrigues in Manchuria and Northern China from 1919 to 1940. He was a military advisor to the Manchurian Warlord Chang Tso-lin and after his fall began to lay the groundwork for the invasion of Manchuria by the Japanese Army in 1931. After the invasion he organised the creation of the new state of Manchukuo and sponsored its new emperor Pu- Yi, leading to his coronation in 1934. When the new Empire of Manchukuo was firmly established he turned his attention to Northern China. For the next few years he plotted to set up a separatist state in the five Northern Provinces of China using local warlords as his pawns. After service as an army commander during the Sino-Japanese War in 1937 he served in various capacities in Malaya and then Japan up to 1945. He was found guilty of war crimes by the International Military Tribunal for the Far East in 1948 and hanged in December of that year.

Major-General Kita Seiichi

From September 1937 placed in command of the Special Sections 'Tokumu-bu' which were responsible for carrying out political activities in the sphere of the Japanese North China Area Army. Behind efforts to recruit Ts'ao K'un and Wu P'ei-fu, the former heads of the Chihli Clique during the Warlord period.

Bibliography

Articles

Anon "Japan Faces Russia in Manchuria" (*National Geographic Magazine*, November 1942)

Insignia Magazine, issues 11,12 & 16

Steele, A. T. "On the Mongol Border" (*Asia Magazine*, August 1936)

Tamura, Toshio "The Full Story of the Manchurian River Defence Fleet" (*Ships of the World*, 1966)

Wang Li-chuan "Adventures of a Patriotic Bandit in Manchuria" (*Asia Magazine*, June 1936)

Books

Boyle, John Hunter *China and Japan at War 1937–1945: The Politics of Collaboration* (Stanford, CA: Stanford University Press, 1972)

Brackman, Arnold. C. *The Last Emperor* (New York: Carroll & Graf Publishers Inc, 1991) (originally published: New York: Charles Scribner's Sons, 1975)

Bueschel, Richard. M*., Nakajima Ki. 27A – B Manchu Ki. 79A -B in Japanese Army Air

Force, Manchukuo, IPSF, CACAF, PLAAF and CAF Service (New York: Airco-Aircam Aviation Series No. 20, Airco Publishing Company, 1970)*

Bunker, Gerald. E *The Peace Conspiracy: Wang Ching-wei and the China War 1937–1941* (Cambridge, MA: Harvard University Press, 1972)

Coox, Alvin. D. *Nomonhan – Japan Against Russia, 1939* (Stanford, CA: Stanford University Press, 1985)

Dreyer, Edward. L. *China At War 1901–1949* (London: Longman, 1995)

Fleming, Peter *One's Company – A Journey to China* (London: Jonathan Cape, 1934)

Forman, Harrison *Report From Red China* (New York: Henry Holt & Co, 1945)

Fuller, Richard & Ron Gregory *Military Swords Of Japan 1868–1945* (London: Arms & Armour Press, 1987)

Fuller, Richard *Shokan Hirohito's Samurai* (London: Arms & Armour Press, 1992)

Glantz, LTC David. M. *Leavenworth Papers No 7: August Storm: The Soviet 1945 Strategic Offensive in Manchuria* (Fort Leavenworth, KS: Combat Studies Institute, 1983)

Green, O. M. *China's Struggle With The Dictators* (London: Hutchinson & Co, 1940)

Jowett, Philip *Chinese Civil War Armies 1911 – 1949* (Oxford: Osprey, 1997)

Li Lincoln *The Japanese Army in North China 1937–1941: Problems Of Political & Economic Control* (London: Oxford University Press, 1975)

Lindt, A. R. *Special Correspondent – With Bandit and General in Manchuria* (London: Cobden-Sanderson, 1933)

Morley, James William (ed.) *The China Quagmire – Japan's Expansion on the Asian Continent 1933–1941* (New York: Columbia University Press, 1983)

Munday, Madeleine *Rice Bowl Broken* (London: Hutchinson & Co, 1940)

Peterson, W. *Orders and Medals of Japan and Associated States* (Chicago, IL: Orders & Medals Society Of America, 1967)

Smedley, Agnes *Battle Hymn of China* (New York: Alfred. A. Knopf, 1943)

Stephen, John. J. *The Russian Fascists, Tragedy and Farce in Exile 1925–1945* (London: Hamish Hamilton, 1978)

Tipton, Laurance *Chinese Escapade* (London: Macmillan & Co, 1949)

Wen-hsin Yeh (ed.) *Wartime Shanghai* (London: Routledge, 1998)